# TARZAN ECONOMICS

# TARZAN ECONOMICS

## Eight Principles for Pivoting Through Disruption

WILL PAGE

SIMON & SCHUSTER

London · New York · Sydney · Toronto · New Delhi

First published in Great Britain by Simon & Schuster UK Ltd, 2021



1 3 5 7 9 10 8 6 4 2

Simon & Schuster UK Ltd
1st Floor
222 Gray's Inn Road
London WC1X 8HB

www.simonandschuster.co.uk
www.simonandschuster.com.au
www.simonandschuster.co.in

Simon & Schuster Australia, Sydney
Simon & Schuster India, New Delhi



A CIP catalogue record for this book
is available from the British Library

Hardback ISBN: 978-1-4711-9091-9
Trade Paperback ISBN: 978-1-4711-9092-6
eBook ISBN: 978-1-4711-9093-3

Typeset in Perpetua by M Rules

Printed and bound by CPI Group (UK) Ltd, Croydon, CR0 4YY

FSC
www.fsc.org
MIX
Paper from
responsible sources
FSC® C020471

*To David and Isabel Page*
*Thanks for standing by me.*

*With thanks to the staff and patrons at the British Library, London School of Economics and Kentish Town swimming pool, where this book was written.*

'While music moves to the rhythm of the composer, words move at the pace of the reader'

DAVID SAFIR, economist, October 2019

'Tarzan Economics captures the conundrum we now face post-Covid-19. We cling to this old vine that keeps us off the jungle floor. At the same time, we lack the confidence to swing for the new vine. The trick is figuring out when to let go. This book is your alarm call as the old vine might let go of you'

JIM GRIFFIN, technologist, August 2020

# CONTENTS

# PROLOGUE

## We All Have a Napster Moment Ahead: Can You See Yours?

I joined Spotify in 2012, during the summer of the London Olympics, and on my first day in the job I was asked to contribute to the global recorded music industry's annual yearbook, where I found myself struggling to find something that would capture the readers' imaginations. Back then, the industry narrative was like a broken record (pun intended): CDs were down, piracy was up, downloads were failing to plug the gap and streaming was all but a 'rounding error' on global record labels' accounts.

I was stuck for ideas, then a friend introduced me to a colleague, Chris Tynan, who back then was one of our lonely data scientists. He had helped build some of the company's first-ever data dashboards, which allowed Spotify staff to visualise how listeners were listening. Tynan would always teach us a lesson when 'pulling data' out of the engine room; he would look you square in the face and ask: 'What are you going to do when I give it to you?' He wanted to teach us to apply common sense before getting lost in the complexity – a lesson I want to transfer over the next three hundred or so pages.

We cobbled together a really simple idea – and 'pulled data' to produce a chart of the top albums of the year on our streaming platform. The music industry is unique in its addiction to charts, as they make the popular visible and the visible more popular, and this chart would be a crowd-pleaser.

Our chart placed Belgian–Australian pop star Gotye's *Making Mirrors* album at number one. Gotye exploded to fame during the year before thanks to the success of the single 'Somebody That I Used to Know', a track I'm convinced was produced to sound good on Apple Mac laptops due to its hollow sound. Lower down the table, we saw Lana Del Rey's *Born to Die* album ranked a distant eighth.

That's when we realised what we were going to do with the data. We have all grown up listening to albums, some of which we admire as a 'body of work' while others are discarded as 'one hit wonders'. We knew that the album would have 'killer' songs as well as 'filler' songs. As streaming measures consumption – as opposed to album sales, which counted transactions – we realised we could use that knowledge to make a more accurate list.

My statistically minded colleagues came up with a simple trick to find out. Using the median concept – the midpoint in a data set – we re-ranked the album chart based on the median track – so if there are eleven songs on every album, we would rank the album based on the popularity of the sixth most popular track. This was our way of finding out how much of the album was consumed, not sold. It would reduce the distortion of hit singles and lift the lid to learn how this 'body of work' was actually consumed. It was our way of finding out if the album was all killer, or just full of filler.

What we learned was that Gotye's album wasn't just knocked off the top spot, it dropped out of the Top 10 like it had fallen off a cliff. Conversely, Lana Del Rey's album shot up the charts, from eighth place to number one. Thanks to streaming lifting the lid on consumption, we learned that Gotye was a 'one-hit wonder' – everyone knew and loved 'Somebody That I Used to Know', but to this day I've yet to meet anyone who can name a second Gotye track. For Lana Del Rey, she didn't just have the hits 'Video Games' and 'Born to Die'. Her fans saw her album as a body of work – giving similar levels of attention to 'Blue Jeans' and 'Off to the Races' and many more.

From statistics to economics, I contemplated a commercial application of the data. If a festival promoter was considering booking both acts to perform on their main stage, and approached me for my advice on the billing, I'd recommend giving Gotye just four minutes and four seconds (the time it takes to stream his one hit), whereas Lana Del Rey should have a full hour with the option to bolt another hour on top for encores – as we knew all her fans loved all of her songs.

From show business to the business of shows, this switch from selling physical albums and downloads to monetising consumption of streaming saw artists pivot to the new rules. As songs were monetised only when they were streamed for more than thirty seconds and compensated at the same rate regardless of their duration, we started to notice that hits were becoming shorter and their choruses being moved to the front. Anthems of yesteryear, like U2's 'Where the Streets Have No Name', which takes almost two minutes before the vocals arrive, would be wasting their time and losing our attention in this new world.

The songwriters' rule for survival was simple: don't bore us, get us to the chorus. Shorter songs reflected shorter attention spans. The album used to be the climax but now it's the conclusion; it tells fans there will be no more events for the next few years. It asks for no more attention. The fans' anticipation that would arise from a band being 'in the studio' preparing their next masterpiece has been replaced by a shoulder-shrug that the band must have gone on sabbatical, and attention needs to be spent elsewhere. The music industry achieved two feats that no one ever thought it would or could or should – it's become more valuable; it's also become less intimate. As David Bowie predicted way back in 2002, 'music [has become] like running water', i.e. always there so no need to care.

This dilemma touches on attention economics, which, as you'll learn later, is the first 'fork in the road' we all need to navigate. For now, this switch between only knowing how something is sold to lifting the lid on understanding how it is consumed is key. It felt pervasive back then, even more so now. Ubiquitous, even. So many lids needed lifting. Knowing how many people joined a gym in January to work off their festive excess does not tell you how many of those people actually used the gym, nor how they use it. Knowing how many cars were sold in last quarter does not tell you anything about how those cars are being used now or for what purpose. Knowing that the housing market is heating up or cooling off tells us little about who is living in those houses and how they are living. Knowing how many newspapers were distributed to newsagents and kiosks tells us little about how many were sold and even less about how many were read – newspaper circulation was always measured on how many were returned back to the distribution warehouse not on how many were sold.

In established markets we may think we know a lot, but the reality is that we actually know very little. Peter Drucker put it well: 'The customer rarely buys what the company thinks it is selling.' That's why you need this book – it makes you look afresh at what you think you know. Once you have that clearer picture, you can learn better how and when to move on, to pivot through the disruption we are all facing in these surreal times.

Should you currently be holding a physical copy of *Tarzan Economics* in your hands, then you're holding a 'product' that has served the book industry well over the centuries. Publishers know lots about how books sell but little about if and how they are consumed. The book industry knows how to market books, signalling quality through previews and quotes, but it does not really know how those books are read – unless, of course, they are e-books sold via Kindle or its competitors.

Which is the point for publishers: e-books tell you what traditional books can't. Traditional book publishers do not know if the reader viewed every word or where they stopped. Worse still, even if they did – just because they read it does not mean they enjoyed it.

This lesson was hammered home to me when one veteran book publisher told me that his successful business operated on the following rule of thumb: 80 per cent of books sold were not read by the purchaser. That's to say that every year he set out his budget knowing eight out of ten books that were shipped would find their way onto a glass table, a dusty bookshelf or would be a gift for someone else. I challenged him to justify a business with that much breakage, to which he replied: 'That's why we like to say a record collection defines who you are, and a book collection defines who you really want to be.' Wise words.

What we learn from the music business tells us so much more about who we really are than other media industries; music is important not only because it was first to suffer and first to recover, but because it was the first to discover who we really are. Throughout this book, music is featured as an example of change. After all, it was first – the canary in the digital mine.

While the list of industries not able to perform such a simple statistical trick as our Gotye and Lana Del Rey chart is virtually endless, times are changing. Fitness apps are telling us about our actual performance, not our membership. Smart cars are saying where they've travelled, not just how they were sold. Devices like Alexa and Google Home are revealing how we are living in our homes, not just who bought them and for how much. Traditional newspapers are embracing the internet, and new platforms are monetising based on time spent reading. Even the rise of e-books and audio books finally tell the publisher (or retailer) how much is being consumed, and at what pace, rather than how many copies were sold.

But they are all playing catch-up with music. Music was 'first in, first out' with digital disruption – giving it a twenty-year head start on all other parts of society. Thanks to streaming, the music industry is not only reaching new highs in terms of revenue and reach – there are more smartphones in circulation than there ever were Walkman CD-players – but it is doing so knowing how its content is being consumed. Streaming tells us how often songs were listened to, the source of those streams, the saves and skips and most importantly the sharing. Music is recovering and we know more than ever why. This is now a business that knows everything – and I mean everything – about how its art is being consumed, not sold. It's a paradigm shift.

Music matters because it got there first and that is why all of us have so much to learn from music. This book will help you catch up.

# INTRODUCTION

## My Job is to Help You See Around Corners

Your decision to invest your scarce attention in this book suggests you are open to new ideas. Disruption starts with an idea, for example getting from A to B in a way that is faster and more efficient than the old way, a rather minimal disruption by comparison with those that truly enable us to do things we could never do before.

We're focused on disruption that is almost indistinguishable from magic, like radio waves and electrification in the 1920s, and the 1990s embrace of the digital delivery of art. Game changers that redefine rules, flipping products into global services, like vehicles into custom global transportation options on demand.

Navigating disruption requires the confidence of knowing when to let go of old ideas and grab on to new ones. Swinging from the old to the new is what technologist Jim Griffin referred to in his address to the 2009 Supernova conference in San Francisco as 'Tarzan economics'. As he reflected on the music industry's response to the illegal file-sharing site Napster and the countless imitators that followed, he said, 'We cling to this vine that keeps us off the jungle floor. Yet, at the same time, we swing for the next vine, because we want to be propelled forward. The trick is figuring out when – when to let go of that old vine and when to embrace that new vine.'

Like a good Speyside sherry-cask malt whisky, Griffin's observation has aged well. Twenty years ago the music industry faced a massive disruption. It screwed up its response to that disruption for a decade, but then it worked out how to pivot and thrive. Today, countless industries – both on- and offline – find themselves staring down the barrel of a similarly disruptive gun, and this book will help you understand how you can skip the decade of screwing up in response and go right to the thriving.

Pivoting means knowing when to let go of what you've got used to holding on to as continuing to hold on will only make matters worse. Reaching out to the new vine will involve staring into darkness and facing your fear of the unknown. This book will instil the confidence needed to let go.

The Covid-19 crisis has accelerated disruptive change that was already underway. The high street was already in decline, and those who hadn't experimented with online shopping before the crisis will have had to by now – and many of them won't be going back to the high street once we've returned to business as normal. At one point during the crisis, the use of video conferencing pushed the value of Zoom to more than the world's seven biggest airlines and even overtook the behemoth General Electric. The seeds of such change were sown before the coronavirus – Tarzan Economics was creeping up on all our lives.

Consider three professions that students used to gravitate towards to earn the biggest salaries: accountancy, banking and law, all now replaced by data science, software engineering and product management.*

* Allana Akhtar and Joey Hadden, 'The 25 highest-paying entry-level jobs for college grads', *Business Insider*, June 2020.

Accountants are seeing apps appear on smartphones that will serve the customer better, faster and at less cost than their profession ever could. Companies like Stripe, with its service Stripe Atlas, aim not just to disrupt the accounting supply chain, but to displace it – removing lengthy paperwork, legal complexity and numerous fees and making it possible to form a company in days, not months.

If you are an accounting student, pivoting through disruption means realising that your profession will be drastically different when you finish your qualification to when you began. The determination to hold on to the old vine in the hope that the problem goes away, or will only replace the most menial of tasks, would be in vain. The ambitions of disruptors entering this space go far beyond basic bookkeeping.

At the other end of the career ladder, if you're responsible for an organisation and overseeing thousands of employees, you need to know that ignoring your Napster moment, by clinging on to the old vine because it continues to pay your bills, will only make the challenge of letting go harder and push the new vine further out of reach.

Bankers, too, now must face their own Tarzan Economics as new entrants eat away at their picnic like digital ants. For all the financial booms and busts we've seen in recent years, there has been wilful ignorance about how banks make money, and how money is made in the first place. Students are rarely taught about fractional reserve lending (how a bank can hold one dollar but loan out ten), and professionals rarely challenge their own finance department's claims that their treasury tools have made millions by asking them to explain who lost those millions in return. We used to celebrate banks declaring profits but now the mood has changed – we want to know how those profits were made.

Companies like Revolut and TransferWise have explicitly attacked the fee structure that made those predictable profits possible. These invisible fees levied on consumer transactions, such as moving money from one's dollar to one's sterling account and losing three per cent of its value in the process, have typically provided the revenue that subsidises everything else a bank does – including going to the casino with its investment arm.

Law is another profession that once topped graduate career league tables but now finds itself creaking under the strain of disruption. Technology has spent much of the past two decades trying to disrupt and 'Napsterise' the legal profession, yet law firms remain either oblivious or opposed to real change. For evidence, look no further than a typical legal department's organisational structure and count how many assistants-of-assistants you can spot. Do not be surprised to find that a third of a costly legal department's headcount are non-lawyers, meaning where there's smoke there's fire (or organisational fat that technology can trim).

There are signs that things are beginning to change. The first drop of blood to emerge is the early adoption of products like DocuSign and Fastcase. At a fundamental level, the 'product' of the legal profession is trust. DocuSign digitises trust. Fastcase is also making inroads and its legal data service that reads and writes arguments based on outcome analysis is as well. These will do far more than get lawyers past their sacred obsession with touching paper.

Tarzan Economics plays out as lawyers cling on to the old vine in vain. But the disruptors that are 'Napsterising' this profession are viral by design; if I use DocuSign, then all my clients have to use it (or countersign it) too. This 'network effect' means adoption will keep pace with disruption. Individuals, organisations and institutions that fail to embrace this new technology will struggle with scaling their ideas. For a typical start-up with four employees that grows to four hundred and then four thousand – do not be surprised if the costly legal department could easily become outsized and make up a tenth of the workforce. Those who are able to reach out to the new vine of legal technology should, on the other hand, be able to cut that ratio – and the costs that come with it – in half.

Fear of the unknown has and will continue to lead to resistance to reach out to the new vine, but that fear is misplaced: technology is disruptive to the business of law, not to lawyers themselves – lawyers will always be needed: humans are fallible, imperfect and will f**k up.

Law, banking and accountancy are just three professions who need this book; I could easily name a hundred more. It could be the partners who sit atop such organisations, or the students aspiring to be employed by them. Learning how to pivot through disruption needs the confidence of knowing when to move: when holding on to the old vine is unsustainable and when reaching out to the new vine is essential.

## MUSIC MATTERS BECAUSE IT GOT THERE FIRST

This is why knowing music's story of letting go of the old and reaching out to the new will enable you to use this book to pivot through disruption yourself. Music got there first. Music was the first to suffer, and the first to recover, from the forces of deep technological disruption, making it something we can all learn from.

Let's go back two decades to appreciate just how profound the scale of disruption was that the industry experienced. In June 2000, *The Economist* published an article titled 'Napster's wake-up call' with the subheading 'It's time for the record labels to embrace the Internet wholeheartedly'. The article concluded that the success of illegal piracy sites like Napster was 'in response to and an indictment of' the industry's hesitations about pivoting to a digital future. In the ten years that followed, the industry spent millions fighting change while losing billions in revenue. As we'll learn in later chapters, the inconvenient truth that haunted the industry during that first decade of disruption was that it was easier for consumers to steal music than it was to purchase it.

It took ten years of staring into a financial abyss for the industry to stop hesitating and start pivoting – to let go of ownership of CDs and downloads and embrace the access model of subscription and streaming. Spotify was launched with a single clear mission: build something that's better than stealing and the people will come. Today, the International Federation of the Phonographic Industry has reported in their 2020 Global Music Report that over 340 million people pay a monthly fee to access music legally just like *The Economist* article proposed back at the turn of the millennium.

I was lucky enough to enter the music industry when it was just beginning its revolutionary pivot. I was living a Batman lifestyle in my home town of Edinburgh, Scotland. A government economist by day (wearing the required charcoal-black suit, blue shirt and red tie) and DJ–journalist by night, writing about Philadelphia hip hop and Brazilian funk for the tastemaker magazine *Straight No Chaser*.

The origins of my journey in music took a teenage detour from passive-listener to active-promoter thanks to a lyric from the New York-based hip hop band Jungle Brothers in their song 'In Dayz 2 Come' from the 1989 album *Done by the Forces of Nature*. The lyric captured the importance of getting their music and message across to as wide an audience as possible without diluting its integrity, without crossing into the mainstream. Rapper Mike Gee (Michael Small), who penned the lyric just over three decades ago, reflected on its deeper meaning:

> 'I wanted to present myself in the humblest manner and speak the truth from my heart so people could understand it, feel it, use it. Everyone back then was talking about the music industry as a scheme; rap music had evolved, from being purely about the show to more about the business, from an art form to a game. Sure, to stay in the game, our records gotta sell but I don't wanna sell my soul just to sell records.'

Those words took me and my musical journey off Main Street and down a side street; away from the centre and left of the middle. The role of a DJ was to get music across without crossing over and diluting its artistic integrity. To keep a dance floor dancing without resorting to watered-down music from the mainstream. The role of a 'rockonomist' would be similar – to transfer the lessons that needed to be learned without diluting its message or losing its crowd.

From partying like it's 1989 to searching for a suitable job description in 2006, I was a rockonomics wannabe, willing to do anything to get a foot in the door somewhere to change the business I loved. At the time, there was no demand for economics in the music industry. There wasn't even much written about it. All I had to hand was a wonderful 'bible' by Don Passman (*All You Need to Know About the Music Business*) that helped me get my head around the alphabet soup of acronyms the industry was littered with and the spaghetti of royalties that flowed through the system.

I had sent my CV to countless organisations, and if I was lucky I got a letter of rejection back. My hand was hurting from all the knocking on doors, and my head was hurting as none of them would open.

Then, on 16 March 2006, I left the government offices after a dull-as-dishwater day debating the details of local income tax and decided to board a number 35 bus to get home. It was there that I picked up a discarded copy of the *Financial Times*. I don't usually pick up discarded newspapers on Edinburgh's buses but in the case of the *FT* the benefits outweigh the costs. There I was, transfixed by an opinion-piece on the penultimate page titled 'Digital Ants Wreck the Music Industry's Picnic' by Adam Singer, the then-CEO of the Performing Right Society.

Bingo! I had stumbled on someone else thinking about the same problems I was. My father raised me never to be shy about approaching people (as the worst they can say is along the lines of 'back-off'), so I wrote Singer a letter challenging him on the contents of his article. Within a couple of days he called me: 'Send me a note of no more than a thousand words on what you think the problem is and I'll get you down from Edinburgh to London and we can meet up in person so you can explain your solution.'

Sensing that I was finally knocking on a door that was already ajar, I spent that evening perched on a stool in Sandy Bell's, a local Edinburgh bar famous for its folk music and where comedian Billy Connolly once performed as one of the two Humblebums, determined to have my response in Singer's inbox the next day. My note was titled 'Why Paper Didn't Die Out Along with the Typewriter'. The observation was that just as we use more paper than ever, even though we no longer use typewriters, music would be no different as the CD fast became redundant. Separating the medium (typewriter) from the message (words on paper) was what I had to explain to Adam Singer if I was to stand a chance of getting to meet him. I wanted to challenge the many doomsayers predicting the end of the music business with a solution that meant changing how music was distributed. We needed to learn from piracy, not fight it.

Within a fortnight of picking up that newspaper on a bus, I was boarding a train to London's King's Cross station to rendezvous with Adam Singer in his executive office at the Performing Right Society. The day before leaving I got lucky again, as I fortunately stumbled across a working paper by the late Alan Krueger co-authored with Marie Connolly, titled 'Rockonomics', which explored the economics of ticket touts (or scalpers). This was a blessing, and by the time the train arrived in London I had worn out two highlighter pens taking notes.

In what looked and felt like a glass house located in the middle of his management team he grilled me thoroughly for hours, probing what it would take to stop the digital ants from eating his music-industry picnic. Our conversation led me to merging my two passions of economics and music, scratching my head for five academic years of lectures I had attended to weld lessons learned from my past to a business I wanted to fix right now.

This stretched from designing auctions for pricing music catalogues – something that the industry had not explored in its hundred-year existence – to exploring how to get the 'bundle' back, as the ants were cherry-picking a couple of hits from the iTunes picnic for 79 pence apiece instead of gorging on entire albums for £10.

As we explored the thorny topic of piracy, I pointed out that many of the actions taken to date, such as suing the customer or disconnecting them from the internet, were self-defeating: swimming against the tide of the customer would not grow digital revenues. Why? Because they wouldn't have access to the internet – obviously. Singer ratcheted up the pivotal thinking by drawing out an astute observation: 'No piracy means you have a product nobody wants.'

We continued to express mutual bemusement that the industry was investing in anti-piracy campaigns that were being shown in cinemas as this was bordering on stupidity – targeting those who are willing to pay for a cinema ticket with negative messages was an own goal as (a) you put them off coming back and (b) they weren't the ones stealing movies anyway. He agreed with this inconvenient truth but knew persuading others around him wouldn't be easy.

I took the five-hour train back to Edinburgh and all I could think about was problems that need solving. The next day, Singer called me back, inviting me to become the first-ever chief economist of the Performing Right Society. After knocking on countless doors, one had finally opened wider than I could ever have imagined. Convincing people to pivot, however, would mean (a) teaching them a lot of inconvenient truths, and (b) avoiding getting fired in the process.

I got lucky! I kept my job and was able to bring a new way of thinking that helped steer the copyright industry through the turbulence and towards a recovery. Now I want to reach anyone and everyone who finds digital disruption taking hold in their lives and help them to find new solutions or suggest new ways of thinking.

### THERE WAS ECONOMICS LONG BEFORE THERE WERE ECONOMISTS

Having the word 'economics' in the title of this book suggests that some prior education in the dismal science is required to enjoy it. To right that wrong, let me be clear: prior knowledge of economics is not a prerequisite for reading this book. As much as my profession would like me not to say this, perfectly rational economics exists totally independently of economists. You know more economics than you realise.

My introduction to economics happened during my pre-teenage years on the football pitch – not a 'soccer pitch' with bags down for goalposts, but the American football pitch. That's because British television had decided to take the bold step of broadcasting highlights of the previous week's American football on Sunday evenings at an hour early enough for my parents to allow me to watch it. I was hooked.

Suddenly, I had discovered a whole new sport. Subconsciously – thanks to the stop-start nature producing easily countable moments that were not found in soccer or rugby – I was immersing myself in statistics. This is what made me an economist. Looking back on those early years, I wasn't aware of probability theory, but I was busy calculating the options facing a quarterback on third down and eight. I would have had no idea what a key performance indicator (KPI) was, but I was wondering why coaches viewed a six-yard gain by a running back as more valuable than the same gain by a wide receiver.

I would have failed to spell the word 'asymmetries' correctly but knowing that an average quarterback with an extra second of time was worth more than a superstar quarterback without it taught me why the offensive tackle (tasked with giving the quarterback more time) was the second-highest-paid player on the field.

I set myself the task of establishing which American football team had the best fans and my untrained economic mind was looking across columns of data showing stadium capacity, city population, teams-per-city and even stadiums-per-team.

The LA Raiders might have had one of the biggest stadiums, but it was America's biggest city that also hosted a second team, and I needed to control for that. My enquiring mind led to having a letter published in a leading sports magazine requesting that they supply all the necessary columns on the data points needed to answer my own question.

Just as you would compare the size of two different economies today by dividing by population to draw a 'per capita' comparison, I was normalising data long before I knew what it was.

This book asks only that you apply some common sense. Common sense was at the heart of how economics was taught to me. My father, a maths teacher, taught me how to teach economics from the age of eleven – long before I had the chance to study it. 'Look at your audience,' he would often say, 'and then spot the least interested person in that room and focus on teaching economics to them; the rest will follow.' His fundamental belief: *The people who need to learn about economics most are those who*

(a) don't think they will understand it;
(b) don't want to understand it; but
(c) have to understand it.

This is not an economics book for economists, nor is it a music business book for industry aficionados. They'll enjoy the ride, sure. This is a book for everyone who feels their business is facing challenges and wants to find a new way to discover the solutions. Unfortunately, due to Covid-19, everyone means everyone – we're all in this predicament together.

## READING ACROSS NOT DOWN

When I was suited-and-booted working in government we had this bible we called the Green Book, which taught us how to think – literally! It gave clear, imperious guidance on how to construct a costs-benefit analysis and even prescribed specific values to complete the calculation. When it came to big investment decisions, it would tell you whether to proceed or to stay put. The Green Book wasn't just a framework, it was a frame of mind. It was more than structured thinking; it was a straitjacket. But it taught me a valuable lesson.

For instance, we would sketch out the costs and benefits of investing in a new public swimming pool. The framework would guide us through the calculation of the upfront and operational costs and then place values on the benefits – the tax revenue generated, jobs created and the economic activity caused by its construction. Tasked with building a model on a spreadsheet, we would read down the column of data to see if the benefits outweighed the costs and construction could begin.

I realised then the importance of reframing the question to address the broader problem(s) involved and get you a better answer. The benefits of investing in a swimming pool are that they make people healthier, which in turn achieves far more than the labour employed in running the pool and the tax revenue generated. A more exercised public helps reduce the potential cost to the National Health Service (NHS). So spending money on a swimming pool (one column of data) helps reduce the cost of the NHS (a separate column of data). But as the Department of Health & Social Care doesn't control the sports budget, it doesn't frame the question. And as the Department for Digital, Culture, Media & Sport doesn't control the health budget, it doesn't need to consider the answer.

Two departments, or two columns, like ships passing in the night. This lesson stuck because I see it everywhere – especially in the arts, which have long struggled to explain their value to the bean counters in government. Why invest in a museum? Because it can inspire us to learn, not because it can recover its costs by visitor numbers. Why invest in music education for children in primary schools? Because it can improve mathematical attainment when they enter secondary education. Why invest in the arts? Because it can increase participation in democracy, not just put bums on seats in a publicly funded theatre. The closer you look, the more all the adjacent columns relate to one another.

This book starts by showing how the music industry held on to the old vine for a damaging first decade and then reached out to the new vine and swung into a successful second decade that is the envy of everyone now staring into their own Napster moment. It will prepare you to learn how to swing from the old to the new.

*Tarzan Economics* pushes back against clickbait titles like 'The one rule that will change all your lives' and recognises that there's no one rule and that we're all different, presenting instead eight transferable rules (or principles) and then recognising they will apply differently to different people. We'll conclude with an expression I coined as Spotify was preparing to go public – 'builders and farmers' – to show how this book will mean different things to different people. Builders create what farmers can't and farmers scale what builders can't. By the end of this book you'll be better placed to understand who you are when applying the eight principles to pivoting through disruption, and you'll be able to pivot faster than any individual, organisation or institution you choose to help.

When I was writing this book, many prospective publishers

suggested each of these eight principles could be its own book. It's a well-known trick: picking an idea and stretching it to 200 pages. But that didn't wash with me, because it wouldn't wash with you. I applied the lessons I learned from the one-hit wonder Gotye and the steady hitmaker Lana Del Rey – determined to ensure that you would consume all of my chapters, not just one! As we'll discuss later, attention is scarce, and readers can quickly sense when an author is wasting their time 'flogging a dead horse'. And as attention becomes even more scarce, those types of books are increasingly destined for the back of the shop. Instead, you have here eight rich principles that can stand alone, threaded together in a path that's meant to help you put them into action – each of them killer, and not one filler.

This book will help you assess your situation, teach you to ask the right questions about your lives, organisations and governments, highlight the challenges faced and help provide solutions so you know when to make the leap to the next vine – and, just as importantly, pick the right one to grab hold of. Once you exit the other side of the next 300 pages, you'll realise not only how fast-paced technological disruption is but also how unstable the status quo is – like a bicycle, it falls over if it doesn't move forward.

Buckle up.

# I

# TARZAN ECONOMICS

## Let's Party Like It's 1999

Twenty years ago, when compact disc sales were scaling new heights (and doing so at ever-higher prices), record-industry executives could weigh their profits on scales. This isn't just a figure of speech – label executives would regularly buy and sell stacks of CDs based on their weight, rather than their music. So predictable was the insatiable demand for a disc in a plastic case that each pallet of CDs sold translated into predictable quantities of cash to calculate their profits.

Pallets of CDs carried virtually no data whatsoever. Labels didn't even care if it was the Stones or the Killers, just whether it was stones or kilos. Yet while it is easy to mock how business was done back then, the music industry did more business in the era of CDs than it has done since. By 2000 the global value of the music industry was close to $25 billion. Twenty years on, the value of the recorded music industry is just over a tenth off reaching that peak – and that's before we adjust for inflation.

The hilarious 2008 novel *Kill Your Friends* puts you inside the minds of egotistical talent scouts during the peak-CD-era 1990s with a story of how a major-label A&R manager would respond to the question 'What music do you like?' The author likens this to 'asking an arbitrageur what kind of commodities he likes. Or saying to an investment banker, 'Hey what's your favourite currency?' The music industry was reaching its peak and was about to find out how far down it had to travel. It might have known what it was worth (or at least, how much it weighed), but it had no idea how much it could lose.

To understand why the old vine was so hard to let go of (and why people are still nostalgic about it today), we need to appreciate just how excessively crazy the good times were, with emphasis on the word 'excess'. Label executives would take helicopters to their private jets. Analytics back then was once described to me bluntly, using a simple bar chart: 'You give me one bar that's bigger than another bar and I'll sell the shit out of it.' The excesses came down to a combination of the scarcity of physical CD products (unlike digital files, there can only be so many), the leverage that came with the ability to control their supply and a sprinkle of fear and greed topped off with line after line of cocaine. I'll never forget learning the expression 'so bent it's straight' as a way of capturing how the old vine held itself together. Here are three of my greatest hits so you can learn why such excesses apply to more than just music.

## PAYOLA WAS SO BENT IT WAS STRAIGHT

The first scam is 'payola', wherein record labels would pay an 'independent radio promoter' to get their new songs played on radio stations so they could draw a crowd and achieve a profitable return in sales. The word 'independent' in the job title of independent radio promoter matters. He (and it was always a he) was neither an employee of a label nor of the radio station and was free to pick his first partner in this two-way negotiation. Contrary to how payola is often perceived, he would consistently pick the radio station first to ask if they intended to put a forthcoming hit record on heavy rotation. If the station replied 'Sure, we love that record, we're going to play it all day once it's out', that was all he needed to know.

Next he would go to the label and auction the slot, pitching: 'If you lay out twenty thousand dollars, I reckon we can get this record on heavy rotation with the biggest local radio-station network.' The song was going to be played even if the promoter hadn't been involved, but his knowledge of one side's intentions allowed him to play off the naivety of the other. The money was paid over to the independent promoter, the station received a handsome kickback for trading its insider knowledge and the music was played without any distortion of market forces that payola is often thought to create. The label paid to play what was already going to be played.

## GIVEN THE RULES, CHARTS WERE SO BENT THEY WERE STRAIGHT

The second scam is known as chart-hyping – promotional techniques used by record labels to 'hype the chart' and get a song into the Top 40, as the gap between 41 and 40 is way bigger than 40 and 39. Once in the charts, momentum would carry you upwards. One label executive famously claimed that the most important form of transportation was the 'bandwagon' – as everyone wanted to be on it! Charts made the bandwagon more visible, and therefore more popular.

Long before electronic point-of-sale systems provided universal data on what songs the public was purchasing, chart companies had to deal with imperfect information – asking a select few shops to report their sales and extrapolating from the surveys. (Shamefully, television and radio measurements still resort to similar extrapolative techniques today.)

For a record label to hype its song into the charts, all it needed to know was which shops the chart company was surveying and then send in fake buyers to purchase multiple quantities of the record to ramp up demand. Better still, these canny promoters often had intimate relationships with the select few influential retailers, offering anything from free goods to holidays to get their co-operation. A pencil mark in the diary to indicate a sale was all that was needed to move the needle. Once a song had charted, it would get the promotional momentum needed to produce a positive return on investment.

## THE RULES FOR CERTIFICATION WERE SO BENT THEY WERE STRAIGHT

The third example of warped behaviour is certification, where albums were awarded gold and platinum status upon reaching a sales threshold of 500,000 and 1 million sales respectively. To understand how this process got bent out of shape, we need to differentiate between shipments (what labels delivered to retailers) and sales (what customers purchased). Certification was based on the former, not the latter. What went unsold was returned to the label's warehouse with no downside for the retailers. The undercurrent that led to over-shipments was the 'sale or return' stance retailers took: if the label asked the retailer 'How many Guns N' Roses albums do you want?', the retailer would reply with 'How many will you give me?' More was better than some.

Record label executive bonuses, meanwhile, were based on shipments, not sales. If the label manufactured and distributed a million copies of a new record it would qualify for platinum certification and executives would hit the jackpot. If that record didn't sell (what was known as a 'stiff') and the retailer returned half a million copies, this would obviously affect the label's finances, but not the platinum certification or the bonus of the executive. This is the origin of the expression 'ship platinum, return gold'.

These are three of my greatest hits in the long list of music-business skulduggery, and I could name a hundred more – but this type of thing isn't confined to music. Political lobbyists have always had their own version of payola, where they accept cash from wealthy donors in exchange for exclusive access to politicians they were going to meet anyway. Financial traders have long played their own game of chart hyping, knowing when to go long on a stock that is about to enter a market within a market such as the FTSE 100 or Dow Jones Industrial Average, and when to short it just before it falls out. And company directors who focus solely on quarterly earnings will often design their own certification system for determining executive pay, setting short-term targets that are easy to reach but can cause pain long after bonuses have been paid out.

Music is a microcosm for good (and bad) behaviour everywhere. The reason the industry was able to game its own system was control of a market, control of a crowd and (most importantly) the copyright. In both legal matters and conventional economics, syntax matters. Copyright stands for the right to control copying.

This right came to a sudden and alarming halt when the music industry and its customers woke up to Napster in June 1999. Overnight, millions of fans found themselves able to swap and exchange music files using the novel MP3 format. If you had a fast-enough internet connection, Napster would allow you to download any pop song within seconds without spending a penny. Within ten months of its launch, Napster had over 10 million users and had spawned many copycats.

Rather than 'embrace the internet wholeheartedly' (as *The Economist* suggested), the record labels embarked on a decade-long journey of trying to reject the changes it brought. In so doing, they also rejected the opportunities the internet could bring. Instead of granting popular digital models like Napster a licence to make them legitimate, the labels used litigation to fight them, for fear of upsetting the revenues that were still pouring in from those pallets of CDs.

In late 1999, the Recording Industry Association of America (RIAA), representing the record labels of the United States, successfully sued Napster, claiming it had facilitated piracy of music on an unprecedented scale. In 2002, the RIAA sued the illegal file-sharing site Madster (formerly Aimster), and the Metro-Goldwyn-Mayer Studios Inc. (MGM) sued Grokster, another file-sharing site, the following year. Soon after, the RIAA labels sued the developers of LimeWire. It was the Whack-A-Mole school of litigation, and the moles kept popping up. The energy (not to mention the money) the lawyers and lobbyists spent trying to whack them created an unwanted side effect: increased consumer awareness of the incredible 'free lunch' services the file-sharing sites provided. When the Motion Picture Association of America (MPAA) went after the BitTorrent tracker The Pirate Bay in its home country of Sweden in 2006, the media backlash was so huge it inspired a feature film aptly titled *TPB AFK: The Pirate Bay Away From Keyboard*.

While Whack-A-Mole was playing out among the illegal streaming services, in 2004 the RIAA also embarked on its most controversial strategy: suing individual consumers. By the spring of 2007, the RIAA admitted that more than 18,000 individuals had been sued by its member companies and news reports showed the number as of October 2007 to be at least 30,000. If the litigation route was doing a bad job at losing this unwinnable battle, the public relations offensive was about to get much worse.

In 2004, the US recording industry pivoted from litigation against teenagers to engaging with them by partnering with Apple and the soft drink giant Pepsi to promote 100 million free download codes on the fledgling iTunes service – one free download with every winning bottle purchased. The television ad campaign was set to Green Day's uber-hip cover of 'I Fought the Law', originally penned by Sonny Curtis and performed by his band The Crickets. It's been covered by many bands, including The Clash, and featured lingering close-ups of pensive kids who had been prosecuted for illegal file-sharing, bannered with words like 'incriminated', 'accused' and 'busted' in convict-style fonts. Let that be a lesson to any thirsty teenager watching: these kids had broken the law, and they hadn't won.

The ad concluded with a teenage girl sitting by her Apple laptop, describing herself as one of the kids who was prosecuted for downloading music from the internet. She leans back from her computer with confidence and says: 'I'm here to announce, in front of everyone, we're still going to download music free off of the internet,' before declaring 'and there's not a thing anyone can do about it' and chuckling the commercial to its conclusion. The difference: this former music thief would hereby be downloading her music legally.

The idea was to fight free with free. Pepsi would legally give songs away from the iTunes store. But the download code bargain had a catch: the music may have been made free, but the Pepsi was not. Sugary soft drinks were the loss leader to rescue copyright from the thieves that surrounded it. Yet the promotion didn't increase the sales of Pepsi. Not because the kids didn't want free music – they just didn't need to buy a bottle of Pepsi to get it.

These kids were crafty: by simply walking into a grocery store, grabbing a bottle from the fridge cabinet and angling it against the light, you could read the code underneath the cap, note it down and get the music literally for free. No need to spend money on Pepsi or damage your teeth any further. As the teenage star of the advert predicted, they would still download music for free and there wasn't a thing anybody could do about it – not even the soft drinks industry.

For an industry that was fast running out of ideas to fight what the consumer clearly wanted – easy, frictionless access to digital music – it was a terrible outcome. Every time execs came up with a new idea to counter digital disruption, they wound up shooting themselves in the foot. File-sharing had become big business, but this market for free goods was without a viable business model. To other creative industries, it was digital anarchy, and fear crept in that it would soon spread to destroy their incomes. They had reason to be frightened. As the internet pipes got bigger, so did the size of files that could be transferred – putting high-resolution audio, television and film next in line.

It looked like a tug-of-war: consumers wanted frictionless access to all the world's music, and the industry wanted to retain control. Consumers were happily swinging to the digital vine that offered faster, cheaper, neater and cooler access to all the world's music, whereas the industry clung on to the old vine and aggressively refused to take part.

Rather than grasp the new vine of opportunity, the music industry redoubled its resistance and the situation worsened.

Piracy was out of control, and recorded music revenues were cratering. Adding insult to injury, the industry's chosen response – attacking the consumer – was creating a PR backlash. Some of the individuals targeted by the RIAA were economically vulnerable, and the settlements extracted would only prove profitable to the law firms leading the prosecutions. For outside observers, this type of behaviour wasn't going to win many hearts and would persuade even fewer minds. The industry had got itself stuck in sinking sand, spending millions on litigation, losing billions in revenue, and losing its cool – which is not a good look in the music industry.

It was during this chaotic time that I was trying to get into the music business. I was knocking on any door I could to see if a business seemingly being run by lawyers would even consider hiring an economist. It was a losing battle and learning why the labels didn't employ any economists was a painful process.

My first job interview was with a major label that was part of the same corporate structure as a well-known hardware device maker. When I arrived at reception, I saw a billboard poster of the hardware device maker's own laptop towering above me, promoting features similar to that of its competitor Apple, namely: ripping, mixing and burning music.

I took the lift to the 34th floor to meet the music division of this corporate giant. It was just me, an economist, hoping to invent a job description (as I had tired of waiting for one), facing three lawyers well aware that their industry was rapidly losing every legal battle. This conversation, I thought to myself, was going to be interesting.

They first asked me what I thought was the biggest challenge facing their company. My mind travelled back down the elevator to the billboard poster that greeted me at reception. 'Your greatest challenge is your own laptop,' I answered. Realising I was already stepping on eggshells, I continued: 'You advertise your latest laptop by promoting the latest features of ripping, mixing and burning, yet you are suing the customer for doing just that – ripping, mixing and burning.' That was when the interview concluded.

My first lesson as an aspiring 'rockonomist' was that there are consequences to pointing out inconvenient truths. It was naive of the company to ignore that its own hardware marketing campaign promoted the same piracy for which it was suing consumers. But there are better ways, I learned, to open a conversation with a potential employer. It was also a lesson in just how much disarray the recorded music industry had got itself into.

I quickly realised that if I were to finally break in, dealing with inconvenient truths would become my business. To create my ideal job in the face of resistance, I needed an argument that could be my trump card. Then, back in Scotland, among a stack of out-of-date books about traditional media economics, I found it: a poorly edited interview with the Los Angeles-based company BigChampagne. What this company was doing taught me that even if I was struggling to get a job as an economist, the industry simply couldn't get by without economics.

BigChampagne measured everything, from traditional charts to digital streams and even illegal file-sharing activity. That impressed me, but it was who they were selling this data to that impressed me more. Among BigChampagne's clients were the promotional departments at the big record labels. While the lawyers were suing the pirates out of existence, the labels were paying for BigChampagne's data on the behaviour of those same pirates. It wasn't just that the left hand was not speaking to the right hand; it was worse – the left hand was valuing something that the right was being paid to punish. BigChampagne's co-founder and CEO Eric Garland had a mantra: 'Popular is popular wherever it is popular.' If you were popular on illegal file-sharing sites, you would also become popular on legal venues like iTunes – and vice versa. BigChampagne made visible the legitimate popularity previously hidden within these new digital Peer-to-Peer (P2P) platforms, and thereby helped to make the visible become more popular. I needed something to justify hiring an economist in the music industry, and finally I had found it.

As Tarzan Economics well understands, suing the consumer for file-sharing may seem like a good idea but, as we'll return to later, the opposite of a good idea can also be a good idea. And in this case that meant that using the data generated by this illegal activity to promote artists could also be a winning strategy. If only the two departments in the same company talked to each other, they could have discovered this themselves. But then they wouldn't have needed an economist.

Learning that data on music piracy existed, and that it was being used by the record labels, reminded me of how people often respond to an upward trend in crime statistics. There are usually three camps: the majority will say that crime is on the up. The second, the minority, recognises that the rise could be down to improvements in reporting crime or, better still, increasing the rate of catching criminals. The third, an outlier, chooses to 'read the small print' to ascertain if the definition of what constitutes a crime has changed during the period observed. BigChampagne's ability to measure crime led to the same split decision: if piracy of a particular artist was increasing, the lawyers would be getting worried about intellectual property being stolen, whereas the promotion departments would recognise that they had a hit on their hands.

Ten years after Napster launched, the industry was in despair, with estimates suggesting there were forty illegal downloads for every legal download. Efforts to deter piracy were evidently doing more harm than good. The industry had spent a decade thinking it could force this problem to go away, but instead it just got bigger. Something had to give. At some point, the industry needed to let go of its old business model and grab hold of a new one, or, as *The Economist* suggested a decade earlier, 'embrace the internet wholeheartedly'.

This is where the wider applicability of Tarzan Economics really comes into play as a framework for navigating us from moments of staring into the abyss to movements where you force disruption as opposed to having it forced upon you. As industry technologist Jim Griffin put it in 2009: 'We cling to this vine that keeps us off the jungle floor [ . . . ] The trick is figuring out when to let go of that old vine and when to embrace that new vine.' The industry was desperate to hold on to its old vine yet not willing to swing to the new vine. It wasn't yet ready to monetise the activity it was trying to criminalise.

At the root of this was a lack of understanding of where the value lay in those pallets of music. There are countless examples of how we often struggle to define the nature of what we're buying and selling. I proposed a surprisingly simple framework to help us do that, a framework that reveals the true nature of the goods being traded.

The framework focused on four different categories of goods – public, private, common and toll. A 'private good' is one for which two conditions hold. First, the good is excludable. This means the owner of the good can deny others access (build a fence) or the law can build a legal fence by creating enforceable property rights in the good (criminalising theft). Second, consumption of the good is what's termed rivalrous (or scarce). That is, if I consume the good, you can't, and vice versa. A meal in a restaurant is a private good – you can only access it in terms defined by the restaurant (so it's excludable), and if I order the meal you can't have it (so, it's rivalrous).

A 'public good', by contrast, is non-excludable and non-rivalrous – national defence is a good example. If the nation is protected against foreign invaders, it is very difficult to exclude particular persons from the protection. And if I get the benefits of a strong national defence, it doesn't interfere with you getting the same benefits. Government intervention is often justified in the name of providing a public good, as free markets often don't work with these types of goods – if a good is non-excludable and non-scarce, then nobody will pay for it.

Although anti-piracy campaigns from the music and film industries have tried to link piracy with theft, intellectual property is not a pure private good. The law can create excludability for information goods, but information goods are not rivalrous. If I download an MP3 file it doesn't affect your ability to do so and vice versa. How do we categorise goods like recorded music that satisfy enforceability but are not scarce?

Toll goods can extract value from consumers because the good creates value that can be captured by restricting access. A highway toll is a good example: it is both non-rivalrous (anyone can use it without diminishing others' usage providing traffic is manageable) but excludable (access can be restricted).

You will have noticed we're missing a corner of the matrix here – goods that are non-excludable, but still rivalrous. Those are 'common pool goods'. The stock of fish in the ocean may be a common pool good, assuming it is either impossible or too costly to enforce fishing limits. Common pool goods are often referred to as the 'tragedy of the commons' because unrestricted access to a resource such as fish stocks ultimately dooms the resource because of over-exploitation. This occurs because the benefits of exploitation accrue to individuals, while the costs of exploitation are distributed across all those exploiting the resource. Our current climate crisis is a very good example of this.*

**PUBLIC, PRIVATE, TOLL AND COMMON GOODS**

| | *Excludable* | *Non-Excludable* |
|---|---|---|
| *Rivalrous* | **Private Good** e.g. food, clothing, furniture | **Common Pool Good** e.g. the fish in the sea |
| *Non-Rivalrous* | **Toll Good or Club Good** e.g. bridges, toll roads | **Public Good** e.g. national defence |

*Source: Author's adaptation*

The matrix underlines the first of our three inconvenient truths that continue to challenge the media industries: digital content is not rivalrous, and never will be, no matter how cheap an MP3 file may become. Copyright law gives me the authority to try to exclude you from making copies of my writings, but it does not make your use of the information – reading the words in this book – rivalrous.

The second inconvenient truth is just how 'non-excludable' recorded music has become. As an illustration, it took three

* There is one footnote to the matrix – the 'club good'. This is a good that has an optimal number of consumers. If too many consume the good, the joint value of the group will be reduced because of crowding effects. The term 'club good' is used because the nature of most clubs is that members can share the benefits, but non-members can be excluded.

years to sell 1 billion tracks on iTunes, whereas BigChampagne estimated that during the same period around 1 billion tracks were being traded on P2P networks every month.

The third inconvenient truth was that the industry had unbundled itself by licensing the Apple iTunes model and allowing consumers to cherry-pick one or two tracks for 79 pence (or 99 cents) each as opposed to paying a whopping £7.99 ($9.99) for the album. The impact of this is well known, but what isn't is that it was never supposed to happen. The original iTunes licensing agreement was supposed to be a controlled experiment within the niche Apple user base. When Steve Jobs stunned the market by putting iTunes on the mass-market Windows personal computers in October 2003, later describing it as 'like giving a glass of ice water to somebody in hell', labels realised unbundling had gone mainstream.

In adapting to digital distribution, the music industry faced this exact challenge: how do we extract revenue from rampant piracy on P2P networks when the files being traded are neither excludable nor rivalrous in consumption? As we've already discussed, the first decade of digital disruption saw the recording industry try to solve this problem by tightly gripping on to the old vine of their traditional business model, under the belief that they could create some form of excludability and scarcity in these new digital markets.

Let's put the matrix to work to see how digital distribution changed the nature of music as a good in the market. Before digital platforms, the only two options for consumers were either paying for physical CDs or concert tickets, or attending free open performances that were limited by the venue's attendance limits. Digital distribution opened up two non-rivalrous options – rights-managed legal downloads or MP3 files traded on P2P platforms.

This posed a problem for the music industry. For consumers, illegal P2P offered everything for free, as a non-excludable, non-rivalrous asset. Meanwhile the legal route required paying for limited access to files with limited transferable value – a tough sales pitch for any marketing department!

Let's revisit the framework to show what happened to copyright when it lost the right to control copying:

***PUBLIC, PRIVATE, TOLL AND COMMON GOODS***

| | *Excludable* | *Non-Excludable* |
| --- | --- | --- |
| *Rivalrous* | **A physical CD or concert ticket**<br>The in-store security guard forces you to pay | **A free open-air concert**<br>At risk of cancellation due to overcrowding |
| *Non-Rivalrous* | **Digital music files**<br>Non-transferable Digital Rights Management (DRM) files | **MP3 files traded on P2P**<br>Unlimited and transferable |

*Source: Author*

The industry needed to somehow rescue music from public good status (where markets typically fail as no one needs to pay) and give up on the notion that it could ever return to a private good status (as scarcity had been lost for ever). Rather than selling a physical product that qualified as a pure private good, they had to accept the need to reinvent the market and impose a toll on accessing content that would never again be scarce.

Spotify did just that and got the £9.99 ($9.99) bundle back by introducing an 'option value' of what you could listen to, not what you did actually purchase. This moved the recording industry away from actual CD sales and towards a more actuarial model of option and risk where the bundles value was less about what you did with it and more about what you could do with it. The beauty of this simple framework remains as powerful today as it did back then; it showed not only an industry in which something had to give, but also that the market for its goods had changed irrevocably, and how it could reposition itself to deal with this disruption.

This is the biggest swing in the history of recorded music, and there's much to learn from why – and particularly *when* – it happened. But in order to understand what Spotify and streaming accomplished, we need to understand a concept central to how the music business (and many other businesses) sees the world, a deeply flawed and rather silly-sounding acronym: ARPU.

ARPU stands for Average Revenue Per User. It is a simple valuation of how much income is generated by a company's customers. In the case of the music industry, this would capture how much the average music-buyer spends each period on owning recorded music. It sounds simple but ARPU metrics can cause as many problems as they solve. For the music industry, one of the reasons why the first decade of digital disruption was so damaging was because of its failure to properly understand its own ARPU, and countless businesses and institutions have made the same mistake since.

At the core of the record industry's fear of pivoting to digital music was the fear that digital distribution would cannibalise existing revenues from CD and download sales: the old vine of ownership may have been dying, but it still produced an

ARPU that was preferable to what you could expect from the new vine of access. Why would you even contemplate letting go of what you had, when what you would need to cling on to instead would make you worse off?

The fear kicked in as initial attempts to launch legal alternatives to Napster failed – sites like Pressplay and Sony Connect (backed by a consortia of the major record labels) are still fondly remembered as the worst websites of all time. That fear was compounded by every subsequent failed attempt from the music labels to compete with the P2P sites. Measuring traditional ARPU wasn't giving them the confidence they needed to make the leap.

A protective mindset had developed: retaining those remaining lucrative music buyers (who were sometimes referred to as '£50-a-month man') was clearly more valuable than gambling on them being willing to spend £120 ($120) a year on an 'all-you-can-eat' Spotify subscription instead. Critics of the 'toll good' model of music streaming argued vehemently that letting go of their 'private good' status meant turning music buyers into streamers was forcing record labels to swap analogue dollars for digital dimes.

At the heart of this fear was the definition of the consumer, or music buyer. The average spend of '£50-a-month man' may have looked higher than with a subscription model, but that was hiding an important fact: although ARPU was high for those who were still purchasing music, the total number of people doing so was falling fast.

MusicWatch, a respected consultancy, has tracked developments in these key metrics for the United States across the two disruptive decades. (Note: a remarkably similar story exists for the UK.) Their ARPU data over time illuminates just how stubbornly the music industry clung to its 'old vine' of ownership.

Back in 1999, when Napster launched, over 170 million

**US MUSIC BUYERS AND THEIR AVERAGE SPEND**

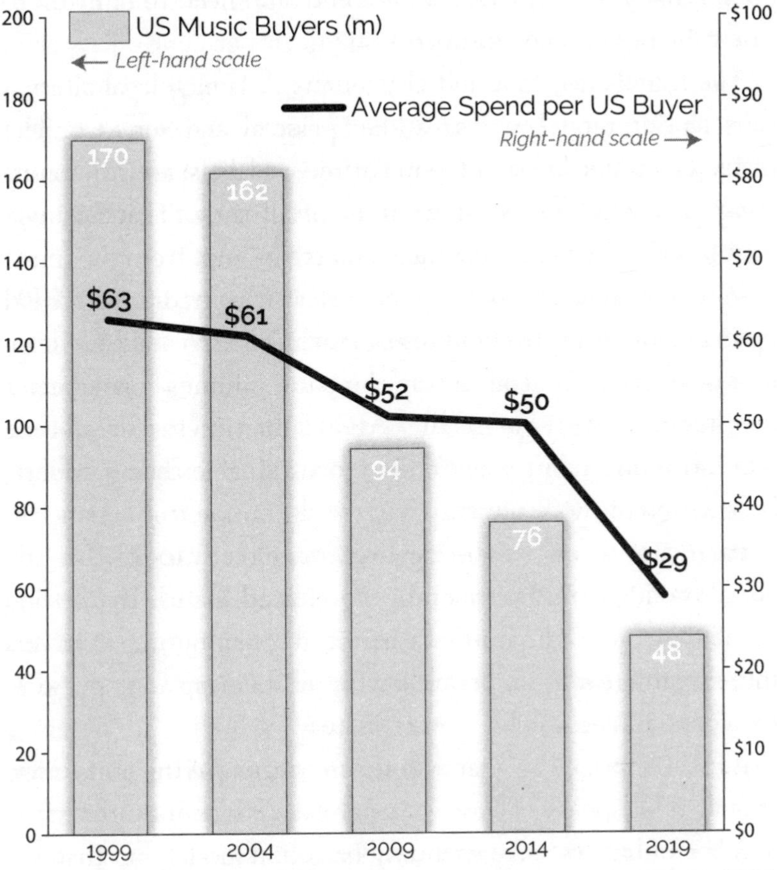


Source: MusicWatch, Inc.

Americans bought CDs and the average spend per buyer was \$63 per annum. Though individuals surely varied in how much they spent, what is striking is that the vast majority of those over-thirteen-year-olds bought something as opposed to nothing – they were ones, not zeros. In the ten years that followed, music moved from a private to a public good thanks to Napster and other P2P sites. When the labels started suing customers, inadvertently raising awareness of illegal P2P platforms, both reach and revenue collapsed. The share of Americans who bought music fell by over 40 per cent to less than 100 million. Their average spend dropped to $52, 20 per cent off its peak in 2000, and less than half that of the ARPU generated by a subscription model with an agreed price of $120 per year. The majority of the US adult population was now giving record companies zero. Fears about cannibalisation were increasingly misplaced; you cannot cannibalise zero.*

When the majority of the population isn't buying, you should optimise for reach rather than revenue. Growing your audience in a new market – converting the zeros to ones – is a better long-term strategy for scaling ARPU than trying to squeeze more revenue from a dwindling market of existing buyers. Now let go of those old bar charts and grab on to the new.

Paying for access rather than ownership really took off in July 2011 when Spotify launched in the United States. By the end of that year, MIDiA, another respected consultancy, estimated there were 4.5 million people paying an average of $75 per year to access all the world's music instead of buying it. By 2019, that had ballooned to 93 million Americans paying an average annual retail price of $81 – 55 per cent more than the same number of buyers were spending back in 2009.

The rising bars in the chart below illustrates how the industry reaped the reward from reaching out to the new vine.

The subscribers captured in this chart don't show the whole picture, however. Accounting for what's termed sub-account holders – members of a family plan – today there are over 110

* This fearing of cannibalisation has an important precedent. In 1994, the Blockbuster chain began making SEGA games available for rental, much to the annoyance of the gaming giant's sales teams. However, these fears were misplaced as sales went up soon afterwards.

**US MUSIC SUBSCRIBERS AND THEIR AVERAGE SPEND**

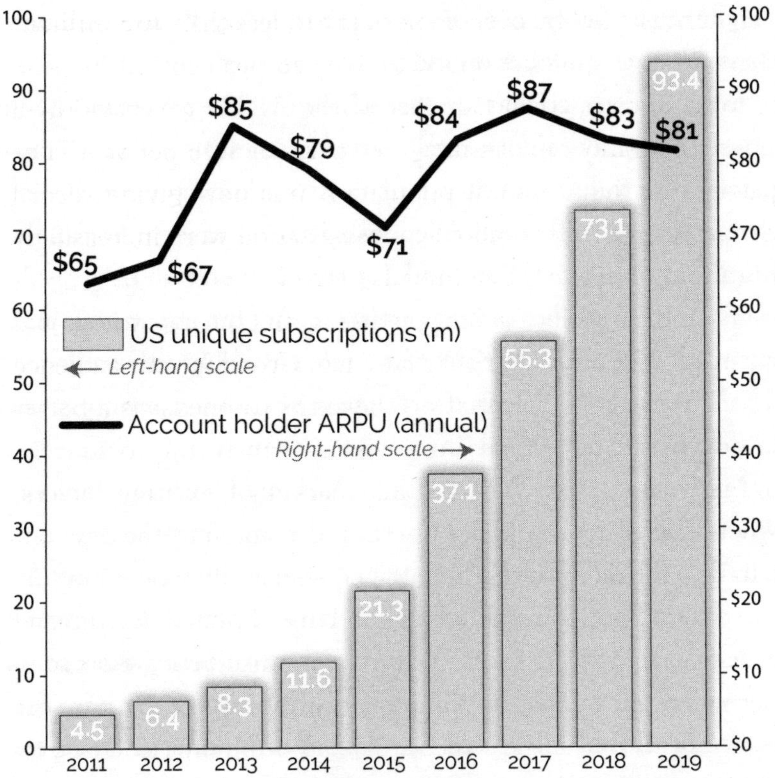


*Source: MIDiA*

million Americans enjoying the benefits of account holders paying for something that always has been and always will be voluntary to pay. In addition, there's an array of advertising services such as YouTube that are free to the consumer and compensate the rights holder. Put these two formats together and you have an American music industry that's grown at double-digit rates for the past four years – a feat many other media sectors can view only with envy.

*

ARPU and discussion of broader trends in listening fall under the umbrella of macroeconomics. But we're also going to need to get into the microeconomics of pivoting. And microeconomics is about the impact on individual creators.

Even if your consumers are changing their behaviour en masse, you may see partners – artists, in music's case – comparing unit values in old-versus-new markets and concluding that letting go of that old vine looked like a bad idea. For all the headlines of subscription models driving double-digit growth, even more headlines convey artists' concerns about how they got paid. The most famous came from Radiohead's frontman Thom Yorke, who referred to the new vine of streaming as 'the last desperate fart of a dying corpse'.

Like many artists, Yorke was disillusioned with a new model where the unit value was a fraction of a cent per stream, compared to the old model where the equivalent unit value was £10 per album. But this was a bad comparison, and bad comparisons lead to bad mistakes. Winning an argument with £10 on one side, and £0.005 on the other, is impossible. Unless, that is, we break out of the old framework and understand all the potential unit values of a music listener.

We'll call this framework the hierarchy of exploitation, illustrated in the diagram overleaf.

On either end of the illustration sit the two extremes of music consumption. To the left is the passive consumption of FM radio, which is a one-to-many broadcast model, with no individual interactions by consumers. To the right of this illustration is the highly interactive action of retail, where the consumer 'exhausts' the intellectual property by offering their money to own content, whether as a CD or download. To underline the importance of ownership, the purchaser can even sell a CD on the second-hand market for a capital gain and not

**HIERARCHY OF EXPLOITATION**

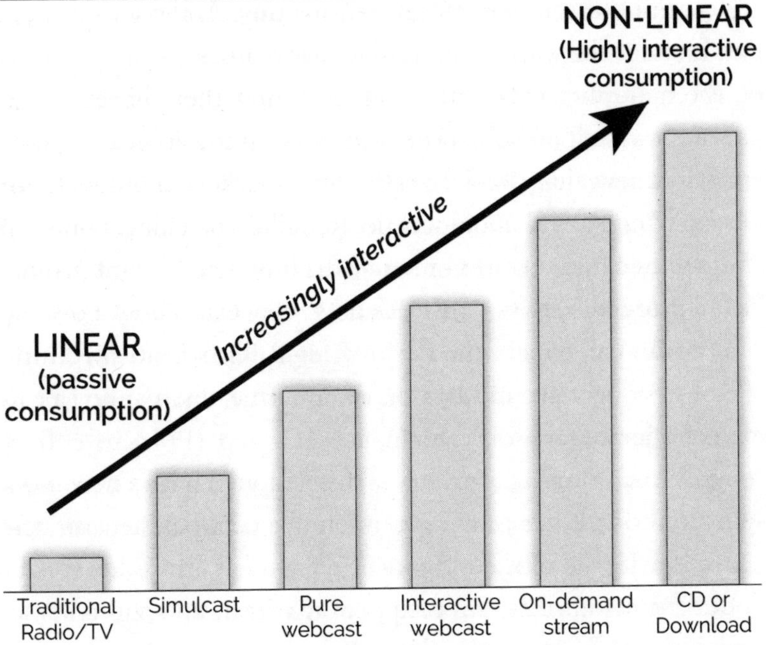


*Source: Author*

have to pay anyone else. In between these two traditional forms of exploitation (transient radio listening and download-to-own) are what we can call the new entrants – the various forms of streaming music – arranged from left to right according to their respective levels of interactivity. The height of each bar tells us how much more 'unit value' is derived from each.

The closer the customer feels to a sense of ownership ('this is my playlist') and the more value they realise, the more the rights holder should be rewarded. The less the sense of ownership ('this is my streaming service's own playlist'), the less the rights holder should be rewarded. This is the hierarchy of consumption. So, the newer, more interactive digital platforms should have provided more revenue for artists than radio airplay did.

To calm the critics of the streaming model, I would suggest looking at it this way: in most countries, when a song is played on the radio, both the artist and the songwriter get paid. The use of the word 'most' captures an inconvenient truth, as there are still a few that don't compensate artists, including North Korea, Zimbabwe, Democratic Republic of Congo and (of course) the United States of America. If we take the UK's most listened-to radio show – BBC Radio 2's *Breakfast Show* – then the songwriter can expect the Performing Right Society for Music (PRS) to collect around £90 on their behalf, and the artist can expect Phonographic Performance Limited (PPL) to collect roughly £60. Stare at a royalty statement which lists £150 for a spin alongside £0.005 for a stream and you can understand the fear of letting go of the old vine.

But the economics don't support that fear. A 'spin' on BBC Radio 2's *Breakfast Show* will reach 8 million people; you need therefore to divide the £150 by the 8 million pairs of ears to get a comparative unit value per listener, and this results in £0.00002 – which is less than half a percent of the £0.005 that you would get from one unique person on a streaming service. What's more, this is not an either/or comparison as those who listen to it on the radio may be more inclined to stream it on Spotify. To bring this calculation full circle, had those 8 million listeners streamed the song on Spotify (which is not beyond the realms of possibility), a cheque of £40,000 would be paid across to the artist and songwriter – not £150. 'Not too shabby' as some Americans like to say.

The hierarchy in our earlier graph explains this – radio is a more passive form of exposure than interactive streaming, as you get what you're given. If you don't like the DJ's taste in music, then tough. At the other end of the hierarchy, if you don't like that song on streaming then you can skip it and, providing you do so in the first thirty seconds, the artist won't receive a dime. Therefore, radio pays less, and interactive streaming pays more.

For all the criticism of the 'per-listener value' of streaming, what was missing was the microeconomics of the hierarchy of exploitation – if you want more control over the goods being sold, you need to pay for it. When we compare the new vine of streaming to CD sales, we have no idea how often the CD was played – just like we have no idea if books are actually read. When we compare it with radio, we need to capture the value of each listener, not the aggregate value of them all. Radio is a broadcast, a one-to-many experience, whereas streaming is a narrowcast, not a broadcast – it measures ones, not many ones at once.

Hindsight can fool you into thinking you have perfect vision. The success of Spotify and music streaming has led many to suggest that the music industry's experience would be easy to replicate. Of course, it's not that simple. To use that old adage from a Scottish tourist office: 'If you wanted to get somewhere, you wouldn't start from here.' I've often heard people say, 'Why doesn't every industry just "do a Spotify"?' Why don't all industries that are based on intellectual property throw their collective hats into an 'all-you-can-eat' model and enjoy similar double-digit growth rates? As we have learnt, you need to dig deep into the specific macro- and microeconomics of your industry to gain the confidence to swing from the old to the new. That isn't easy. And we haven't even taken into account one of the most important elements of the music industry's experience – the role of culture.

It is worth learning the cultural reasons why the music industry's transformation happened at a different pace, and in different ways, in each respective country. The stories of Sweden and Germany illustrate the extremes. The first moved first, the second moved last. Sweden (and its neighbour Norway) can lay claim to being the birthplace of streaming. Both countries have a reputation for being early adopters when it comes to new technologies. Norway was the first country to switch off all FM radio stations in 2018, and while Sweden already functions in a cashless environment it will probably go further and become the first country to give up on cash completely.

The same trend occurred in music. Sweden was an early adopter of piracy – Swedes were responsible for building some of the most powerful piracy sites like uTorrent, The Pirate Bay and Kazaa. Indeed, many of the engineers who built them switched from 'poacher to gamekeeper' and moved over to build Spotify. After all, if you want to build something that's both legal and better than piracy, it helps if you hire the people who built the best piracy sites. Hal Varian, chief economist at Google and co-author of *Information Rules*, has a simple rule for choosing future strategies – 'To forecast the future look at what rich people do and scale it.' My adaptation of his maxim is 'Look at what Sweden is doing and just scale that instead.'

Sweden's quickness to adopt is, I believe, an outgrowth of its culture. Free-market economics argues for fostering a risk-taking entrepreneurial culture by removing the societal safety net. Without the state safety net to catch you when you fall, the logic goes, people are encouraged to be more entrepreneurial – to take a risk and start a new business rather than play it safe and rely on the state. The fact that this leads to a widening gap between rich and poor is just a function of this risk-taking mentality – winners get to win big.

But my observations of Swedes make me think that the opposite of this idea may also be a good idea. Sweden has a robust social safety net, yet it produces the same level of entrepreneurial activity as countries without. Sweden is renowned for how it supports both maternity and paternity leave and the childcare it provides to help parents once they're back at work. But Sweden also offers support that allows workers to simply not work. Swedish employment law allows staff to take sabbaticals to pursue education or even to try launching their own start-up. Should that start-up fail, they can then return to their previous role in their old company.

Pivoting through disruption involves spotting how more safety nets may actually mean more risk-taking. And with less inequality between rich and poor, there are more chances a Swede's new idea reaches a critical mass as more people can afford it.

Swedes took to streaming and Spotify from 2009, a full ten years after Napster launched in the United States. By September 2010 Spotify was celebrating its 10 millionth user. Sweden was viewed by the labels and publishers as the golden child of the global music industry, standing alone in reporting growing revenues while everywhere else was in terminal decline. Sweden had completed swinging from the old to the new by 2012, with 60 per cent of the Swedish music market's revenues coming from streaming.

The same year, Spotify launched in Germany, where the music market was still three-quarters dominated by the ownership of CDs, with downloads comprising the majority of the remainder. While some Swedish record labels were eschewing this physical format entirely, their German counterparts were experiencing unwavering demand. Germany held on to the old vine of CDs for longer than any other European market. Germany's tendency to be a late mover was not restricted to music. While high-street bookstores such as Waterstones and Barnes & Noble were losing out to Amazon in most major Western markets, Germans continued to flock to their high-street bookshop, Thalia. Even German home-DVD sales had been virtually flat as late as 2011, whereas my local charity shops in North London had even stopped accepting them.

In Germany a newspaper still means an actual printed product involving paper, whereas in most other markets the way of consuming news had already transitioned to the smartphone or iPad. If you arrived at a German airport as recently as 2018, you wouldn't have been surprised if the taxi driver only accepted cash; in Sweden most drivers had moved on to only accepting cards.

A telling way to show the different dynamics of these two countries is to look at the percentage of the population that was addressable (i.e. unique – someone with two phones can't be counted twice), smartphone-enabled (BlackBerry phones don't count) and financially inclusive (with a debit or credit card). After all, without a smartphone or a credit card, there's little chance of subscribing to a streaming service.

Omdia, a consultancy, has modelled the addressable market in both countries since Spotify's original launch. The chart below shows that, by the time Spotify launched in Germany in 2012, almost half the Swedish population was 'addressable' (in possession of a smartphone and a debit or credit card) whereas only a quarter of Germans ticked the same three boxes – a remarkable difference given the similar geographies and economies.

By 2019, however, Germany had drawn level with Sweden (with two-thirds of its population addressable), pointing to a 'late adopters, great implementers' culture – where those who move late can often catch up fast. The lesson of Tarzan Economics is to consider the forces that dictate when a country reaches out to the new vine to propel itself forward: is it the demand for streaming, supply of smartphones, or is it more to do with culture? Some markets will swing slower and more belatedly than others. But they all work out how to let go.

***TOTAL ADDRESSABLE MARKET AS % OF POPULATION***

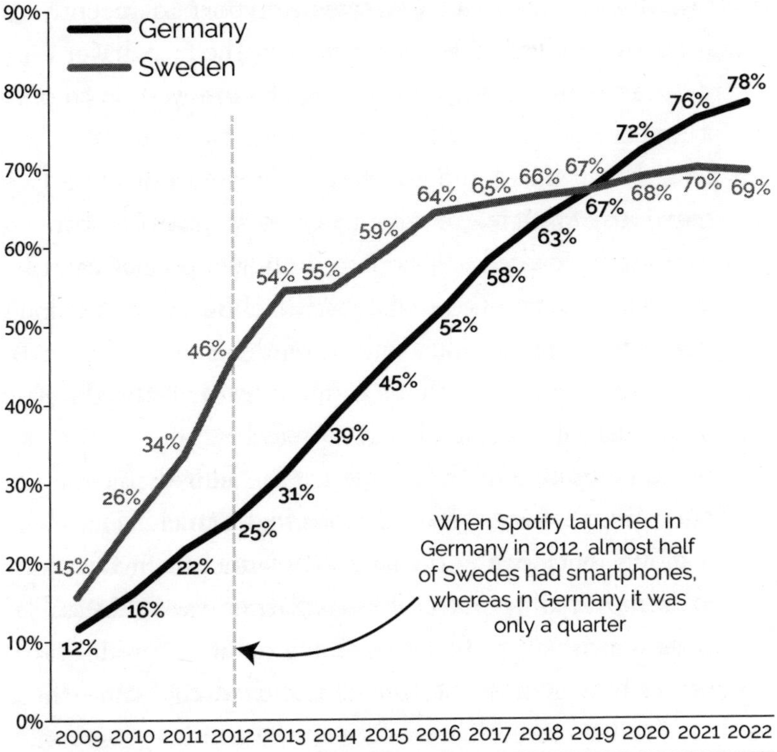


*Source: OMDIA*

**GLOBALISATION BUT NOT AS WE KNOW IT**

The music industry is growing again – much to the envy of many other industries. Recorded music revenues passed $20 billion in 2019 and are now just 14 per cent off their 2001 peak. The global value of copyright, which factors in the revenues to songwriter-collecting societies and publishers, passed $30 billion in 2018 and may never have been higher. The future is bright and it's global: there are 7.6 billion people on the planet and not many of them don't like music – so how will this global recovery story play out?

Classical economics teaches us that poor countries are supposed to catch up with rich countries due to the marginal productivity of capital – a dollar in an emerging market goes further than it does in the established ones. That logic is controversial for two reasons: firstly it may not be true, and secondly it may even go in reverse – the more there is globalisation the more the rich widen the gap on the poor due to free movement of capital and labour.

Music matters because it got there first, thanks to globalisation of streaming, where both the music being made and the customer are transcending borders. These forces should unleash globalisation of a global business – causing America's dominance to wane. Yet the reverse has happened – since the launch of Spotify in the United States in 2011 the business has got bigger (up by a fifth) and more American (up from a quarter to now over a third).

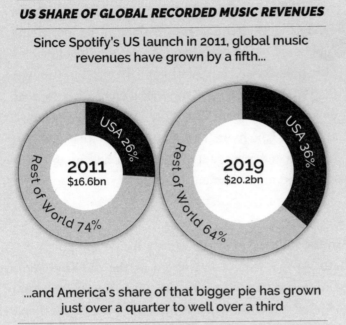

### *US SHARE OF GLOBAL RECORDED MUSIC REVENUES*

Since Spotify's US launch in 2011, global music revenues have grown by a fifth...

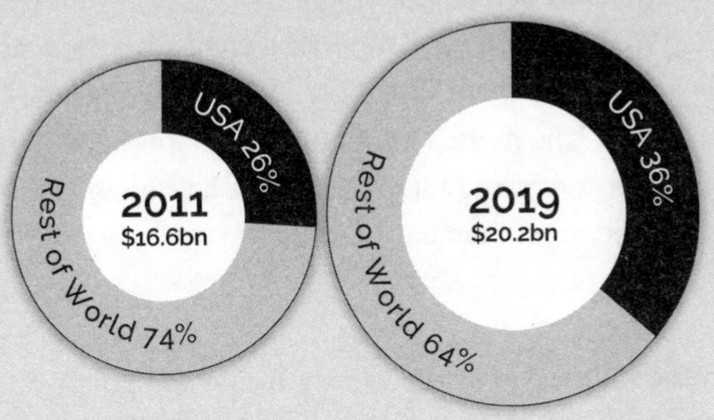


...and America's share of that bigger pie has grown just over a quarter to well over a third

*Source: IFPI*

There are some obvious reasons why this has happened – America is the biggest market, and it has grown at one of the fastest rates. The exchange rate may have helped too, as the dollar has risen steadily against a basket of currencies since 2011. Also the slowdown in Japan – which hasn't changed in value in over four years as it remains dominated by CD buyers – will have boosted American's global hegemony. But economics can only tell you so much, culture can tell you so much more.

A less obvious reason is that streaming playlists come without borders and the growing 'melting pot' of multicultural America can be viewed as both a cause and effect. The fact that there are so many cultures inside the United States – Asians, Africans, South Americans – all streaming music which originates from outside – K-pop, Afrobeats, Reggaeton – means that globalisation is happening within borders as well as across them. The more internally globalised a country is, the more it benefits from globalisation (i.e. America is the biggest and most globalised, and has benefited more than any other).

*

The music industry was the canary in the mine, but it taught itself to replace fear of letting go of the old vine and found the confidence to grab on to the new vine of streaming and kick-started a recovery that is now the envy of everyone else. Music recovered first because it got hit first. This wasn't intentional. The internet in the late 1990s was like a river that was relentlessly rising; it didn't choose who it flooded. It was the changing nature of the good being sold – non-excludable and non-scarce – that swept music up before anyone else. As the pipes of the internet became fatter, the tide rose further. Now (especially as we come to terms with the Covid-19 hangover) everyone is feeling the river around their feet. Now we all need to know when to let go.

Music won its war when it stopped fighting it. Beating piracy was never going to work unless you beat it at its own game. Stacking up the macro, micro and cultural arguments allowed the industry to let go of the old vine and swing: for reach, not revenue. Understanding how that happened will help you understand your own Tarzan dilemma, so you too can build the confidence to propel yourself forward. The confidence to know that holding on for too long only makes matters worse.

Music's 'first to suffer, first to recover' journey is clearly pervasive when you look around and see that so many other sectors are now feeling the river rise around their feet. Media sectors like newspapers, cinema and public-service broadcasting are all guilty of holding on. Why do we refer to the 'box office' or 'newspapers' any more? When YouTube footage is embedded into a public broadcast, just who is the public broadcaster?

That rising river travels beyond media, be it professional services like finance, which is staring down a 'blockchain barrel' of its own making, or a government that struggles to measure the digital disruption that surrounds it. Tarzan Economics is so pervasive that nearly everyone still needs confidence to know when to let go and overcome fear of the unknown. We've just learned that the confidence needed isn't so difficult to find.

We're all now finding ourselves facing a Napster moment. Tarzan Economics empowers anyone with confidence to stare into the darkness knowing there's light at the end of the tunnel, the confidence that disruption can be beaten at its own game. But the battle doesn't end there. Tarzan Economics also prepared the music industry for the next war: the war (fought primarily in the mind) being waged by merchants fighting for our increasingly scarce time and attention.

# 2

# PAYING ATTENTION

Swedes are natural early adopters; they instinctively like to get there first. They embraced illegal piracy first; dispensed with CDs first; engaged with legal streaming first; and now they're on track to get rid of cash before anyone else. They also got to the chorus first. As streaming took off in Sweden, two things started to happen: songs got shorter and the chorus got moved to the front.

I first noticed this when I entered Spotify's Stockholm reception back in 2012. Playing in the background was the music of Avicii (Tim Bergling), which had me hooked from the opening note. There was a serious buzz about Avicii inside Spotify; a hometown hero, the hope was that if either Spotify or Avicii exploded, the other would fall into the 'slipstream' and explode with it. Avicii's songs were catchy as hell, grabbing listeners from the outset with the chorus and never letting go.

I wasn't used to being hooked so quickly.

As a failed guitar player who never got further than stealing my big brother's Ibanez six-string (only for it to be returned with interest and injury), I had grown up with a different type of song structure: one that grew over time, building to a climax with a predictable verse-chorus-verse-chorus sequence followed by a guitar solo, then back to a climatic chorus before the final fade. Bon Jovi's 1986 anthem 'Livin' on a Prayer' – co-written by Desmond Child along with Jon Bon Jovi and Richie Sambora – was (and still is) a masterclass in this style of songwriting: a 4-minute-and-9-second yardstick by which to judge all other anthems. The band could be a distant dot on the horizon for thousands of fans in a packed stadium but when they sung that climatic last chorus – intimacy prevailed. They sang it to you.

The reason why that chorus works so well can be found in the key change at 3 minutes 23 seconds into the song, or what songwriters refer to as modulation – Bon Jovi jumps an entire minor-third up from the previous choruses. And that key change knocks listeners off balance so resoundingly because of its timing – as Todd Kemp of Belmont University points out, that pause before the chorus has an unexpected three beats rather than four.* For a non-technical description of modulation, try swigging back several pints of strong gassy lager (or a couple of bottles of plonk) and perform 'Livin' on a Prayer' at your local karaoke – you may draw attention for your efforts after 3 minutes and 23 seconds of vocal effort, but from that mother of all key changes onwards the crowd will disperse with pained face-palm aplenty as you fail miserably to reach that note. And that's the point. Many pop songs today are done and dusted by 3 minutes and 23 seconds.

Songs are getting shorter. Dan Kopf of Quartz points out that from 2013 to 2018 the average song on the *Billboard* Hot 100 fell from 3 minutes and 50 seconds to about 3 minutes and 30 seconds. Six per cent of hit songs were 2 minutes 30

* Todd A, 'The Perfect Illusion of a well-executed key change', *Medium*, September 2016

seconds or shorter in 2018. From hip hop to country, songs keep shrinking.*

Choruses are starting sooner, too. Analysis by *The Economist* and *Billboard* magazine reveals a striking trend. In the past, the number of hits with a chorus that began in the first fifteen seconds would hover at between 10 and 20 per cent. In 2018, that spiked to 40 per cent and shows little sign of subsiding. *The Economist* points to the first notes of Shawn Mendes's 'Señorita', which gets you to the chorus within the first 15 seconds and is a fixture throughout the song's 3 minutes 10 seconds.†

My gut reaction to all of this is that any aspiring songwriter would be 'livin' on a prayer' to think that today's attention spans could be stretched any further than 3 minutes and 23 seconds – the aforementioned tipping point in Bon Jovi's anthem. (As a music fan this is concerning, but it does mean fewer embarrassing key changes at the karaoke!)

What's changed? To answer that, we're going to talk about attention economics. Let's break that term down. Start with attention. Soundlounge CEO Ruth Simmons, who (along with Nigel Elderton of peermusic) helped pioneer the use of music in television commercials back in the 1980s, looks to children today to understand the attention spans of tomorrow. She has identified three stages in marketing to a child's attention: promise (5 seconds); anticipation (15–20 seconds); and the commitment (anything beyond 30 seconds). Point being, the seller has, at most, 30 seconds to make a promise, create anticipation and secure a commitment before the listener moves on. Hit songwriter Crispin Hunt points out that musical pleasure is about recognition: a song frames a melody, and when

* Kopf, Dan, 'The economics of streaming is making songs shorter' *Quartz*, 17 January 2019.

† 'The economics of streaming is changing pop songs', *The Economist*, October 2019.

the listener hears it repeated, the brain releases endorphins. Combine Simmons and Hunt, and you can conclude that starting with the chorus is going to be the best use of the 30 seconds of listener attention that you can count on.

The other part of attention economics is the economics. If rights holders only get paid after a song has been played for 30 seconds, then you need to hook a listener and keep them listening past the 30-second mark. What's more, if songs don't pay out any more for lasting any longer, it's entirely rational to write shorter songs: if a listener has a finite attention span, best to cram as many songs as you can into that tiny window. Canny writers write shorter tunes.

We've been here before, where the business affected the show (or the tail wagged the dog). The first iteration of the phonograph could only hold about two to three minutes of music. It is said Puccini used to deliberately write arias that could be cut into three-minute segments that could fit on one side of a 78 rpm disc, arguably making him the first ever pop writer. Elderton notes that during the late 1950s and early 1960s, the average duration of American pop songs fell to 2 minutes and 30 seconds. As the mafia owned and controlled jukeboxes across America, they insisted that a record was limited to 2 minutes 30 seconds, allowing them to boost their take-per-machine considerably.

Music is not the only medium that's changing its output to try to capture more of our attention. You see similar tactics employed by Netflix, YouTube advertisers and social media platforms. In a media landscape that has never been more crowded, the 'attention merchants' (as we'll come to understand them) have had to develop new tools to capture our attention – even when we don't want to give it to them. A&R executive and former Geffen Records CEO Neil Jacobson asks 'What price is your undivided attention?' when valuing the counterfactual of screening-out all other distractions; as we'll learn later, virtual reality (VR) is in pole position to find out the answer.

I now know why I can still remember hearing Avicii for the first time while waiting in Spotify's Stockholm reception a decade ago. He may have been born in 1989 (and tragically took his own life in 2018) but he still lived by the old mantra that was writ large on the staircase of the Brill Building, the home of many of the great songwriters in New York in the 1960s: 'Please don't bore us, get to the chorus.'

Boredom is so passé. Those who can remember life before the smartphone will recall how we used to occupy our downtime by gazing out of windows past the pile of stuff smartphones have replaced: cameras, hi-fi equipment, fax machines, televisions, books/e-readers, radios, typewriters, audio recorders, VCRs and more – a room full of stuff.

It was something we all did when we had nothing else to consume our attention. Today, we no longer stare through a piece of glass, but into one – our phones. Boredom simply isn't an option any more. The device that consumes so much of our attention shuttles endlessly between our pocket or bag and the palm of our hands. Even if the battery dies, we stare impatiently at the screen until it recharges enough for us to dive back in to the endless streams of content behind the black glass.

When it was hard to build distribution networks for content, media companies relied on boredom to increase the value of their products. Record companies asked artists to obey a strictly limited release schedule, and television channels were not always on air twenty-four hours a day. We now have enough competition for our scarce attention to make boredom a thing of the past. Digital has turned the supply-and-demand dynamics of media distribution on its head, from a surplus of boredom to a deficit of attention.

The big technology platforms understand this and optimise their products to make the acquisition of our attention feel frictionless: YouTube's Auto Play function loops video after video, sucking us into longer and longer viewing sessions; Instagram stories are ranked by recency, so we have to keep opening the app to check for updates from accounts you follow. Twitter and Facebook give us an eternal scroll of links, videos and posts. These streams of content are endless, but our attention is not. An oft-quoted (and heavily disputed) Microsoft study in 2015 suggested that, due to digital lifestyles, the human attention span had fallen to 8 seconds – less than that of a goldfish.* That infamous study is now older than the lifespan of most goldfish, and attention spans have probably got shorter since.

We may feel that our attention is a private good: scarce yet excludable, and under our control. But we're wrong. Author Tim Wu summed it up perfectly in his book *The Attention Merchants: The Epic Scramble to Get Inside Our Heads*. He says these merchants have hijacked our attention, effectively removing the excludability, increasing the scarcity and taking it out of our own control. As each of the new platforms seeks to monopolise our attention, none of them have considered the problems created when we exhaust this resource, something we will have all felt when we've spent too long looking at our screens.

A useful metaphor for understanding how scarce our attention has become is fossil fuels. We know that oil is scarce, but we don't know how scarce it is. We've had estimates in the past, but those estimates become obsolete with each new discovery. In 1919, David White, chief geologist of the United

* Andrew Littfield, 'No, you don't have the attention span of a goldfish', *Ceros*, January 2019.

States Geological Survey, wrote, 'the peak of production will soon be passed, possibly within three years'. The idea of 'peak oil' – that the rate of oil production would peak and irreversibly decline – is still disputed. The moment when oil reaches its peak has been debated ever since. A counterargument to 'peak oil' is that, thanks in part to technological progress, we know of more oil in the world today than we ever have before, and we continue to discover more at an increasing rate. Oil may be scarce, but its scarcity is unknown. We can switch this analogy from 'peak oil' to 'peak attention', as we are painfully aware of how scarce our attention spans are, but we don't know just how scarce; one could argue we are now entering a 'fracking era' of attention.

A good example is in your hands right now – provided you purchased the physical copy of this book. You will have a good idea of how long it will take you to read this book and would probably agree that there will be little else that could occupy your attention while reading it. But you also know there are more time-efficient ways to get the contents of this book into your head – such as on audiobook or even a podcast.

Reading books eats into scarce attention – often resulting in a zero-sum game, in which there is a clear winner (the object you spend your attention on) and a loser (everything else you could have spent your attention on). But consuming books using other mediums, such as audiobooks and podcasts, might not be the same kind of zero-sum game. There are some forms of attention – listening, rather than watching – that can be combined with other activities, like jogging, at the same time.

When we have to focus on one activity – like getting lost in a good book – we remember that our attention is limited and therefore scarce. As such, we may plan to use our attention carefully and deliberately, like selecting a particularly good read for a holiday or a long-haul flight. If we use a different kind of attention – like listening to audiobooks or podcasts – we can raise the amount of available attention, as we can do other things while we listen.

This means we can fit more books into our everyday life than we could if we only read them. The book industry has realised this and is pivoting in a way that creates more opportunities for readers. Digitisation has unintentionally, and successfully, been fracking for new forms of attention for book publishers, and it's radically changing their business models as a result.

The history of how we measure attention shows us that companies don't just compete within their own industries – but with anyone or anything that might conceivably take up a consumer's scarce time. If you have a traditional economic lens that looks at a single industry, it will measure the market share within that industry and miss the fact that competition for our attention comes from all angles. A television broadcaster doesn't just compete with other broadcasters, but also books, radio, board games, music, computer games, cinema, and even simpler pleasures, like going for a walk.

If the attention economy is a kind of commons, then the huge number of competitors for our attention creates a tragedy of the commons – more content and competition will ultimately exhaust, and potentially over-exploit, our attention. But this tragedy presents an opportunity for a new kind of competition, based not on creating more content, but on helping consumers make more effective use of their attention. One of the most surprising examples of this comes from the analogue world of the nineteenth century.

As well as writing books like *Huckleberry Finn*, Mark Twain was an inventor and publishing entrepreneur. Just as digital networks have created a surplus of content in the twenty-first century, the new technologies of railways and cheap printing processes in the nineteenth century led to an overwhelming surplus of popular magazines, catalogues and newspapers. Readers needed a way to organise and control this huge influx of content, and this was where Twain's innovation came in.

He developed and patented pre-gummed scrapbooks – blank books with columns to help readers clip and organise the content they were reading into subjects like 'home', 'cookery', 'fashion', 'news' or 'religion'. Twain produced different versions of the scrapbooks for different audiences, including authors, children and pastors, and even druggists' prescription books. The patent on his scrapbook earned him more than

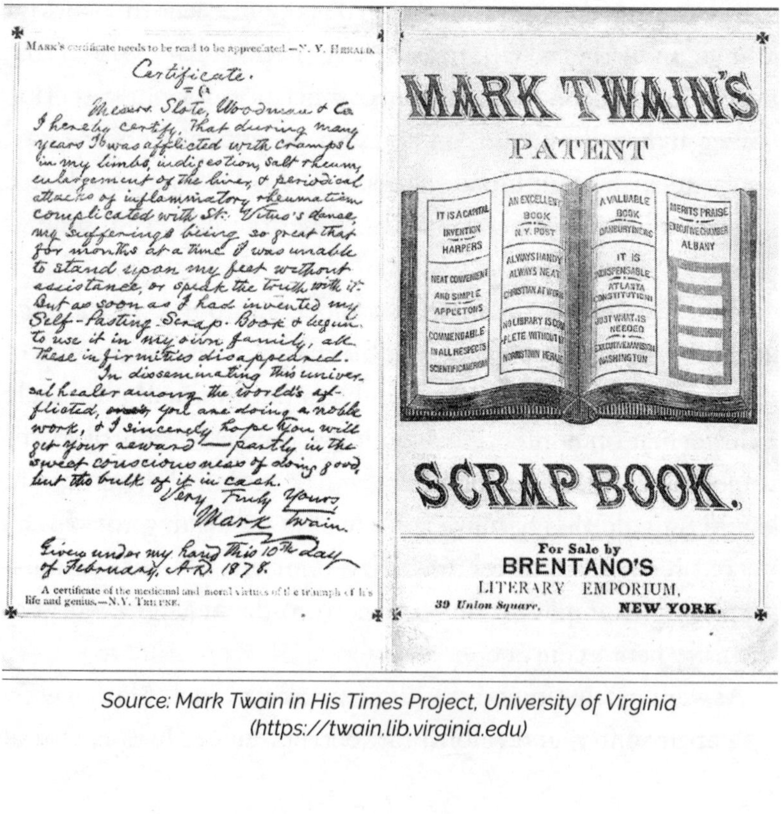


*Source: Mark Twain in His Times Project, University of Virginia (https://twain.lib.virginia.edu)*

$50,000 during his lifetime, almost a quarter of the earnings from all his books.

There is a direct line between scrapbooks and the rise of social media. Early blogging tools like Blogger are identifiably similar to Twain's scrapbooks, providing readers with simple tools for collecting, presenting and commenting on the huge surfeit of content that emerged as the internet exploded.

In the last ten years, tools like Twitter and Facebook have scaled these digital scrapbooks into global networks, driven not by the careful curation of individuals, but by algorithms that capture data from our every click and swipe. Scrapbooks, in the Facebook newsfeed era, are not only a tool for dealing with an overwhelming supply of content, but also the source of the overwhelming supply itself. They are a never-ending stream of ready-gummed strips, capturing headlines, images and videos, like flies sticking to flypaper.

Twain's scrapbook was a blank space in a noisy world of print, giving audiences the time and space to choose what they wanted to spend their attention on. Facebook is like a scrapbook that is already filled with an endless supply of content, giving us hardly any opportunity to pause and reflect. Twitter takes it one step further, converting our attention from a private good into a public good for others to consume and for the platform to monetise.

If Twain realised there was an economic imbalance – a wealth of information competing for a limited amount of attention – and exploited this opportunity by patenting his scrapbook, he could only do this because there was a metric to measure this scarce resource of attention. The companies sending books, catalogues and newspapers into homes across America needed to know how many people their materials were reaching, and if they were getting their attention or going straight into the bin.

The need to measure audience attention goes back centuries

before Twain, even before content was packaged up and distributed in physical objects like books. Attention metrics were important back in the Roman Empire, where applause was a way for leaders to measure the impact of their speeches on their citizens. In her essay 'A Brief History of Applause', Megan Garber explains that 'one of the chief methods politicians used to evaluate their standing with the people was by gauging the greetings they got when they entered the arena'. Astute leaders would read the applause – its volume, duration and pattern – for clues about their political fortunes. Garber continues, describing clapping as the only available metric when 'all we had was hands':

> Applause, participatory and observational at the same time, was an early form of mass media, connecting people to each other and to their leaders, instantly and visually and, of course, audibly. It was public sentiment analysis, revealing the affinities and desires of networked people. It was the qualified self giving way to the quantified crowd. It was big data before data got big.*

By the nineteenth century, applause was such an important metric of attention that there were professional 'claques' – groups of people paid by theatre owners to applaud, laugh or cry at the appropriate points in the show. If you were a theatrical entrepreneur, the roar of the crowd was the most valuable form of advertising. Audiences leaving an enthusiastically received performance would recommend it to their friends. The claque emerged as a way of gaming this response – of

* Megan Gerber, 'A Brief History of Applause, the "Big Data" of the Ancient World', *The Atlantic*, 15 March 2013.

manipulating attention – and ensuring that the audience would go away feeling the show had been a success.

In the early twentieth century, the rise of broadcast networks like radio raised new problems for measuring attention. Radio wasn't a physical product, like a book or newspaper, and it didn't involve people coming to the same location, like theatre, opera or cinema. As audiences bought radios to listen to in their living rooms, they became an audience that could be neither seen nor heard.

Writer and media researcher Matt Locke has described this as a fundamental moment in the history of attention metrics. Radio broadcasts had no direct feedback loop, no physical connection between the broadcaster and the audience. As Locke describes it, the race to develop new ways of measuring attention was a race to learn 'how to measure ghosts'. The man we have to thank for solving the challenge is Arthur C. Nielsen, founder of the metrics company that still bears his name nearly a century later. Nielsen was obsessed with measurement. He once said to his son, who would later inherit the Nielsen company, 'If you can put a number on it, then you can know something.' Broadcasters had struggled to prove to potential advertisers that people were listening to their shows. Nielsen solved this problem using a device called the 'Audimeter', a slowly turning paper roll that automatically marked the frequency and time when listeners turned on their radios. Once completed, the paper rolls would be sent back to Nielsen's teams for analysis, and turned into listening numbers, or 'ratings' for the broadcasters.

The word 'solved' needs a caveat – as we'll discuss later, all Nielsen knew was whether the radio was on and what station was being transmitted; he didn't know if you were paying attention. Caveats aside, it was important to both broadcasters and advertisers that the ratings were developed by a neutral organisation like Nielsen, who was paid by both sides to provide the service but had no stake in the meaning of the resulting numbers.

As radio gave way to television, Nielsen shifted his technology to the new broadcast medium and his company became a household name in the United States for broadcast ratings. But as technology changed the world of broadcasting, Nielsen's approach to measuring ghosts had to change as well. The explosion of formats and devices used for watching video content has made tracking it harder. Watching 'television' has expanded from a limited number of scheduled channels in a box in your living room to accessing an endless number of videos across multiple platforms, devices and contexts, on demand, at any time of the day.

These changes have made it harder for an organisation like Nielsen to measure attention – especially when new entrants and advertisers have nothing to gain from a neutral and transparent middle party. Digital technology platforms like Google and Facebook not only control the algorithms that decide what content is shown to audiences, but also the measurement of the audience's attention to advertisers. This has been a controversial development often referred to as 'marking your own homework', but the tech platforms' monopoly on our digital attention has meant that advertisers have little power to argue.

Facebook's introduction of the 'Like' button in February 2009 added a crucial new attention metric to their already powerful news feed – the modern-day equivalent of Mark Twain's scrapbook. Traditional metrics of attention measured what we watched, and how long we watched it for, but measuring whether we liked it was a much harder process, requiring research with small focus groups. The Like button gave Facebook not just metrics about what people watched (even when hosting other platforms' video content), but how they felt about it – an incredibly powerful combination of metrics, tracking one of the largest global audiences ever assembled by a single media company.

The level of targeting this enabled was an advertiser's dream, but it wasn't just restricted to our individual Likes. When Facebook launched its Graph API in 2010, it gave access not just to one user's activities, but showed how these were connected to all their friends' activities. In fact, even if someone wasn't on Facebook at all, you could piece together a reasonable profile of them just by extrapolating data from people they were connected to.

The story of the Like has turned sour, with a string of well-documented scandals about fake metrics, fake users, fake news and the selling of data to nefarious third parties. Although Facebook gives advertisers access to unimaginable scale and detail, when all this data is controlled by one company it's impossible to check its veracity independently.

Facebook broke with traditional media market models by disintermediating the 'neutral church' of measurement middlemen like Nielsen and selling its metrics directly to the advertisers. Yet perhaps intermediaries like Nielsen play a crucial role in keeping attention economics fair and transparent. Facebook's motto was 'move fast and break things', but sometimes the things they break are valuable links in the chain.

If the early years of broadcasting cut the feedback loop between creators and audiences, turning us into ghosts, it took the rise of social media in the early part of this century for audiences to find a voice again. This brief history of attention shows us that once metrics are defined, attention can be measured and, once measured – whether through claps, ratings or Likes – it can become a market.

With attention economics it is important to not only maximise attention but also to do it efficiently. In conventional economics, improving efficiency means improving productivity. This can be done by getting more out of the same, the same out of less or – at the extreme – more out of less.

In 2006, Spotify set upon a journey to help the music industry pivot back to profits by understanding the status quo when piracy reigned supreme. Spotify didn't just offer a legal alternative to illegal MP3 sites; it offered a more attention-efficient alternative. At that time, when illegal P2P sites were at their peak, one of the reasons why stealing trumped purchasing was that file-sharing was more efficient (and therefore required less attention) than purchasing music legally. To convert a consumer from hugely popular but illegal sites like Napster, uTorrent and The Pirate Bay to the legal and licensed venue of Spotify meant reducing the time it took to access and listen to a song. Spotify engineers understood this and created new metrics to measure attention efficiency. Their target was for the play button on Spotify to start playing a chosen track within 285 milliseconds, because their understanding of the human perception of 'instant' was 250 milliseconds. Start a track within this narrow time frame and the brain cannot spot any delay.

Improving the efficiency of the demands on our attention made Spotify more valuable – so much so that people were willing to pay for what they would otherwise have got for free. This metric helped Spotify beat piracy at its own game, by giving the consumer instant access to over 60 million songs in a faster, more convenient and, most importantly, more attention-efficient manner than stealing.

We now need to address the stackability of attention – which relates to whether attention that's being asked for (or given) can be exclusive or can be combined with other activities (and if so, what types of activities?). This brings up another interesting question: if it's possible to pay attention to two pieces of content at once, how should we understand the relationship between those two pieces of content? Are they fighting for your attention? Or are they working together to capture your attention? This is a concept we'll call 'contestability'. Contestability means working out who your friends and foes are in your battle for attention. This means mapping the activities and distractions that complement each other, and those that substitute one another.

Are the forms of attention demanding your time complementary, like gin and tonic, or substitutes – competing brands of gin? Sticking with the music industry, we can see that music is a form of gin, with many forms of tonic that can accompany it. Music is a complementary form of attention – you could argue that music depends on being complementary, as listening to music without other forms of activities or distraction often makes it less enjoyable. Netflix and its like are arguably more substitutional – more akin to competing brands of gin – as it would be hard to listen to music while also watching Netflix.

When we are binge-watching, we're giving Netflix a monopoly on our attention – and probably for longer periods than we might have intended. Eyes demand more attention than ears. Restricting this idea of contestability to eyes and ears is an over-simplification. Listening and watching can also be substituted or complemented by reading, playing and communicating. To understand the contestability of attention requires the ability to monitor and measure the many ways attention can be consumed.

In this multi-layered framework there is no single measure of attention. Instead we need a range of metrics to assess how much attention, and what kind of attention, we're getting from our audience. These could include active attention (dwell time), passive attention (out of focus) and inferred attention (implied by behaviour). Not one of these metrics directly reflects value – long dwell times could be a positive indicator, suggesting a high degree of engagement from the audience, or it could mean the audience is unsuccessfully searching for something. For example, one of Google's core objectives for its search function is focused on how little (as opposed to how much) attention a user must pay before finding what they're looking for. Less time spent searching means a better-performing search engine. This is why Google was such a breakthrough product when it launched, compared with portal search engines (like Yahoo!) that tried to get users to spend as much time on their site as possible.

There has been surprisingly little research done on monitoring and measuring the contestability of different kinds of attention. Individuals, firms and governments would all benefit from a framework that allows them to step back, look at the wider picture, and construct a map of all the brands of gin and tonic in our attention economy.

Luckily, thanks to a long-forgotten 2010 study published by the UK telecoms regulator Ofcom in their report 'The Consumer's Digital Day', we may have one. Their simple yet powerful framework compares five forms of attention – watch, listen, play, read, communicate – using survey response to rank the relative importance of those activities and the relative attention paid to them.*

It is this insightful trade-off between 'attention paid' and 'importance of' that brings the economics of attention to life.

* Ofcom summarised the methodology for this chart as follows: along the X-axis, each time a media activity was undertaken during the seven days, respondents were asked to score the attention they paid on a scale of 1 to 5, where 5 was 'all of their attention'. Along the Y-axis, in the attitudinal survey undertaken at the end of the survey period, respondents were asked how important each media activity was to them, using a scale of 1 to 10, where 1 is not important at all and 10 is very important.

**ATTENTION VS. IMPORTANCE OF MEDIA AND COMMUNICATIONS ACTIVITIES**

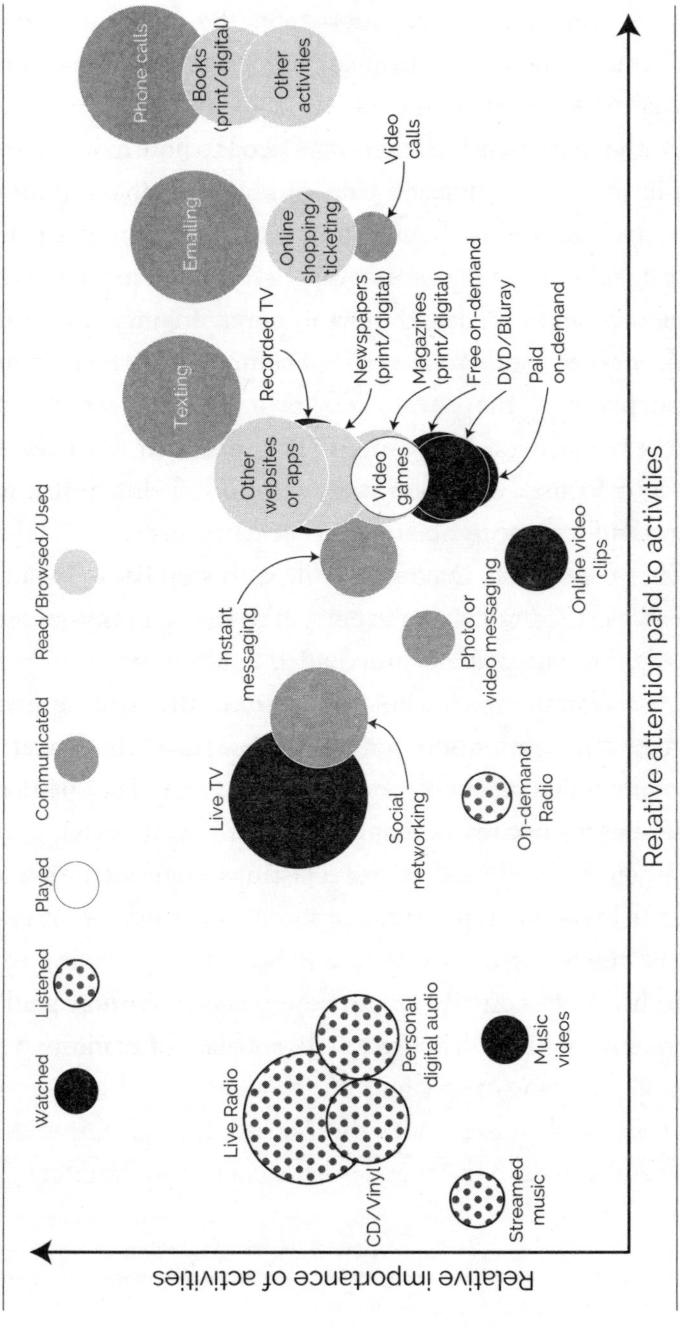


*Source: Ofcom, 'The Consumer's Digital Day: A research report by Ofcom and GfK' (Ofcom, 2010)*

It explains how we allocate our attention and allows us to identify complements and substitutes. By doing so, almost by accident, it uncovers previously hidden truths about how the media works in our real lives.

In the north-east corner of Ofcom's framework, in the quadrant of high attention paid and high relative importance, you have the circles of communication and reading. Emailing, phone calls, texting, messaging or reading require a lot of attention, and are clearly very important to the user as they rank high on both relative importance and attention given. Unsurprisingly, they involve a fellow human being on the other side of the attention exchange. Those are activities competing for your focused attention; they're often like a gin that leaves no room for an accompanying tonic.

The centre of Ofcom's grid is occupied by watching activities. Live television events, like live sports, are seen as important, but don't capture all our attention. On-demand video-streaming sits lower and further to the right, meaning it demands more attention, but is less important. Binge-watching a documentary about tigers in captivity may take up a lot of time, but it's not really that important.

When Netflix CEO Reed Hastings suggested that sleep was his biggest competitor, stating 'You get a show or a movie you're really dying to watch, and you end up staying up late at night, so we actually compete with sleep', he may well have been envisaging a framework like this.* The more Netflix monopolises our time and shifts north-east, gaining both attention and importance, the more all other activities will feel pressured into the south-west corner as contestability plays

* Rina Raphael, 'Netflix CEO Reed Hastings: Sleep is Our Competition', *Fastcompany*, November 2018.

out. The more Netflix reaches out to grab the attention of the future, the more their competitors will lose their grip.

At the other extreme, the south-west corner of low attention and low importance, is music. Whether it is via streaming, videos or radio, music demands relatively little attention and is less important than personal communication. More important activities, such as dancing and socialising, can be consumed while consuming music. The Ofcom study was carried out in 2010, and a lot has changed since, but music being a valuable tonic to all other distractions has remained a constant.

One current attention-grabber that's missing from this 2010 Ofcom chart is podcasts. In the decade since, podcasts have exploded in both volume – with over 2 million shows and 45 million episodes – and value – with blockbuster content and studios being acquired for nine-figure sums of money. The global podcast audience may now be approaching 500 million yet the name 'podcast' predates the Ofcom chart. 'Pod' refers to the iPod, and 'cast' is tied to broadcast, namely the RSS distribution format. Since both iPods and RSS feeds are more or less obsolete, podcasts have a branding problem – especially so in some of the biggest podcasting markets, where the iPod barely entered, like Brazil and Indonesia. What's more, while there is a word for a podcast creator (podcaster) and podcast apps (podcatcher), there isn't one for devout podcast fanatics, like cinephile or booklover. This is a market that is still finding its feet.

The medium's secret sauce for capturing attention, which was already scarce when it emerged on the scene, is the inherent intimacy that accompanies focused, opt-in listening, often during solitary moments like commuting to work or doing chores around the house. Intimacy has a physical component too, in that you're actually putting headphones inside your skull, through which you're hearing what sounds to your brain like a genuine, intimate conversation between people (whether that's two people talking to each other, or someone talking to you). The success of a podcast or podcaster therefore depends on the ability to utilise that intimacy, combined with a self-assured voice and unique point of view, to establish a genuine sense of companionship with each and every listener to keep them coming back. But podcasts are still by and large the Wild West of attention merchants and lack the editorial skills in time management. A telling joke: 'What's the best way to keep a secret? Put it in the second half of a podcast.'

Of paramount importance is the question of who in this battle for attention are your friends and who are your foes. Streaming music may occupy the bottom left corner of Ofcom's chart, but it can be complemented by friendly activities like emailing and reading in the top right – not just in their respective activities but in the time spent doing them: the more you read, the more you might listen (and vice versa).

At the other extreme are those activities that monopolise attention: these are your foes because they leave no room for anything else. Scarcity gives the monopolist a powerful upper hand. When Netflix wins more attention, everyone else had better prepare to lose. When music wins, many others can win with it. Knowing both your friends and foes in this battle for attention makes you better placed to pivot through disruption.

A natural extension to this framework is to play around with the size of the bubbles – or the reach of the audience. For example, one can envisage an 'appreciation index' that's genre specific – as the audience gets smaller, the appreciation index should go up as the remaining population will love it more. In radio circles, this is referred to as a 'Howard Stern effect': the outspoken US talk-show presenter lost audience as he moved from terrestrial radio to Sirius but was able to increase his earning power as a presenter from the remaining audience due to their increased loyalty.

There are quality-versus-quantity trade-offs to consider as well as the fact that people are more likely to pay attention when crowds are intimate than when they are vast – music fans in a cosy jazz bar pay more attention than festival-goers in a muddy field. More people paying attention could result in less attention that each is willing to give.

Ten years on, this little-known framework buried inside the pages of a long-forgotten Ofcom document doesn't just tell us how consumers allocated their attention back then but how contestability will play out tomorrow.

**WE'RE ALL IN COMPETITION WITH PYJAMAS**

Many events-oriented businesses have been slow to respond to the ever more enticing comfort and convenience offered by a sofa, Netflix and pyjamas. One piece of evidence here is the distinctly American pastime of tailgating, wherein sports fans drink beer and cook BBQs from the back of their cars in stadium parking lots, where they can hear the cheers when their team win and get home sooner when they lose. The failure here is that sports teams aren't in the business of hosting makeshift barbecues; they want to sell tickets. Every fan that's passionate enough to leave home and spend hours in a parking lot but who does not enter the stadium is arguably a missed opportunity. And the largest hurdle standing in the way of these fans entering the stadium is the high prices of not just tickets, but beers, hot dogs and other concessions, where unit prices often exceed that of a monthly subscription to Netflix.

One team that is proactively bucking this trend and making sure their stadium stays full – despite the growing allure of sitting at home in one's pyjamas – is the Atlanta Falcons. The club has made big investments in providing fans with a ritzy stadium, including high-quality grub at an affordable price. Atlanta's finest pizza purveyors, for instance, charge exactly what they would downtown. Water bottles that once cost $6 have been slashed by two-thirds. All told, the Falcons report that in the last three years prices inside the stadium have remained flat across the board, and in some cases have fallen, yet ARPU has risen 16% as merchandise sales have increased 90%. By making sure fans enter the stadium, the club gets out of its own way and enables itself to capitalize on having won their attention.

One needs to look no further than the recent past of the gaming industry to see how contestability of attention will play out in the future. Gaming has constantly had to innovate to win attention, often by replicating reality and occasionally by influencing it. Gaming has always been the tail that can wag the attention merchants' dog.

Let's stick with American football, which has always been intrinsically linked to television. Zach Seward, co-founder of Quartz, calculates that an average game lasts 3 hours and 12 minutes, but if you tally up the time when the ball is actually in play, the action amounts to a mere 11 minutes. The game is a sideshow to the commercial breaks, as there are over twenty of them containing more than a hundred adverts. If that isn't off-putting enough, the Jacksonville Jaguars, a perennially poor-performing team, would charge $40 for a season ticket holder to see the game, and more than that to enter their Fantasy Football League lounge once inside!

One of the reasons live American football has been able to successfully vie for attention (so it can sell all those advert spots) is that it followed what was happening in gaming, especially with EA Sports flagship video game Madden NFL. The camera angles developed in the game, such as the cable-cam, which flies overhead, were developed on Madden NFL in the late 1990s, then adopted by the real game a decade later – a cable-cam tail that wagged the dog.

On the flip side, the animated yellow line that's imposed on the screen to indicate how many yards a team needs to progress to in order to get back to 'first down and ten' was developed by the TV networks first and adopted by the Madden game two years later – the 'first down' dog wagging the tail.

It's not just American football tails, nor is it just America's dogs, that are wagging here. A lot of the World Series of Poker (WSOP) camera angles, including the one underneath the table that shows the cards that the player is privately holding, were taken from South Korea's TV production of StarCraft eSports in the late 1990s and early 2000s. So, in that case, another physical 'sport' (poker) was the tail wagging the South Korean eSports dog.

What differentiates gaming from bingeing Netflix is the amount of voluntary effort that is required to engage with the content, and the gradual but certain advancement in skills that is an inherent part of most gaming experiences. The famed psychologist Mihaly Csikszentmihalyi put forward a model that could explain such deep engagement with games as a state of 'Flow': 'When goals are clear, feedback relevant, and challenges and skills are in balance, attention becomes ordered and fully invested.'

Csikszentmihalyi presented a model of optimal engagement that is widely applicable to game design. When games are too challenging for an individual's skills, they create anxiety, but when they are too easy, they create boredom. The trick for game design, therefore, is to first present challenges that match the optimal skill level, and then increase the difficulty of the challenges as the skill level progresses over time.

***FLOW THEORY***

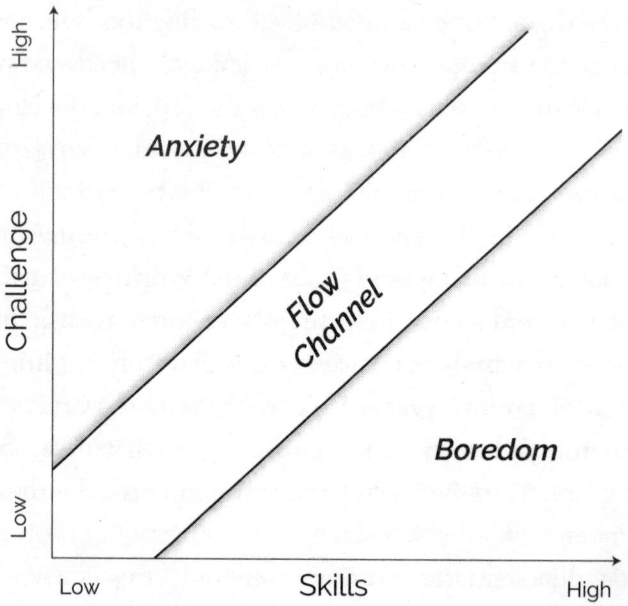


*Source: Csikszentmihalyi, Mihaly, Flow:* The Psychology of Optimal Experience *(Harper Perennial Modern Classics, 2008)*

We can see Csikszentmihalyi's theory at work every thirty seconds (literally and visually!) when we use TikTok. One of the things that stands out in the TikTok experience is that the user has to swipe in order to go to the next video. Compare this to the automatic playing of the next episode on Netflix. By making people swipe, TikTok is ensuring that people pay attention to the app every 30 seconds, which arguably constitutes more engagement than autoplay on Netflix, where the content is probably playing in the background. This solidifies Flow theory: adding a little amount of effort that is within the competency range of the users is actually a good thing, because it ensures sustained attention.

Then, along came Covid-19: gaming's 'black swan' moment.

Thanks to Covid, we all find ourselves staring into a Napster moment and that affects everything – including our attention. Given what our principle on 'paying attention' teaches about maximising value over attention, it should come as no surprise that computer games emerged from this global crisis bigger than ever – in both attention and monetary terms. Adults who hadn't played a game in decades have returned to doing so – often having invested in consoles to get through the 2020 global lockdown. Kids who used to discuss their day outside the school gates did so on Fortnite instead. As the music industry celebrated reaching 341 million digital subscribers around the world after twenty years of blood sweat and tears, it needed to remember that Fortnite amassed 350 million users in just three years. Moreover, the average time spent streaming music was under two hours a day while the average duration a gamer would spend playing Animal Crossing was approximately nine hours!

Why are games winning? No form of media is designed to work

with our scarce attention like games, which are built from scratch to accomplish longitudinal entertainment via effort and reward. Be it the craving for more points, for mastering the next level or even watching the experts play on eSports and aspiring to attain their level of proficiency, gaming is uniquely designed with deliberate triggers that facilitate long-term motivation to 'consume' that type of content – triggers that audio and video don't have.

At the beginning of this chapter we were confronted with a question: What price is your undivided attention? The question was not about how much your attention is worth, but how much more it is worth if it forces you to screen out other distractions. This is where virtual reality (VR) games move to the fore, as they demand your undivided attention. Yet like the boy who cried wolf, VR has promised much but failed to deliver on numerous occasions. This time, the wolf is at the door, as we're now seeing hardware getting cheaper and better. Wires are disappearing, as is latency.

When viewed through the lens of attention economics, VR is well placed to win the battle for attention as it has set its sights on becoming a 'first-class experience'. The desire to 'upgrade' is something that's innate in many of us – we believe in better and enjoy media more when it gets better – and it's now a question of when, not if, VR will become a worthwhile upgrade for the mass market. 'It's like taking a vacation,' said Seth Gerson of the leading VR developer Survios when reflecting on what the VR experience competes with. 'Night clubs have "velvet ropes" for their VIP lounges and now the media has it too – and we don't even need to change the [VR] initials!'

One factor working in VR's favour is the depreciating value of alternatives, be it a cinema with someone texting on a bright screen next to you or a sport that hasn't innovated its rules in years. Let's revisit the challenges facing American football.

Parents would prefer their kids not play the game through fear of concussion or injury. The rigid rules, like the predictable extra point, threaten to bore viewers and push them to other activities. The NFL governing authorities could change this – by making the game safer and more exciting – but it takes a lot of time and has to happen gradually due to the rules and regulations already in place. In VR, conversely, there are no legacy effects – developers can make the game more exciting and, if need be, safer – in months, not years. Two similar ships – one real, the other virtual – are effectively passing each other in the night.

VR may make inroads into American football and other sports, but the developers have their sights set on a much bigger prize: Hollywood. Film studios are unenviable places to be right now, with so many rules and regulations as to what you can and can't do with cast, staff and location, compounded by the devastating impact of Covid-19 on the production cycle. VR circumvents all these hurdles. It can easily adapt to distance-working and requires no approvals.

Games are becoming as valuable as anything Hollywood can produce, and will soon be drawing bigger crowds.* As with music streaming's ability to draw a crowd before radio and television (reversing the traditional order of events, which we'll explore in the next chapter), the tipping point will soon be found in the order of events – soon we can anticipate games to move first, and Hollywood second.

*

There's a reason why this chapter is called Paying Attention. As Nir Eyal, author of the illuminating book *Indistractable: How to*

* IDG Consulting, a games industry market-research and analyst firm, sees the value of gaming overtaking that of linear television, home entertainment and box office to become the number one vertical in media by 2021.

*Control Your Attention and Choose Your Life* points out, 'our time and focus have value'. The syntax matters too: in English, we 'pay'; in Spanish we 'lend'; in French we 'make'; and in Swedish we 'give'. As English is (still) the largest language in the world, (if you count both native and non-native speakers), and many English speakers are monolingual, the rest of the world will need to get increasingly used to the currency of 'paying'.

Paying attention is tough these days: attention is a scarce resource and everyone wants more of it, meaning something has to give. Think of your attention constraint this way: when you're driving and the weather turns really bad, why is it you switch the radio off? Because you can only consume so much, and the demands of paying attention to what's outside your vehicle cancel out the ability to pay attention to the entertainment inside. When we reach our ceiling, something has to give.

As there are only so many hours in the day, when one attention merchant wins our undivided attention, it leaves less for the others competing for it. But it's not always a zero-sum. Knowing when you are competing with friends or foes is the crucial missing piece of this puzzle.

Contestability is already well understood by the leaders of the tech platforms who deploy strategies to ensure that their devices and products can secure our attention. They either create barriers to competition within their technology ecosystems or buy up potential competitors before they have a chance to disrupt them. Facebook bought Instagram and then WhatsApp. When younger audiences left Facebook, they didn't leave their attention behind. Facebook won the war of attention, but now faces an endless battle of screening out (and where possible buying out) distractions.

Given these myriad companies, organisations and individuals constantly pounding on our door, demanding our attention, and given the sophisticated tools that they've developed to capture our attention even if we won't give it freely, it would seem a miracle that any of us can give focused attention to anything. Yet we do. Each of us has a favourite song we listen to incessantly, a TV show we binge-watch, even a social media platform we feel we couldn't live without. And occasionally we still bundle our attention together with the attention of a bunch of other people and bestow it on one particular cultural artefact. Those are the ones we call 'hits' – the number one songs, blockbuster films, killer apps. In a world where attention is in such high demand, how do some people still succeed in drawing a crowd?

# 3

# DRAWING A CROWD

When your day is done and it's time to down tools and head home, it pays to be nice to your fellow night-owl colleagues and call by their desk to say goodbye. You never know what you'll learn as you make for the exit. These moments of camaraderie create a unique atmosphere, where small nuggets of knowledge are shared in a way that is rarely possible during the madness of the working day.

It's the sharing of those 'wee gems', passed on at a time when you least expect them, that can prove the most illuminating. These moments can force you to pivot your entire direction of thought. I learned that lesson late one cold dark winter evening in December 2015.

A year earlier, I had stumbled across a dispute about a quirky song titled 'All About That Bass' released by Meghan Trainor in 2014. The headlines declared that the song was the first to enter the UK charts without a physical or digital sale, doing so on streaming alone.

Since singles charts were first conceived, in 1952 in the UK, they have been based on unit sales. In 2014, the changing behaviours of music audiences meant they had to pivot, uncomfortably, to accommodate streams. The industry agreed to a chart metric using a ratio of 100:1 – one hundred streams equating to one sale. (I saw this as converting the future of streams into the past of sales and called it fax-equivalent-emails.) Meghan Trainor's song had accidentally appeared on streaming services like Spotify a week before it was available to download on iTunes. It had unintentionally drawn a crowd that was large enough to take it into the Top 40.

My inquisitive mind took me to the United States, where the song had been deemed a 'sleeper hit' – a track that takes an unusually long time to top the charts. It debuted on the Hot 100 singles chart at the end of July and climbed to the top spot by early September, replacing Taylor Swift's 'Shake It Off', making Trainor the twenty-first female artist in history to top the chart with her debut release. A 'sleeper hit' had happened without intent. And I intended to find out why.

'All About That Bass' is performed in a throwback style reminiscent of the 1950s and 1960s. The chorus is catchy, and people of all ages and stages are drawn to its rhythm. When you first hear it, you feel like you already know it, which makes you want to hear it again. Fiend for data that I am, I went back through the anatomy of a hit. How could a 'sleeper hit' in the United States take over a month to sleepwalk to the top of the charts?

The only leading indicator I could find for the success of 'All About That Bass' was that it had performed well on Shazam. Before Shazam, if you heard a song on your car radio that you liked, you had to hope that you were still in the car when the DJs got around to telling you what the song was. With Shazam, all you needed to do was whip out your phone and, with the press of a button, or what Shazam termed 'a tag', the app would display the name and artist of whatever song is playing. It was the bridge between lean-back discovery on radio and lean-forward recovery on your own device.

It also made no sense as a leading indicator of the success of 'All About That Bass'. If you were going to tag a song on Shazam, you first had to hear the song playing out in the world. And 'All About That Bass' flipped the order of events on its head: from radio to Shazam and then sales and streams to Shazam leading, sales and streams following and radio picking up the rear. It wasn't playing on any car sound system. So, where had those Shazam tags come from? I had no idea, and neither, some research suggested to me, did anybody else.

The problem ate at me for a full year. It would have persisted to this day had I not taken the long route out of the office so I could say farewell to some colleagues.

Spotify's London office overlooked the city's famous Regent Street. Crowds were gathering for last-minute festive shopping, admiring the Christmas lights that draped above them. I had been working far too late and was close to putting out all the fires I needed to, so finally I left for home. The office had about a hundred desks, and by that time of night only a small handful were occupied. On a whim, I decided to say farewell to everyone who was also staying late. As I made for the door, I saw a friend, Emily ffrench Blake, who had been travelling across America for several weeks and was busy following up with meetings in the time zones she had left behind. Not wanting to disturb her rhythm, I muttered 'Don't work too late' as I made for the exit.

As I waited for the elevator to arrive, Emily called me over: 'Pagey, come back! I need to show you something I learned in Seattle last week. It's the missing piece in your Meghan Trainor puzzle!' pointing to slide decks awash with jottings and note-taking. She had been working with Starbucks in their Seattle HQ.

I asked her why a track that was close to two years old was such a hot topic in Seattle, especially in meetings with a coffee company. She hastily pulled out more paperwork, covered in even more notes and jottings: 'Starbucks are one of the biggest sources of Shazams in the States.' She was angling at a novel idea: had 'All About the Bass' been played in store, accounting for the early spike in Shazams of the track? Emily's thesis was that Starbucks' sheer number of coffee shops effectively made it the biggest radio station in the United States. This sounded like baloney; Starbucks sells coffee – it does not break new music.

But Emily ffrench Blake was street-smart and there was visible excitement on her face.

'Look, Pagey, these numbers don't lie. A large US FM radio station may reach 6 to 7 million listeners in a month. Now look at Starbucks: in the US alone we're talking about 14,000 stores and around 40 million customers. All those customers spend time queuing to place their order, waiting to receive their order and even more time spent slurping their coffee – that's a dwell time of close to half an hour per person and they're hearing music in the store throughout. If they like what they're hearing, they'll Shazam it.'

Now I was beginning to join the dots: I went back to Shazam to find out the time of day those Meghan Trainor tags took place. The data backed it up convincingly. Across time zones, the Shazam tagging happened between 8 a.m. and 10 a.m. – peak period for people queuing, ordering and slurping their 'morning joe'. Starbucks was effectively one big radio station, just not in the form we normally considered. Emily had pivoted my thinking. The ability to draw a crowd was no longer limited to conventional channels like radio and television – a crowd is a crowd wherever it gathers (even if disparately). And crowds are all we seek – a gathering of people with attention to spend.

A music industry that had spent half a century obsessing about the impact of radio pluggers (staff solely responsible for getting songs played on radio) was now contemplating replacing them with streaming playlist-pluggers. Meghan Trainor made me realise we may need to think about Starbucks pluggers too! If labels want to have hits, they need to understand the many varied means by which hits are created.

I still reflect on leaving the office that late December evening back in 2015. It's my favourite example of why we need to 'be prepared to re-examine our reasoning', something we'll learn more about in our eighth principle on Big Data, Big Mistakes, as we had all this data but couldn't see where it was being drawn from. It's also a good reminder to take the time to be nice to your fellow night-owl office colleagues as you make for the exit.

The challenge we all face in trying to draw a crowd is that there is now so much more of everything. There are more books, with the United States reporting over 850,000 new titles being published annually. There is more television, with over five hundred scripted series being shown in the US in 2019. There are more artists, more songs, and more ways for people to listen at any time of day. In the fight to draw a crowd we're facing increasingly larger rooms that are getting increasingly more crowded, and it's becoming ever more difficult to reach the people standing at the back.

Measuring exactly how crowded the music room has become since Columbia records put out the first vinyl album in 1948 involves some 'guesstimation'. From 1948 through 1958, 13,000 albums were issued, an average of 1,200 albums a year – although it would have been scarcer on the front end and bulkier at the back end of that period. In 1967 there was a step change in the supply side, as albums became a more important part of the music industry's supply chain. *Billboard* magazine estimated that by 1970 around 5,000 albums came out per year.

Fast forward to the SoundScan era, where hard data is available: by the mid-1990s, 27,000 albums a year were coming out annually; by the late 1990s that was up to 30,000; and by around 2005 it was about 60,000. In 2010, with downloads peaking and streaming ready to take off, there were about 90,000 albums released and, as streaming lowered the barriers to entry, this reached 127,000 a year by 2013.

Today, streaming companies are adding almost 55,000 unique songs a day; that's easily a million songs a month, which scales up to over a million albums a year. As streaming enters new markets, especially India, China and Africa, this number can be expected to grow further and faster in the near future. From about 30,000 albums being released each year in the 1990s to over a million being released today, the room is barely recognisable from its past and the rules need to be rewritten.

Drawing crowds is how hits happen, and there is truth in the old adage 'where there's a hit there's a writ' (i.e. many will claim to be part, or the sole cause of, its success). We'll now turn to how crowds were drawn in the past, and the lessons of the past that help us navigate how hits will happen in the future.

We can use the concept of the Keynesian Beauty Contest to help us understand how the role of the gatekeeper has changed in recent years. In 1936, the economist John Maynard Keynes compared selecting investments to making choices in newspaper beauty contests. These contests involved newspapers publishing photos of hundreds of beautiful women. They would then ask readers to send in their opinions of which women were the most beautiful, and the reader whose choices most closely matched the six most popular women would win a prize. Keynes wrote:

> It is not a case of choosing those [faces] which, to the best of one's judgment, are really the prettiest, nor even those which the average opinion genuinely thinks the prettiest. We have reached the third degree where we devote our intelligences to anticipating what average opinion expects the average opinion to be.

In other words, you could win the contest if you could correctly guess what everyone else thought that everyone else thought. Winning was not about beating the system but being the system. Art and commerce have a lot in common here as the cyclical patterns of each can be volatile – if a particular genre of music or book appears to be what the judges want today, labels and publishers alike will congregate their investment decisions around this genre tomorrow. If a particular stock appears attractive as markets close, then a herd of individual investors will congregate around similar stocks when markets reopen. But those rules have changed. Today's harsh reality is that winning over the judges doesn't necessarily win over the consumers.

Tarzan Economics means letting go of the 'one-to-many' broadcast model that gatekeepers could control and getting to grips with multiple 'one-to-one' relationships that platforms enable. Those judges in the beauty contest can no longer influence the views and opinions of others, as the audience, whose opinions they were trying to anticipate, now have an opinion of their own. The judges (or gatekeepers) of the past have lost their primacy, as they were not designed to be influential in the world of abundant choice available to consumers today.

The loss of the gatekeepers has ramifications far beyond the music world – from culture to journalism to politics. Much of our understanding of the world has historically been moderated by gatekeepers, and there's a feeling that a world without them can't have much to do with the world that came before. But there are some basic realities of drawing crowds that remain unchanged, and we can get at two of them by looking at two businesses from an era when the gatekeepers were still very much keeping the gates: Tupperware and Tower Records.

## EMOTIONAL CONTAGION

Sir Peter Bazalgette, the television executive who famously brought *Big Brother* to British TV screens at the turn of the millennium, mastered the art of making content go viral by making reality television more than just a mirror of our lives. In his recent book *The Empathy Instinct* he explores the psychology of what attracts attention and encourages it to spread. Acknowledging that men and women have more similarities than differences, he argues that empathy is the exception – not only are women better at it than men, but babies are, too. One of the earliest signs of what he refers to as emotional contagion (and the first stirring of his broader theme of empathy) is when one baby cries at another infant's wailing. Typically, girls do this before boys. Even in adulthood, women are more likely to yawn when they see someone else yawn – another act of emotional contagion. Bazalgette suggests there is a 'follow the leader' dynamic to our attention – that we react when someone else has reacted, and we respond when someone else is responsive. Bazalgette shows why emotional contagion matters when making things go viral, with the rising currency of today's social media influencers adding fuel to his fire.*

As markets have become increasingly crowded, you need more than just recognition from your audience to move up the pecking order of popularity. You need to go viral. Virality occurs when your reach expands as each new user shares your content with more people. The people who like your thing can't just like it, they need to share it. Virality is often embedded into a product's functionality; merely using such a product causes it to spread. Facebook is an obvious example, as signing up to the platform motivates you to invite all your friends to use it too. Ditto for payment platforms and legal software, as adopting new invoicing software means that all your suppliers need to adopt it – the incentive being that they want to get paid.

The term 'viral' may sound like something born in Silicon Valley in the noughties, with websites like Hot-or-Not (where people would upload their photos to be ranked by an audience) or email services like Hotmail (which cleverly added an invitation to join Hotmail at the bottom of every user's email). But the origins of viral growth go back to the years immediately after the Second World War, when an American single mother demonstrated what it would take for ideas to spread.

In 1946, inventor Earl Silas Tupper had designed a wonder

* The original manager of the Rolling Stones, Andrew Loog Oldham, acted out his own form of emotional contagion in 1965, from the back of the theatre where the band would perform. As the band came onstage, he noticed that if he crouched down to be out of sight and screamed in a high-pitched voice, then everyone else would scream with him. The rest, as they say, is rock and roll history.

bowl with an airtight seal for keeping food fresh. The sealed lip was an innovation in American kitchens, helping families store leftovers for much longer and more conveniently. Before Tupper's invention, the housewives, who did the vast majority of the cooking, would often stretch their shower caps over their leftovers, which was ugly and undesirable.

Tupperware should have been an easy sell, given that the alternative was a shower cap, but an extensive marketing campaign using newspapers and in-store displays failed to draw a crowd as the product was neither attractive to the eye nor was it obvious how it could be used. Top-down advertising might have offered reach, but it couldn't create engagement – an assurance that, once purchased, the product would have a purpose – as consumers didn't understand what to do with Tupper's wonder bowl. Sealing the lid to 'lock in freshness' wasn't an easy task and fumbling with such a new object left customers frustrated. Of the few customers who purchased Tupper's wonder bowl, many returned the item claiming the lid didn't fit.

This is where Brownie Wise, a single mother from Dearborn, Michigan, enters the story. She worked as a distributor for Stanley Home Products and noticed that Tupperware would be ideal for home demonstrations. Wise demonstrated her retailer instinct and de-prioritised all other Stanley Home Products, focusing purely on what she called her 'Poly-T parties'. Within a decade, Wise had established a social network of ladies across America, hosting what became known as Tupperware Parties to demonstrate how these plastic products worked. 'Get rid of those shower caps and turn those leftovers into makeovers' was the rallying cry of the Tupperware sales force.

Each Tupperware seller relied on her social network of sympathetic friends, neighbours and relatives to arrange a gathering. The pool of people willing to host such an event would be self-selecting in an advantageous way: it would be those who already had strong networks most prone to put themselves forward as sellers. Each party hostess invited women from her social circle to attend, then invited friends to host their own parties with guests from their own social networks – a form of word of mouth that would allow both the word 'Tupperware' and how to use its features to spread from living room to living room across America. Smart sellers would identify attributes that would signal smart hostesses – just like how we search social media to find 'influencers' today.

Wise's Tupper-training manual was fifty years ahead of its time in its insights for how ideas spread across a network: 'Three people must gain at every party: the dealer (through sales), the hostess (through status) and the guests (through social interaction).' Tupperware parties only worked if all the participants saw it as a win-win, and one of the biggest wins was the fact that a gathering of ladies could support 'one of their own' – the polar opposite of supporting an unknown salesman knocking on your door.

Thanks to Brownie's crowd-drawing networks, Tupperware sales soared, hitting $25 million in 1954 (more than $238 million in 2020's money). Kat Eschner at the Smithsonian notes that products like the Wonder Bowl, Ice Tups popsicle moulds and the Party Susan compartmentalised serving tray came to represent a new post-war lifestyle that revolved around at-home entertaining and patio parties.* By 1954, there were 20,000 dealers, distributors and managers in the Tupperware network. Technically, none of these people worked for Tupperware – they

* Kat Eschner, 'The Story of Brownie Wise, the Ingenious Marketer Behind the Tupperware Party', *Smithsonian*, April 2018.

were private contractors who collectively acted as the infrastructure between the company and the consumer.

Tupperware's viral success in the 1950s teaches us three lessons. First, virality depends on participants, not products; Earl Tupper's approach of using top-down marketing mechanisms to draw a crowd failed, but Brownie Wise flipped it to draw the crowd from the bottom up. Not only that, she was a first mover in exploiting the benefits of the gig economy, creating flexible work opportunities for those who needed it.

Second, what made the Tupperware party viral was the fact that network effects scaled the business in multiple directions: more sellers meant more parties, which drew in more buyers, which recruited more sellers, and so on. As we'll learn later, Tupperware may well have set the scene for the 'flywheels' that were to come.

Third, Brownie Wise's 1948 training manual stated: 'It is a proven fact that you will sell more to a group of 15 women as a group than you will sell to them individually' – this tapped into the group dynamics of herd mentality, fear of missing out and lowering the social barrier to entry for making a purchase. As groups can quickly identify and share new applications for the product that were previously unknown, this created a cultural value of solving problems for the common good – not dissimilar to the 500-million daily views of 'how to' videos on YouTube.

'There are three kinds of lies: lies, damned lies and statistics.' We need to keep Mark Twain's popular expression close at hand when we tackle the thorny topic of the 'long tail'. In any bricks-and-mortar store there are usually a small number of goods (visible from the shop window) that make up the majority of demand – what we call 'the head' – and a longer list of niche items (usually at the back of the store) that make up a disproportionately small slice of demand – what we call 'the tail'. Scarcity of shelf space in bricks-and-mortar stores meant that an 80/20 rule would take effect, where 80 per cent of demand would come from 20 per cent of the goods, and the remaining 80 per cent of goods would make up only 20 per cent of demand.

*Wired* magazine editor Chris Anderson's famous 2004 essay on the long tail (and 2006 book of the same name) recognised that digital markets offered consumers more choice and argued that the consumer would inevitably exercise that choice. His theory argued that demand would shift from the head, spreading demand away from the 80/20 split further down toward the tail. He claimed that as demand shifted, the tail would both lengthen (more choice) and fatten (more demand for that choice). This would create viable business models for previously niche products and reduce the control on the market that traditional gatekeepers held.

The famous long tail chart overleaf applies Anderson's theory to music. It compares the inventory stocked in a typical bricks-and-mortar retailer at the time of his famous essay to the larger inventory provided by Rhapsody, a streaming service which was licensed around the same time. When Anderson's book was published in 2006, a bricks-and-mortar retailer like Walmart would typically stock 52,000 tracks, bundled up into 4,000 albums, and this would form the 'head' of the total music distribution curve. The additional choice brought by the digital-music streaming services like Rhapsody, which was beginning to find traction at the time, meant a further 3 million tracks were available. (Today, that number has ballooned to over 60 million.) For Chris Anderson's theory of the long tail to work, demand would have to shift away from what was previously offered in the high-street shop, and towards what could be found only on digital services.

## *THE LONG TAIL*

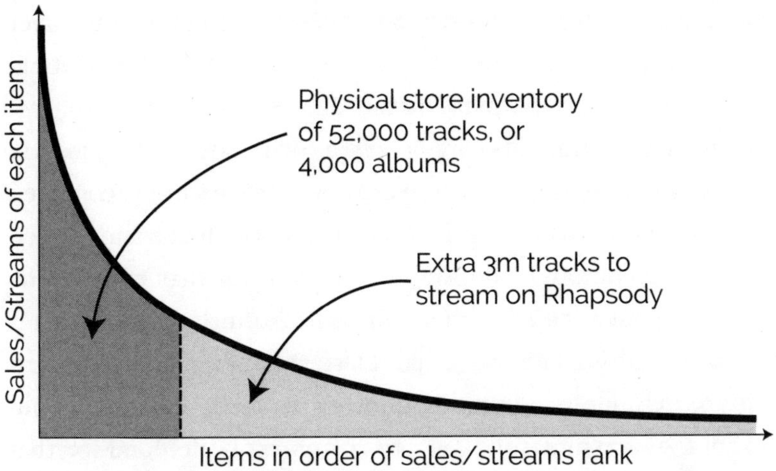


*Source: Adapted from Chris Anderson, 'The Long Tail' (Wired, 2004)*

This shift in demand – away from the hits and towards the niche – is the central thesis of the book *The Long Tail*, captured in its subtitle *Why the Future of Business is Selling Less of More*. On reflection, there is a touch of irony that a book which claimed the future is about selling less of more became a blockbuster. Not just a blockbuster, but a belief. The idea that future riches would be found in offering unlimited choice was appealing for entrepreneurs and investors alike as they had a vested interest in replacing the traditional content-industry gatekeepers – those who influenced and guarded which lucky few products were displayed in shop windows. New businesses were built on this concept, and venture capital flocked to it. Critics of this Long Tail concept included the Harvard professor Anita Elberse, whose 2013 book *Blockbusters: Hit-Making, Risk-Taking, and the Big Business of Entertainment* argued that you needed to pivot back towards the head to succeed – what's termed 'go big or go home'. The irony continued, as her book failed to get the same traction as Anderson's, meaning Elberse's book about hits found itself in the long tail, whereas Anderson's book about the tail found itself in the head!

But as digital markets matured, controversy surrounded Anderson's book and its core beliefs, as demand for hits remained strong, if not stronger than ever. For those seeking to make a living in the long tail, the income they made was failing to live up to expectations. The long tail tapped in to our emotions, generating an altruistic vision of redistributing wealth from the rich to the poor. This longer (and fatter) tail created a picture of a more democratised media industry, where broader selection meant the industry could cater to customers with broader tastes, and artists without a more 'mainstream' appeal could still be part of the industry. And when we don't see evidence conforming to our emotions, we are tempted to criticise the theory, or the platforms tasked with turning the theory into reality.

This controversy and criticism around the long tail theory stems from an unfortunate conflation of percentages and absolute numbers. The confusion can be captured in political discourse around inequality, where you will hear constant references to the privileged 'top 1 per cent' – and how this small percentage of a population can take such a large percentage of the wealth. The same discrepancy carries across to media (where this reference to the top 1 per cent may have originated): blockbusters walk away with all the wealth, leaving a long tail of niche content scraps to live off. When we argue that the rich get richer, or the winner takes all, we need to revisit how we are defining the rich (or those winners) over time.

To avoid the conflation, we need to disentangle the percentages and recalculate absolute values. While some thought that the 80 per cent of music in the long tail would get more popular, instead the whole industry ballooned, and now the 20 per cent in the head constitutes much more music than used to be found in the tail. Some simple number-crunching backs this up: if a streaming service has 4 million artists and 60 million tracks, then 1 per cent of each constitutes 40,000 artists and 600,000 songs – far more choice than the bricks-and-mortar world could even contemplate stocking on its shelves. Anderson's theory suggested that demand would shift down the tail, causing it to get fatter. The mistake was missing how choice under the whole curve would grow instead.

To get to our twist in the tail, we need to go back to the industry heyday of the late 1990s and early noughties – prior to the disruption of digital piracy. The high street had a retailer that offered a vastly different level of choice to the Walmart example Anderson uses: Tower Records.

Tower Records may have come and gone long before the *Wired* article in late-2004 captured our imaginations, but it's time we looked back and realised that Tower Records was serving a kind of 'long tail' way before *Wired* magazine started using the phrase. The tale of Tower Records' long tail begins in 1960, when Russell Solomon opened his first store in Sacramento, California. In the following four decades of boom and bust, Tower expanded its empire to almost two hundred and forty-four stores in eighteen countries. After entering a well-documented tailspin (captured in the documentary aptly titled *All Things Must Pass*), Tower Records filed for bankruptcy in 2004 – the same year Anderson's long tail article was published. It was also the same year that Blockbuster's dominance of the video rental market peaked, before nosediving towards its own bankruptcy six years later.

History has not been kind to either Blockbuster or Tower Records, portraying the retailers as stubborn to change. The truth is that Blockbuster innovated more than most, filing more patents for digital innovation than many of its bricks-and-mortar competitors. Still, the company couldn't let go of its reliance on charging late fees to their loyal consumers – something Netflix noticed and pounced on with a vengeance. Similarly, though Tower Records may have made many mistakes on its roller-coaster ride, it opened Tower.com in 1995, making it one of the earliest adopters of e-commerce.

Tower Records' slogan was 'No Music, No Life' – suggesting music wasn't a choice but a necessity. To satisfy this necessity, the store tried to offer more choice than any of its competitors so it could not only draw a crowd but engage that crowd. A trip to Tower Records needed more than just a lunch break, and the stores were so crowded that queuing to flick through the records was commonplace. Russ Solomon had to optimise the level of choice offered to his customer, based on three variables: supply of new releases, available shelf space and consumer demand. These are the same variables that Walmart and every other retailer faced, but in contrast to them, Tower Records secured more floor space so it could offer a lot more choice – far more than the long tail theory gave them credit for.

Russ Solomon's team was also responsible for taking curation in-house. Not only did they stock the largest selection of music and culture magazines to be found anywhere (catering for the 'head' of every niche interest to be found in the 'tail') but they also innovated with their own monthly magazine entitled *Pulse* that was handed out free in the stores. This was not just a newsletter but a magazine close to the size of *Rolling Stone* and gave the store the keys to curation, similar to a streaming service owning the most popular playlist today.

In 2014, I was fortunate to meet a near-ninety-year-old Russ Solomon and learn about the rule he would apply to each of his two hundred and forty-four stores in eighteen countries. Every time a consumer walked into a Tower Records they would be presented with around 40,000 unique albums across the entire available floor space. For Solomon, this was optimisation. Should the customer not find what they were looking for among those 40,000 unique album titles, then, if there was sufficient demand, Tower Records would order it, based on a 'one-in, one-out' policy – that is, order that title and remove a dormant title that had been at the back of the shelf collecting dust.

For flagship stores like Union Square in New York, Solomon would offer even more choice – stocking 32,000 unique album titles in the classical music section of that store alone. Nevertheless, even 40,000 unique album titles under one roof is a lot of choice, arguably more than enough to satisfy most music aficionados' tastes. Tower Records may have filed for bankruptcy in 2004 but it was already delivering Anderson's long tail concept in every one of its many stores.

I don't use the word 'revelation' lightly, but the following analysis justifies it. Using official US data from MRC Entertainment (formerly Nielsen), we can plot music demand in the calendar year 2019 by selecting four thresholds to measure 'the head' of the distribution – from the top 40, 400, 4,000 and 40,000 unique albums – and separate each by audio streams (Spotify, Apple Music), video streams (YouTube, Vevo), digital albums (iTunes) and physical albums (CD and vinyl).

The top 40,000 bucket is our focus, as that is a comparable sample to the inventory that was offered to customers walking into any one of Tower Records' stores fifteen years earlier. The smaller buckets bring additional colour to the history of the long tail: the Top 40 is a typical limit imposed on a chart; the top 400 is what you might find in today's supermarkets and big box retailers; whereas the top 4,000 is what HMV or Walmart would have typically stocked at the time the long tail caught our imagination back in 2004, making it a useful benchmark for comparing the more limited bricks-and-mortar retailers of the noughties to the unlimited choice on the digital shelf.

Indeed, the results charted below are a revelation. The Top 40 albums comprise between 2 to 3 per cent of total streaming demand (white and light-grey bars), but a tenth of total sales demand (dark grey and black) – suggesting that the sales model is more hit-heavy (as the theory suggests).

Among the top 400 albums, under a fifth of demand comes from streaming (white and light grey), a quarter from downloads (dark grey), and more than a third from CD sales (black) – capturing the natural long tail cut-off point for today's 'stack 'em high, sell 'em cheap' high-street retailers.

A similar pattern emerges from the top 4,000, where half of demand is captured in digital formats but more than two-thirds from physical. Restricted shelf space explains the concentration of demand around the head (just as the theory predicted) but a countervailing force would be that the increased dominance of online physical retail, such as purchasing a CD from Amazon, will widen choice and push this black bar down. Thus far, the long tail theory stands up – the more choice on streaming, the less concentrated demand is around the head, the more is reallocated to the tail.

Finally, when we compare the 'Tower Records Long Tail' of Russ Solomon's 40,000 unique albums to today's digital marketplace, we strike gold! For streaming services that carry over 60 million songs on their service, had they stocked the same level of choice as Tower Records did twenty years ago, that top 40,000 unique albums would have made up between 88 per cent and 95 per cent of all demand.

What this tells us is that the vast majority of today's demand,

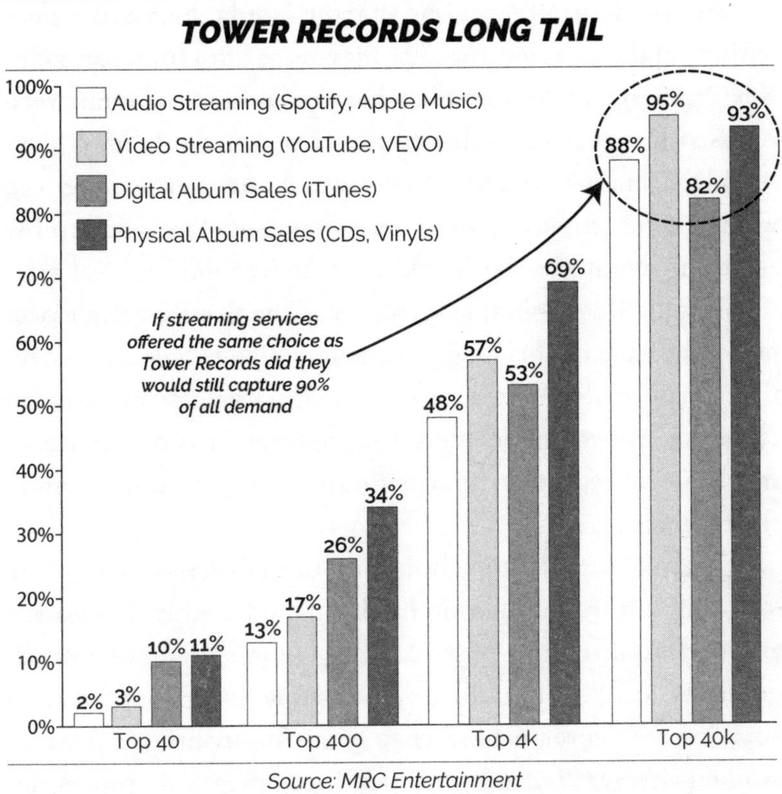


despite the unlimited choice that's on offer, could have been stored in physical form in a typical Tower Records store in the 1990s. A blunt interpretation would say that a streaming platform that carries 60 million unique tracks and absorbs over 55,000 new tracks every day could effectively go without stocking 99.3 per cent of these tracks and still keep 90 per cent of their business!

Before we go any further, there is one big caveat: Tower Records didn't keep a fixed stock of the same 40,000 unique albums – choice may have been limited, but it varied. To reiterate Solomon's retail philosophy, if the store didn't have that rare CD you were looking for, it would order it in and if there was enough demand, take one title out from the 40,000 – they optimised the 40,000 titles that they were limited to carrying. Nevertheless, this was an era where only 30,000 albums were released in a year (a small fraction of which would have been stocked), and it needs to be contrasted with a streaming era where the near-equivalent 30,000 albums (or 300,000 tracks) are being ingested every week.

What did Russ Solomon know that Chris Anderson (and the many advocates of his long tail theory) didn't? Solomon knew that you needed to offer a lot of choice to draw a crowd – more choice than anyone else offered at the time – but he also knew that some is better than none but more is not necessarily better than some.

A lot has been written about the statistics that describe the long tail, but little attention has been paid to Russ Solomon's approach to inventory control management. He may have just got lucky, taking a punt on 40,000 unique titles as opposed to applying any clever data science to justify it. But his method worked. Tower Records expanded its operation around the world and defied the forces of economic gravity by raising prices and increasing demand – although one should also note that it actually was fined for price-fixing in 2002.

US President Harry Truman is widely attributed with the quote: 'Give me a one-handed economist!' His point was that economists abuse the get-out-of-jail-free card by saying 'on one hand this, on the other hand that'. With apologies to President Truman, I must play that card here. On one hand, Tower Records tells us about the benefits of limiting choice. On the other hand, expanding choice provides value, even when the demand to justify it is not immediately visible. It takes two hands to tango.

Imagine you are going to a restaurant with a large group of friends. A plot of the demand for the restaurant's main courses would probably skew heavily towards a few popular dishes, and a longer list of other choices would comprise the long tail. Let's assume those 'blockbuster' hit dishes are steak, chicken and the vegetarian option, and the rest of menu offers twenty other 'long tail' choices. When the restaurant tallies up its sales figures, those three choices will be responsible for over 80 per cent of all the turnover (and, due to discounted buying of ingredients in bulk, even more of the profits).

If that same restaurant were to conduct its own rationalisation exercise, it may look at the long tail and decide to snap it off as unwanted goods. For a dish to earn its place on the menu, surely the demand must justify its inclusion. But if we go beyond money and add factors to the framework like religion or dietary requirements, we would see that cutting vegan, halal or gluten-free dishes, which may be down in the tail, would mean the customers who need those dishes cannot dine at this restaurant.

If those vegan customers cannot dine, then neither can any of their carnivorous friends. The damage from cutting the tail would multiply. Again, understanding the social context of choice is critical to Tarzan Economics. That vegan dish may be down in the tail but, due to the specific characteristics for which it caters, it is worth more than some other dishes generating similar sales. Not all 'tail' content is of equal value.

Selling records is one thing, managing restaurants is another – we need to draw from chapter 1 and remind ourselves about the goods being traded. Food is a renewable resource: if I like a dish, I'll come back again and again for that dish. A CD is a non-renewable resource: once I've bought *Nevermind* at Tower Records, I'm never coming back to buy that album again. So, Tower Records has an incentive to cycle albums in and out of their inventory, which suggests a utility for the 80 per cent of music they weren't stocking. A restaurant doesn't have the same problem: sure, snap off the tail and just sell the extremely popular dishes to willing customers for ever. The incentives are different.

That said, there are many reasons why a restaurant may pivot on such logic and keep their less popular menu items on the list, beyond serving 'niche' markets like people with dietary restrictions. The rest of the menu gives you a chance to experiment with new dishes. It creates a context to reach a broader audience (it might not be a bestseller, but there might be a small but devoted audience for some less popular dishes who themselves bring along people who may order the most popular dishes). Anyone you get in the door helps with the word-of-mouth virality of the restaurant. Plus, choice is something some people value in a restaurant even if they don't exercise it. Option value may appear as a zero when counting transactions, but it can be worth as much as the one's which reached the till.

Nassim Nicholas Taleb discusses this in the chapter 'The Most Intolerant Wins: The Dominance of the Stubborn Minority' in his book *Skin in the Game*. His core argument is that the long tail is comprised of an ensemble that behaves in ways not predicted by the components. What matters more, he argues, are the interactions. More broadly, Taleb wrote:

> Studying individual ants will never (one can safely say never for most such situations), never give us an idea on how the ant colony operates. For that, one needs to understand an ant colony as an ant colony, no less, no more, not a collection of ants. This is called an 'emergent' property of the whole, by

> which parts and whole differ because what matters are the interactions between such parts. And interactions can obey very simple rules.*

Taleb explains his simple rule as follows: a kosher (or halal) eater will never eat non-kosher (or non-halal) food, but a non-kosher eater isn't banned from eating kosher food. Also: a disabled person cannot use the regular bathroom, but a non-disabled person can use the bathroom for disabled people.

Tarzan Economics promotes thinking less about individuals and more about how social networks connect people into a community. The needs of the few are critical in allowing crowds to gather. Taleb argues that society doesn't evolve by consensus – in fact, only a few people are needed to disproportionately move the needle for the whole of it. All it takes is an asymmetry that prevents the few from sharing an experience with the many for the whole group to fall apart. And asymmetries are present in just about everything. The sole vegan who is out dining with a large group of carnivorous friends is just one example.

Veganomics, as you might have seen, pervades the Tower Records long tail. It is the reason why it is unfair to say that today's streaming services could offer just 400,000 tracks (or 40,000 albums – 0.7 per cent of today's choice) yet still retain 90 per cent of the demand. The vast majority of those shopping in the head also venture occasionally down into the tail. To deny this choice may push them away and risk alienating them from a potentially culture-shifting movement.

For the first six months of 2019, MRC Entertainment

* Nassim Nicholas Taleb, *Skin in the Game: Hidden Asymmetries in Daily Life*, Penguin Random House, 2018, p. 69.

reported that almost 40 million songs were streamed in the United States – a long and skinny tail. The top 40,000 albums – about 400,000 tracks – made up 90 per cent of all demand. Meaning 10 per cent of all demand would be music that couldn't be stocked in Tower Records. There are many songs in that skinny 10 per cent of the long tail – 39,400,450 to be precise. That's 39,400,450 vegan dishes successfully served to some customer or other. And with each vegan dish served, a popular dish (or hit song) was probably served alongside it – unless, that is, vegans dine out alone. We can take this a stage further as in 2019 there were 60 million unique songs on the digital shelf and only 40 million were streamed at least once, meaning a further 20 million vegan dishes were on the menu but not served. They may not have got much love, but the option of knowing they were there would have served up some value that made them subscribe in the first place. Veganomics teaches us that money cannot be made in the tail, but you can make money off the tail.

Chris Gardener of the commercial real estate giant CBRE succinctly sums up veganomics by observing that consumers no longer go into a store and ask 'Have you got . . .' – they either expect it to be there due to greater checks prior to a shopping trip or the slightest hint of a perceived risk of something down in the tail not being stocked has already made them default to Amazon. As people's time has become increasingly valuable and consumption has become laser-focused, nobody has the time to risk leaving a shopping mall empty-handed.

Another indirect benefit of veganomics is to broaden participation. Music would traditionally be bucketed into ten genres, from pop down to classical. Sure, there were niche genres, some with baffling titles like 'Intelligent Drum and Bass' (presumably requiring a first-class degree to qualify) but the genre tail was far removed from the head. If a jazz artist proved popular, they'd be reclassified from jazz to pop. Now we have incredible sites like Every Noise at Once which offer a scatterplot of the 4,800-plus musical genres they have listed. The latest genre to be identified is 'Ugandan Tradition'. Awareness of what's in the tail can only help it survive.

This is why veganomics is especially illuminating given the political and social debate about diversity and inclusion. 'Tail snapping' of media content, where attention is pulled towards the lucky few in the head and excludes the many down in the tail is transferable to 'diversity and inclusion' in the wider workplace. Diversity is the easier part of this double-header as its definition is open to interpretation; inclusion is harder as it means leaving no one behind. Inclusivity and tail-snapping are not compatible. The sensitive process of judging if, and how, inclusivity should have scope and limitation is not dissimilar to if, and how, the tail should be snapped. But veganomics helps to remind us of the counterfactual – the cost of excluding the few can adversely impact the many.

### HOW IMDB SERVES VEGANOMICS

You can watch veganomics in action without leaving your sofa! Amazon is remarkably similar to a traditional bricks-and-mortar retailer in that it stocks the head on Prime and sources the tail through the marketplace. But its approach to Prime Video is different, as it plays to veganomics, serving the tail as opposed to snapping it. Amazon's acquisition of IMDb (the world's richest database on film and television) gives it perfect information about what it does and doesn't currently stock – correcting the information asymmetry that so often leads to an underpriced tail, and allowing Amazon to read across the columns of media metadata as well as down them.

If all you had to judge a book by was its cover (or a movie by its stars and director) then that would be limited information. If you knew the expansive 'family tree' of all the actors and production crew, along with an aggregation of reviews and trivia, which IMDb provides, then the information becomes less limited. Surfacing all the 'unsung heroes' who played an undervalued role in capturing our attention corrects the information asymmetry and allows that value to be crystallised.

From reading across the columns of data involved in a film, to discovering the music playing in the background, pressing pause to display the title and a link to the track on Amazon Music, Amazon knows that not all diners want the same dish, and some have specific needs. Maybe you want to watch a movie based on genre (e.g. thriller, romance), but maybe your desired menu is based on actor, director or soundtrack. The names you wish to follow may belong in the head, but their past work might be down in the tail – and Amazon's integration of IMDb makes that discoverable. By reducing friction in the search process, vegan options have never been so easy to find, and never have they uncovered so much value.

*

We all have an innate desire to draw a crowd. As Vanessa Bakewell of Facebook put it so profoundly, we all 'want to go fishing where the fish are'. Money is a motivator, but recognition (and the intimacy of appreciation that comes with it) matters more. The penny dropped for me when Ross Michaels, the manager of the Grammy-award-winning singer Yebba (Abbey Smith) once told me that the comments from the crowds she'd drawn on YouTube mattered more to him than the cash paid over by Amazon, Apple or Spotify.

As with attention, there's a contestability to drawing crowds – in the past we competed in a Keynesian Beauty Contest mindset where judges controlled which crowds could be drawn. Now you have the confidence to let go of that gatekeeper mindset and grab on to the new rules of how crowds are drawn.

The tales of Tupperware and Tower Records act as a call to action for all of us – when top-down marketing failed, Brownie Wise pivoted to a bottom-up viral approach of Tupperware parties. Tower Records taught us that, on one hand, some choice is better than none, but it doesn't necessarily follow that more is better than some. Twenty years on from its bankruptcy, veganomics, on the other hand, taught us that some tail content is worth more than others. Restaurants might make pennies from vegan dishes, but without them they wouldn't make half as many pounds from the hit steak.

We have to instil in our heads that a crowd is a crowd whenever and wherever they are drawn. Radio stations may have drawn crowds towards artists for half a century, but Meghan Trainor taught us that Starbucks can serve the same purpose. We can see this everywhere we look; as platforms scale, new networks are formed and crowds gather from the edge, not the middle. Take, for example, the old vine of how a customer support department would function within a typical firm, often involving a one-to-one relationship with the customer; now crowds are drawn to community pages to share solutions and pre-empt problems. The old vine of top-down communications has been replaced by a new vine of bottom-up social influencers.

This crowd-drawing principle adds to your ability to perform Tarzan Economics when faced with disruption; let go of what no longer works, empowering yourself with what does. Podcasts, which we explored in the previous chapter, are a prime example, as the barriers to entry have been removed and the ability to connect niche interests with niche audiences has been amplified. Notable podcasts like 'The Moth' and 'Do The Right Thing' (and even, on occasion, Freakonomics Radio) are performed live on stages to crowded theatres – turning the cost of content creation into a revenue stream (and flipping the rules of media on their head). Podcasters are harvesting considerable money here – more so, in some cases, than advertising. It's those pivots we all need to learn from and act upon now.

The traditional vine of crowd-drawing has been found withering, and the importance of the intermediaries that creators and other artists have traditionally counted on to draw crowds has been called into question. Especially when they expect the creator to do the crowd-drawing themselves. Anyone practising Tarzan Economics should be asking themselves: are these traditional middlemen still as relevant as before? If I may request a posthumous pardon from President Truman, the answer is: on one hand . . .

# 4

# MAKE OR BUY?

Any parent, guardian or (even) child who has shown some aptitude in writing and performing music will probably be asking two questions: how might my child become the next Billie Eilish (who rose to fame at the age of seventeen); and who do I need to bring on board to help get them there? Not to mention: do I need a record label, a manager, a publisher? If so, which comes first? Or can I just use the power of social media and streaming services instead?

After all, we've learned from chapter 3 how hits can now happen without any intent from the industry gatekeepers, but instead thanks solely to the will of the consumer. This disrupts how we approach 'make or buy' decisions – whether to go it alone or bring in the services of others.

In the past, a parent looking to nurture the next young star would have little choice but to grant control to audience-creating intermediaries. But now the first question those intermediaries will ask is, 'What audience are you bringing me?' Like it or hate it, this catch-22 is our call to action: we all need to learn more about going it alone to pivot through disruption.

There are numerous forces in play that can tip the 'right'

decision in either direction. If we go back to our introduction, we saw how technology has removed the monopoly grip previously delegated to experts like accountants, bankers and lawyers. Apps that perform the necessary bookkeeping, financial transactions and contractual agreements are a thumb-press on a piece of glass away, enabling one to retain control and perform more of these tasks, and become less dependent on others.

Technology can also tip the scales in the other direction, where buying more services in becomes more appealing than making it yourself. Driving your own car, for instance, may have been a rational choice in the past, considering the financial investment that you made in acquiring it. But now, you might choose to sell your car and use a ride-share service like Uber instead, as this allows you to do something more productive with your commute – namely work in the back. Technology adds appeal to buying a ride, rather than making it happen yourself.

But how to know when to make and when to buy?

For an illuminating example of such a decision, let's go back to 2007 and reunite with one of the most famous 'go it alone' decisions in history: Radiohead's *In Rainbows* album. It's a case study with layers of lessons that have a universal application to a question we all face every day – to cede control to others, or to go it alone?

The five founding members of Radiohead met at school in Oxfordshire in 1985, predating the mass adoption of the CD. In 1991, having performed in Oxford's Jericho Tavern under the banner of On a Friday, they recruited Chris Hufford and Bryce Edge as their management team. After signing to EMI, they changed their name to Radiohead, paying homage to a brilliant Talking Heads song written by one of the finest Scottish exports to the US since whiskey: David Byrne. That line-up – five musicians and two managers – has stayed loyal to each other for the last thirty years. The band's loyalty even extends to producer Nigel Godrich, who first worked with the band in 1994 – long before Steve Jobs had ever dreamt up the iPod.

Radiohead have left a lasting legacy to rock music, from the studio to the stage. Their 1997 live performance at Glastonbury, off the back of their seminal *OK Computer* album, cemented the band as one of the world's most important acts. Few performances are more revered, which is astonishing given that the technical problems were so bad they almost walked off the stage. Their thirty-six-year career recently received the ultimate recognition in being inducted into the Rock and Roll Hall of Fame. The band has lived through more disruption probably than any of today's millennials will ever see. They had been signed to the London-based record label EMI since 1991, and by the start of 2007 had delivered six albums (and over 30 million sales).

As work began on their next album, the band found themselves in what Bryce Edge referred to as 'limbo land' – they had fulfilled their commitment to EMI and were legally able to break ties with the label and go it alone, though EMI would retain ownership over the previous six albums. The benefits of exploring that first taste of freedom in over fifteen years was balanced with the cost of losing control of their ownership of the six previous albums. There was a sense of boredom creeping in with what Hufford calls 'the conveyor belt process' of recording and releasing music.

As Radiohead were considering their options, the record industry was in the midst of convulsions. CD sales, which made up 90 per cent of label income, were falling off a cliff; piracy was in the ascendancy; notions that legal downloads of tracks priced at 79 pence (99 cents) would plug the gap were treated like a joke. The situation was so dire that one label executive infamously told his own A&R team, 'The music industry has AIDS, and hopefully we'll die last.'

EMI had recently been acquired by Guy Hands's private equity vehicle, Terra Firma. Anyone who has read the book (or watched the hilarious film) *Barbarians at the Gate* will understand why that was bad news for EMI. For those who haven't, consider how private equity works: buy a house for £100, using £99 of debt and £1 equity, meaning that (so long as the rental income of the house more than covers the cost of financing the debt) selling the house for £101 can double the investors' money in a relatively short amount of time. The challenge at EMI was that Terra Firma's short-term profit goals conflicted with the long-termism needed by musicians to create their art – and it wasn't working out.

There is a wise, old expression in the music business: 'If you want loyalty, get yourself a dog.' Radiohead told EMI to get itself a dog.

The band's managers formed what they called a 'circle of trust', which brought on board a motley crew of experts in publishing, accounting and legal services. In a scene reminiscent of the film *Ocean's 11*, this 'circle of trust' was assembled to execute a caper of a kind nobody had ever done before. Increasing the size of the management team to make-not-buy radically increased the costs of managing Radiohead. Bryce Edge remembers joking with the band that 'We've become the label here, so why don't we get more than our current 20 per cent?'

The band were now in full control of their digital destiny at a time when it was barely clear what the future of digital music would look like. Radiohead weren't even on iTunes. They resented the iTunes model where fans could cherry-pick songs from an album, eroding the artistic value of the music the band had created. And there was no reason to believe that digital music would ever constitute a sustainable business. Meanwhile, the CD industry was dying on the vine. CDs, in Hufford's own words, were just 'an interim pile of bollocks'. At the time, the record labels' approach to digital distribution was a relic of the physical era; they even deducted postage and packaging from iTunes sales.

It wasn't just Hufford who had doubts about the CD model, which made up 90 per cent of the industry's revenues, as there was growing discontentment within the ranks of EMI itself. Simon David Miller, a progressively minded executive within EMI's management team, who witnessed the label's star act set off on their own, was brave enough to later challenge Terra Firma by arguing 'the best thing this label could do right now is stop selling CDs'. Miller was grappling with Tarzan Economics at the time, arguing that the label should let go of what was both sustaining the business yet simultaneously killing it. Only by letting go could EMI reach out to a new vine for its survival.

Radiohead had both the contractual freedom and the confidence in their recording to try something different. Edge would say:

> We would never have played that hand had we not got a great record. One of our fears was being accused of gimmickry. The quality of the record helped drive the decision to release it in the way we did. None of us thought it would make the News at Ten.

Then the proverbial shit hit the fan. On 1 October 2007, Radiohead announced to the world that their highly anticipated new album *In Rainbows* would be made available, effectively for free, through a voluntary pay-what-you-want model. This would be the first phase of a multiphase release strategy that would be unveiled over the next three months but at the time it was the only phase that mattered. Not only that, but after almost two decades with the record label EMI, the band were retaining ownership of the recordings and compositions for the ten songs on *In Rainbows*. Cue an unprecedented global media meltdown.

It wasn't just that Radiohead were releasing an album digitally without major label support. It was that they were releasing an album that customers didn't even have to buy. The music industry unanimously held its breath to see if the experiment was going to change the pillars of intellectual property at a stroke. One of the world's most popular bands was not only going it alone, but they were also giving their music away. Radiohead had done much more than 'make' their own marketing and distribution instead of relying on the label to do it for them – they had removed the need for the consumer to 'buy' it as well!

There was method to the madness. Radiohead were avoiding the traditional staggered promotional cycle (where albums would be released in different markets at different times), ensuring that fans across the internet would have access to the music at the same time, thereby preventing leaks on piracy sites, which had plagued many previous big-name releases. In a clever calculation of the opportunity cost, if fans were determined to steal it anyway, then they might as well take it legally from the band's own site for free.

For Radiohead, the timing was right to test the merits of 'make' over 'buy'. But for a nervous industry, this was a step too close to the cliff's edge – it was gambling the entire future of copyright and the supply chain that it supports. If this worked, would the world ever be the same again?

To really understand what happened with this experiment,

the order of events matters. Shortly after the announcement on 1 October 2007, fans could visit the band's own website and pre-order the album with the option of paying a voluntary price. As the orders came flying in from all around the world, speculation as to what would happen next reached a fever pitch. But the wild conjecture overlooked a key behavioural economic consideration – the time between offer and acquisition. Timing was vitally important to the band's strategy. Bryce explains:

> What was critical to the tip-jar process was the 'thinking time' between the announcement and the launch. There were something like seven days for fans – real fans – to make up their mind as to how much they were willing to donate. The fans that came in early were donating large amounts – hundreds of pounds – so much so that we decided to put a cap on the tip jar and place a ceiling of £99 as the maximum amount fans could contribute. We felt it was right to limit the amount you could pay.

### HOW DO WE KNOW WHEN THE PRICE IS RIGHT?

This 'thinking time' that fans had to decide upon a price opens up a Pandora's Box of economic theory and analysis in the field of auction design, which has since been used to propel numerous tech companies' fortunes.

Before we get into 'auction theory' we need to remind ourselves of the constraints Radiohead were facing.

First, the preparation for the release of *In Rainbows* was being conducted in complete secrecy, which meant there was no public information, nor were there any album reviews – meaning it was of an unknown quality. Second, they were selling MP3 files, which are non-perishable goods. Third, during this 'thinking period' fans were aware of a deluxe CD-box in the pipeline (which we'll examine shortly) but which was not yet available.

The first lesson in what Bryce Edge refers to as 'thinking time' is from Francesca Cornelli, currently dean of the Kellogg School of Management. Cornelli published a paper on 'pay-what-you-want for museum entrance'.* Her thesis was that voluntary donations may actually raise more money on average than charging a fixed price, because wealthy individuals would choose to pay an outsized amount. Poorer individuals, meanwhile, may choose not to participate at all under a fixed price, but could contribute something above zero under a 'pay what you want' system. The availability of public information was critical to Cornelli's study, as potential patrons knew about the museum and the value it brought. In Radiohead's case, there was no information leakage as neither the fans nor the press had prior knowledge about the quality of the record. So, while Cornelli's price discrimination theory has some relevance, it is not a perfect fit.

The second lesson from auction design comes from

* Francesca Cornelli, 'Optimal Selling Procedures with Fixed Costs', *Journal of Economic Theory*, Vol. 71, Issue 1, October 1996, pp.1–30.

a seminal paper on competitive bidding by economists Paul Milgrom and Bob Weber.* They found that, generally, the value of a song to any one person depends on the expectation of the value to others – we enjoy a song more knowing that we will share it with others, a phenomenon sometimes known as a 'watercooler effect'. Milgrom and Weber show how the release of information increases the highest valuations even if the lower valuations remain unchanged. When I learn that you think what I'm passionate about is valuable, I'm going to value it more. This feedback effect captures what makes charts so compelling to the music industry: they make the popular more visible and the visible more popular. Pricing could therefore be designed to be conditional on where an album comes out in the charts, so that fans pay X if it hits number 1, 75 per cent of X if it hits number 2, 50 per cent of X if it reaches number 5, and so on. In Radiohead's case, however, such conditionality would have been impractical as neither the tip-jar model (nor the deluxe CD box set which followed it) were chart eligible – denying the consumer a relative ranking that could influence their payment decision.

If you'll pardon the slight digression, an analogy for the 'Milgrom effect' can be found in the collapse of the Soviet Union, when the Czech government auctioned off a fixed number of shares in state enterprises. As

* Paul R. Milgrom and Robert J. Weber, 'A Theory of Auctions and Competitive Bidding', *Econometrica*, Vol. 50, No.5, September 1982. On 12 October 2020, these two Stanford economists won the Nobel Prize for 'improvements to auction theory and inventions of new auction formats'.

bidders received information that the 'fixed pool' had been oversubscribed, they raised their own bids and asked for more shares. One of the motivations was to resell those former state assets for a profit. While there would be no second-hand market for digital copies of *In Rainbows*, there would be for the deluxe CD box set.

The website Discogs, a dangerously addictive second-hand vinyl auction platform, lists the limited edition deluxe box set and provides key price signals. As of June 2020, there are 7,538 'haves' (owners willing to sell it) and 2,677 'wants' (buyers expressing a desire for it) with a review score of 4.73 out of 5 – high by any standard. Today, the lowest price for the box set offered on the platform is £53, the highest £142 and the median £91 – which, after all these years, is still more than twice the fixed price of £40 the band charged back in the autumn of 2007. This may be due to a collectors' item appreciating in value, or the vinyl format increasing in popularity, or both.

The third and final lesson we can draw from the theory of auctions can be found in Hal Varian's 1994 paper 'Sequential Contributions to Public Goods'* and the more recent 'Public Goods and Private Gifts'.† Varian's analysis builds upon the 'provision point mechanism' and will be familiar to anyone who has used Kickstarter – a platform we'll be exploring shortly.

* Hal Varian, 'Sequential Contributions to Public Goods', *Journal of Public Economics*, Volume 53, Issue 2, February 1994, pp. 165–86.

† Hal Varian, 'Public Goods and Private Gifts', *Mimeo*, 2013.

The seller states they will release the album if they raise enough to cover the costs of creation. Donors contribute a fee, because they want it to be released. The incentive there is to remove the uncertainty and prevent the possibility of the album remaining a dormant zero, as it may never see the light of day. The sequencing of the bidding process is key: if someone else bids a hundred pounds, it suggests that someone other than you thinks it's valuable – similar to the beauty contest discussed in the prior chapter. This ties into the observations from Chris Hufford and Bryce Edge, regarding the early bids for *In Rainbows* being from those willing to pay the most.

Like so much of economics, the theory of auctions will prescribe many assumptions that cannot be replicated in practice. Nevertheless, it gives us a necessary lesson in abstraction about the forces driving Radiohead's strategy – rather than simply assume the seller sets the price, we can ask if the buyer would have offered more if they'd had the choice. The role of information is often treated as a 'given' but we should challenge our thinking by asking why an album with a great review costs the same as one that's been trashed by the media – and what happens to price when there are no reviews in the first place. Finally, Radiohead were going to release the album anyway, making it non-risky and non-exclusive, but sequential bids tell us how that changes when those two conditions are reversed.

All in all, theory can tell us only so much, but with

the benefit of hindsight it can tell us a lot. Where it struggles is factoring in the most important variable of them all – the band and their circle of trust instinctively knew that the album would rock.

Then came download day, or D-day. On the morning of 10 October 2007, Radiohead made available on their website a ZIP file containing the album's ten tracks encoded in MP3 format for their fans to download. This was the first stage in what would turn out to be a five-stage relay race. The format matters, as it wasn't locked by unwanted Digital Rights Management (DRM), which the iTunes store wrapped around their files to make them non-transferable – making the transferable MP3 of *In Rainbows* a superior good.

Two months of intense media scrutiny followed over the average price fans had paid. Chris Hufford recalls how it fluctuated over time: as 'the passive fans came in towards the end of the experiment, the price was brought right down'. This created an unplanned and unconventional risk for the project due to a quirk in copyright; if someone paid zero for the recordings then this would have cost the label and artists money as they still had to pay the publisher and songwriters a royalty for the underlying songs – songwriters who confusingly happened to be the same people as the artist. The recordings may have been available for free, but backstage the songs still had to be paid for, even if the fans paid nothing.

Once the experiment was live, the baton was passed on to the second of the five release formats – a £40 limited box set edition containing the new album on CD and heavyweight double vinyl, along with a second enhanced CD with digital photographs and artwork and a hardback book with more artwork and lyrics.

The box set edition was a high-margin product delivered on a made-to-order basis from the band's own distribution plant. Bryce Edge explained how the economics of charging for the thrill of a luxury complemented the thrill of a bargain – something we will be tackling in chapter 6:

> Having our own merchandise company, WASTE, was critical to the whole project. It gave us options. We produced 100,000 box sets and sold them all directly. What was remarkable was getting them to distribution warehouses around the world in the months prior to its release, to ensure that when we flicked the switch everyone would receive the Disc Box on the same day – yet we still managed to keep all this logistical work a secret from the media and fans alike!

The deluxe box set was shipped from the start of December 2007, with buyers receiving it before Christmas. Radiohead mitigated their risk: there were no returns allowed.

These two go-it-alone options of tip jar and made-to-order disc box also circumvented the music industry's antiquated payment system, which can take months (if not years) to move money from consumer to creator. By adopting modern transactional models of processing payments directly, the band saw all their money within seventy-two hours – meaning they had cashed in their chips long before the third stage of this relay race commenced.

By reducing the price of recorded music effectively to zero and then hiking it back up to £40, Radiohead's strategy tested two extremes of pricing the same ten songs. The third stage was to move the price back to the middle. The conventional CD release hit retail stores at the beginning of 2008 and debuted in the UK and US charts at number 1 – becoming only the tenth independently distributed album to ever top the charts in America. At this stage in the story, neither the tip-jar intake nor the disc-box sales counted towards *In Rainbows*' chart position, making this achievement even more remarkable.

Tip-jar, deluxe and physical formats had all proved popular. With the CD at the top of the charts in markets around the world, the baton would return to digital format, with the band debuting the album on iTunes three days later. Apple, by far the largest of the download stores, wouldn't allow artists to sell an album as a 'hard bundle', but since the full album of *In Rainbows* had already been available as a digital download, there was less for the band to lose by putting it on iTunes. In its debut week on iTunes, *In Rainbows* scaled Apple's album charts in a similar fashion to the CD sales earlier that month. Half a year later, the rest of the band's catalogue would finally join it on the digital shelf.

A year after the launch of *In Rainbows*, Jane Dyball, formerly of Warner Chappell Music Publishing (and part of the band's circle of trust), reported that the album had sold 3 million copies, over half of which were in CD format, in its first year – more than either of their previous two albums. Even the vinyl edition was the bestselling vinyl album of 2008. Radiohead had proved that hit music is a hit regardless of the release format. That proved telling for the fifth and final leg of this journey.

Piracy – files traded on illegal BitTorrent sites – kicked in as soon as the original ZIP file was released on the *In Rainbows* website on 10 October 2007. The album had been released without Digital Rights Management (DRM) protection – anyone who had the file could share it. Piracy wasn't part of the plan, as making the content available legally for free was supposed to eliminate the need for fans to go to illegal MP3 sites. During the two-month tip-jar period, data from

BigChampagne and published in the study 'In Rainbows, On Torrents', co-authored by myself, showed there were two *In Rainbows* files downloaded illegally on BitTorrent networks for every single file taken from the band's website. There were a total of 2.3 million torrented files by 3 November – with torrent users trading a staggering 400,000 copies on just its opening release date of 10 October.

BigChampagne drew a comparison with Panic at the Disco, who released their album around the same time using conventional means. Illegal downloads peaked at only 157,000 in a single week – about a third less than *In Rainbows*' peak day of trading. 'Legal free' was a success, but it was surprisingly overshadowed by 'illegal free'.

Bryce Edge reflects on the popularity of *In Rainbows* across this five-stage experiment by pointing to the sticky behaviour patterns of the consumer: 'It was a great record – it just showed people have buying habits. Back then people still purchased a CD, today they still purchase vinyl.' Inertia similarly helps to explain piracy. People have a tendency to do what they've always done. The keyboards that we type on today are still laid out with QWERTY at the top left, an 1874 design that was deliberately inefficient to slow secretaries down to reduce their mistakes. A hundred and fifty years on, we (and the generations that follow us) will continue to do what we've always done – and type on an inefficient layout of a keyboard. Music fans had been using piracy sites for nearly a decade when *In Rainbows* was launched, and many of them were also 'locked in' to do what they'd always done.

For Brian Message, of ATC Management and another member of the 'circle of trust', the band's bold decision to make and not buy has had a lasting effect:

It was a ballsy move. From that business model point of view, it was of that time. The bravery of it – to take their destiny in their own hands. We raised questions about the role of intermediaries. I think services like AWAL (Artists Without A Label) came out of *In Rainbows*. Labels give you capital, and maybe access to the best slots like the soundtrack to the latest Bond movie. Other than capital, you can get the rest of the services you need elsewhere.

Message recalls how secrecy may have been key to the success of *In Rainbows* but could have easily gone sour: 'We were worried about the press reaction as we hadn't given them the record up front. Our fears about them dissing the record were misplaced – they loved it. We were just f**king lucky.' Message points to the band's US concerts to show how they raised the bar in terms of credibility: 'The real return was seeing the band play out to 20,000 in San Francisco before *In Rainbows* and then 60,000 afterwards.'

Nearly fifteen years on, we're still learning the lessons from the *In Rainbows* experiment. Take, for example, how consumers are willing to pay for the thrill of a bargain (tip jar) and for the thrill of a luxury (disc box). Today, we see that the luxury of purchasing vinyl generates more gross revenue to labels than downloads. Perennially dismissed as a blip not a trend, the resurgence in vinyl is now so great that it has overtaken CD revenues – a real sign of the format-times, especially when you consider this is restricted to the first-hand market and ignore the burgeoning second-hand trades.

To learn another lesson from *In Rainbows*, take the direct artist-to-fan website Bandcamp. It serves over 600,000 artists around the world and has paid out over $650 million to creators. Since 2009 Bandcamp has offered a cleverly framed 'Name

Your Price, No Minimum' protocol for downloads and physical content. It may be niche, but it serves artists who want to take back control of pricing and let their fans decide for themselves, as opposed to buying in to the conventional corporate pricing formula.

In exploring new territory between the creator and consumer in 2007, Radiohead left behind a map that many others have followed.

The conventional tripartite structure of creative industries is formed by creator, editor/publisher and distributor/retailer, and *In Rainbows* is just one of many examples from history showing that competition plays out between the three parties as they vie to maximise their revenue from the whole chain. Publishers, stuck in the middle, tend to have the upper hand, as they alone can hedge their bets and cross-collateralise, offsetting losses on one side to capture gains on the other. A book publisher is in a position to give kickbacks to a distributor; a record label may give favourable deals to the retailer; and a movie distributor may give exclusivity to the cinema and so on. Middle men can rob Peter to pay (or bribe) Paul.

This makes the creator the 'principal' (owner of the work) and the publisher the 'agent' (assigned to maximise the value of the work); both will have their own self-interests that can be aligned through an agreed contract. An advance paid from the agent to the principal signals a commitment that they believe in the commercial value of a piece of work with an unknown quality – the bigger the advance the more the scales tip. Think of it this way: if you owe the bank £100,000 then you have a problem, if you owe them £1 million then they have a problem. What differentiates a principal from an agent is similar to what differentiates a loan shark from a bank, in that the latter has the ability to hedge and spread their bets over many options and across many time periods. Loan sharks, by comparison, often resemble a gambler in a casino whose options are limited to putting all their chips on red.

Disruption can tip the balance of power in this tripartite structure. Examples abound of each side getting the upper hand. On the creator side, many games developers pay the Apple app store a flat tax of 30 per cent on transactions, circumventing the need for a middle-man publisher to get to market. On the distributor side, when Apple publishes the game on their app store, they are taking power away from the intermediary who would have previously published the game for retailers. Power, in this instance, moves away from the middle to either side.

Professional footballers, often derided for their excessive pay, also show how value can migrate away from the publisher and distributor and toward the creator. Arsenal's Mesut Özil (a creator) is paid a reported £350,000 per week – around twice what the UK's prime minister gets paid in a year. Rather than express disgust at the inequality, one can admire how his agent has soaked up all the value that his publisher (Arsenal football club) and distributor (pay-television sports networks) creates, and gets rewarded accordingly. It's not often in life we see the person who does all the work get the lion's share of the reward (although Özil's work rate is questionable).

As we've learned from *In Rainbows*, in this continuous battle for power, when push comes to shove, one of these three players may do their own maths and calculate that it's time to strike out alone. But to make it (do it yourself) successfully, and not buy (bypass conventional intermediaries), they will need to have weighed all the known costs against the expected benefits, and then compare this calculation to the opportunity cost – the value of the road not taken.

All cost-benefit analyses are tricky, but they're particularly tricky in times of disruption. A good cost-benefit analysis will try to take into account all sorts of complex, often ineffable, forces in the real world and reduce them to numbers that can be slotted into a spreadsheet. That process of reduction relies on frameworks and rules derived from cost-benefit analyses of the past. But what if you're looking at an entirely new world? What if the old rules don't apply? To pivot through disruption is to challenge entrenched 'rules' and assumptions.

If the rules of constructing a cost-benefit analysis state, for example, that the value of a property is supposed depreciate over time, then why is it that older houses tend to be worth more than newer ones? If the rules of capturing how money now is worth more than later state that you use the same prescribed discount rate for future values, not even adjusting as central banks worldwide now operate at interest rates close to zero, you need to ask if this naivety exists simply because that's how it's always been done?

The Scottish economist John Kay captured how warped the cost-benefit reasoning can become with his observation that discouraging smoking actually ends up costing the government money in the long run. This is because the cost of additional state pensions through increased life expectancy far exceeds the savings from reduced demand for NHS treatment of smoking-related diseases. (Not to mention the lost tax revenue when the smoker quits.) In Kay's view, economists seem deserving targets for Oscar Wilde's characterisation of the cynic as a 'man who knows the price of everything and the value of nothing'.* Many non-economists know this, ironically giving them a competitive advantage and approaching the costs

* John Kay, 'The price of everything: what people get wrong about cost-benefit analysis', *Prospect Magazine*, March 2019.

and benefits of make-or-buy decisions differently – making rational choices as a result. Knowing that no audience-making middleman is going to invest in you until you have created an audience, makes the calculation a lot simpler – you've got to go it alone regardless.

Something has fundamentally changed in the principal–agent relationship and it goes far beyond music and media. The appeal of buying into intermediaries was that they provided finance upfront and would exercise their gatekeeper power to draw a crowd in return for ownership of the resulting creation. Sign away your copyrights, receive a sizeable cheque in return and the wheels of the crowd-drawing machine would begin to turn, hopefully, in your favour.

These days, the first question intermediaries ask is 'What audience are you bringing?' If the role of creating an audience has shifted back from the agent to the principal, this creates an inconvenient truth for the make-or-buy decision. Why, the principal might ask, should I cede control over my work to an agent, when the first question they ask is 'What audience can I bring to them?' This tension in the relationship between principal and agent is not new, but we need to go back several centuries to see how it has been resolved.

Patronage is the support, encouragement, privilege, or financial aid that one organisation or individual bestows on another. Its origins date back to the Renaissance, when patronage was necessary for European artists, writers and musicians to make a living. A wealthy, powerful patron provided the financial means and political cover for a career in creativity. In return, praise for benefactors littered the pages and canvases of the artists' work. Edmund Burke, an eighteenth-century Anglo-Irish statesman and philosopher, described patronage as 'the tribute that opulence owes to genius' – to flaunt their wealth, the rich buy the one thing they don't possess: creative excellence.

Burke's canny observation proved short-lived, as soon afterwards the emergence of a burgeoning middle class and mass-production technologies brought creative works to the masses and pushed patrons to the fringes. The opulent moved their investments into other areas, and creative geniuses looked for large markets, not wealthy individuals. The end of traditional patronage was the beginning of the entertainment industries we see today.

But thanks to digital disruption, patronage has returned, though perhaps in an unrecognisable form. Patronage has had a modern makeover in which customers have become contributors: giving a few pounds (or dollars) to artists, podcasters, writers and even academics whose work they enjoy.

Patronage still requires 'drawing a crowd', as we explored in the previous chapter, but the way money changes hands is different – instead of releasing content so the customers pay you, they pay you so that you release the content. Varian's provision-point mechanism has found a home in modern models of patronage in that people want to support artists during the creation process not just at the output stage. The trade-off is more nuanced than meets the eye: retaining ownership and self-funding creation while a platform manages your money versus relinquishing ownership and having an intermediary finance it for you and control your money. Because artists need to draw a crowd regardless of these options, patronage obviates the need for intermediaries to play the money-manager role.

Just as there are two-sided platforms disintermediating traditional business models in other industries (like retail and commerce), there is now a competitive market for patronage services. In a crowded market, it's Kickstarter and Patreon who can tell us most about how and why patronage returned, and where it goes next. Kickstarter and Patreon have each made widely accessible the means for customers to give money directly to creators, without the need for an intermediary.

Kickstarter was founded in 2009 and is widely credited with being a pioneer in the modern-day revival of patronage. Creators (principals) use Kickstarter to crowdsource finance for their projects, and their willing backers (agents) face an all-or-nothing risk profile: they are charged only if the campaign reaches its funding goal. Since launch, Kickstarter says it has raised $5.5 billion in total pledges from over 19 million backers, and around 200,000 projects have reached their goal. Kickstarter takes a 5 per cent share for helping to match creators and their patrons. Everything else flows as usual, from the patrons to the creator.

Kickstarter's innovation was realising how patronage could be reinvented in a world of digital, two-sided platforms. The company's stated mission is to 'help bring creative projects to life' and they've succeeded by helping creators to find backers themselves rather than entering the lottery of hoping for a traditional publisher to invest in them.

That one-shot model of patronage accumulates risk over time as each project must find backers on its own, and should it fail then momentum will be lost (and the principal may struggle to find backers for a second try). Even if it succeeds, however, the artist may still need to go back to square one to find more backers to develop a sequel. This stop–start format may help creators get a project off the ground, but it's hard to sustain.

The next logical pivot in patronage is from such one-shot games to continuous games. Patreon was set up in 2013, four years after Kickstarter. It provides business tools for creators to fundraise not just for a single project but as a recurring subscription. The continuous model proved popular in media formats where output frequency is high – such as video blogging ('vlogging') and podcasting – and less so when frequency is low, such as releasing music albums. The transaction costs of this recurring model are higher than Kickstarter at around 8 per cent, but this varies depending on the creator's size and the way they choose to tailor their membership offer. Patreon's membership now claims 6 million monthly active patrons supporting more than 200,000 creators, and over $2 billion paid out since launch, and has gathered significant momentum as a result of Covid-19 as creators search for survival.

To put this achievement into context: if we assume a flat 20 per cent artist royalty, it took the global recorded music industry twelve years to get two billion streaming dollars to trickle down to individual creators, whereas it took Patreon just seven, and as streaming-revenue growth shows signs of slowing down, Patreon is only just getting started – expanding its operations outside the United States, opening a new office in Berlin and adding payment options for euros and British pounds.

## PATRONAGE AND *THE PICKWICK PAPERS*

Our second principle of Paying Attention taught us that the economics of streaming is affecting songwriting – songs get shorter, choruses moved to the front. Our fourth principle, Make or Buy, stumbles upon a much earlier example, the patronage that Charles Dickens pioneered with *The Pickwick Papers*, his first full novel. Contrary to popular belief, Dickens was not paid by the word, he was paid by instalment. At one shilling for each instalment, the final nineteenth instalment being a double-header costing double-as-much, each novel would gross him 20 shillings. Similar to the current music-streaming economics, the model was not 'duration based', meaning the more words, the lower the compensation-per-word. Dickens and his publisher also add light to our first principle of Tarzan Economics in that they optimised for reach over revenue in a way that's akin to the ARPU economics of streaming. Each instalment was a snip when compared to the thirty-shilling price tag for a full-length book – the equivalent of a full week's salary. His addressable market was the many, not the few.

Dickens also taps into our third principle, of Drawing a Crowd, as each instalment creates anticipation for the next, a bottom-up viral word-of-mouth buzz not dissimilar to our tale of Tupperware that came a century later. But it's the model of patronage that is most telling for people wrestling with a make-or-buy decision. As revenue was being drip-fed back to the publisher over the course of the production of the book, the costs of production of one instalment could be recouped before the next went into production. It also allowed for cross-collateralisation, as 'blockbuster' hits could help offset earlier misses. It wasn't just revenue, but feedback too. He never changed plots based on readers' suggestions, as commonly believed, but in *Martin Chuzzlewit* scholars argued that he sent his characters off to America when sales underperformed, and in *David Copperfield* he altered the character of Miss

Mowcher because of a complaint from the woman on whom that character was based. This is not dissimilar to how early access gamers help developers tweak their games before publishing – the evolution of Minecraft being one of the most famous examples. Dickens and his publisher were pioneers in patronage, balancing risk and reward in a way that allowed his creativity to reach more people and achieve more compensation by doing so. A win-win that patronage-platforms today are arguably (and unassumingly) trying to emulate; learning by doing, just like Dickens and his publishers almost two centuries ago.

What explains the recent resurgence in patronage? One reason is that there is a feel-good factor at play; as today's digital patrons realise, they are enabling artistry that would never have seen the light of day under traditional gatekeepers. Patronage affords bragging rights, too, as the artist remains visibly sustained. To offer a personal anecdote to both of these, your author is a patron to the vlogger who goes by the name 'Squidge Rugby' for his long-form analysis of a complex game, something television pundits have to cram into a matter of minutes. My name appears in the credits of every episode – meaning even if I don't watch it, I still get a sense of gratification knowing others have.

But there is another, much deeper, force at play: intimacy. For many of us, the link between consumer and creator is little more than a thumb press on a piece of glass. That's because the internet can scale many things, but it struggles to scale intimacy. There's a desire for the pendulum to swing in the opposite direction, from quantity to quality; from the many to the few; from mass one-way reproduction to a more intimate two-way communication. Estrangement begets intimacy; as we become more alienated, we struggle to feel heard in an increasingly crowded room.

If creators can form membership groups based around models of patronage, they can kill three birds with one stone, drawing a crowd that intermediaries no longer draw, creating finance that would not otherwise be forthcoming and forging intimacy that intermediaries cannot create. Giving doesn't just foster intimacy; intimacy fosters giving. There's something of the Tupperware example in this: when you're confronted by a product in the intimate setting of a friend's home, surrounded by people with whom you have an intimate relationship of trust, all interacting with a product in a personal way, it increases your likelihood of wanting to purchase that product.

In his famous 1935 essay 'The Work of Art in the Age of Mechanical Reproduction' philosopher Walter Benjamin argued that when mass production technologies created the potential for thousands of perfect copies to exist of the same artwork, art lost some of its 'aura' – the direct connection an artwork has to the artist. Almost a hundred years on, consumers are choosing to become patrons to get that 'aura' back. In doing so, they are circumventing the mass-market model and seeking out new ways to get closer to their art and into deeper relationships with the artists they admire.

Patronage is matchmaking two markets. There is a consumer desire to rediscover that 'aura' on one side, and a need for the creator to develop intimacy on the other. The traditional gatekeepers in the middle are not well placed to recover this connection and partly to blame for taking it away.

*

The old vine of making make-or-buy decisions typically meant weighing up the costs and benefits and concluding that doing what you love would be no more than a hobby and doing what you got paid for was an occupation. For musicians this typically meant losing money making their art and making a living by teaching it. Gatekeepers knew this and were able to leverage their crowd-drawing capabilities in the contracts they offered. Getting signed by an intermediary was like throwing a rope down to help the artist escape the dungeon of everyday life. Now the scales have tipped.

Like all history's pioneers, Radiohead's real legacy from *In Rainbows* is not the success of their specific journey – as they came from a position of strength – but how they took the 'ballsy move' to explore new territory and left a map for countless others to follow. They learned priceless lessons about creativity, commerce and crowds by carving out their own route to market, lessons they would never have learned had they employed an intermediary to do it for them. For those seeking to draw a crowd today, doing what Radiohead did and 'making it yourself' becomes the default option as no one is going to help you until you do.

Now, the traditional 'buy option' has lost some of its appeal due to this catch-22; the crowd-gathering intermediary now expects the creator to build their own audience anyway. Meanwhile the 'make' option has become easier thanks to new models of patronage embracing digital platforms where direct and monetisable relationships can be forged at scale. Millennials seeking to draw a crowd today already know this, but for the rest of us it's a wake-up call to knowing when to let go of the default buy option we relied upon in the past.

This make-or-buy dilemma is deeply pervasive, well beyond the first-mover minnows of Kickstarter and Patreon. Relatively speaking these companies are Davids to the Goliaths of YouTube and Facebook, who operate on a truly global scale and can draw crowds that national monopoly companies can only dream of. Being accessible everywhere on global platforms will mean more than being huge somewhere on a national platform.

And it is games of football (on the pitch, not on consoles) where we need to go next. We're seeing the goliaths of YouTube and Facebook flex their patronage muscles working with sporting clubs to develop membership clubs around them. The English Premier League champions Liverpool FC have launched their own premium channel on YouTube to convert their current free subscription base of almost 5 million global subscribers (by comparison, the long-running highlights programme *Match of the Day* reached 7 million in 2018). By opting in to a recurring subscription model, fans of Liverpool get exclusive access to Premier content – not dissimilar to Spotify's freemium economics offering.

The 'club within a club' strategy is relevant to where we go next – the collective. Liverpool play within the English Premier League, a collective structure that centralises the crowd-drawing function of selling lucrative broadcasting and branding rights. The collective makes the league both feasible and valuable, as it is able to negotiate a one-stop-shop licence to acquire some or all of the premiership rights around the world. The downside of having the most-lucrative sports rights on the planet managed by a collective, however, is that the individual club may feel its hands are tied as it is unable to explore new commercial opportunities.

This is what makes Liverpool's YouTube channel such an illuminating example of what we've learned and where we now turn. The most valuable English football club is able to circumvent the collective and extract value directly from its fans. It's found a way of balancing 'make' or 'buy' with their own 'self-interest' and the 'common good' of the collective, and by doing so it will generate revenues outside the collective that will give it leverage to negotiate better terms to continue staying in. As we are about to discover, it's a form of Marxism – but not as you know it.

# 5
# SELF-INTEREST V COMMON GOOD

I first realised I had a book inside me waiting to get out when I observed the changing tone of newspaper editors I met at media conferences. During the first decade of disruption, newspapers would indulge in *Schadenfreude*, mocking the music industry's woes. Record labels and music retailers were labelled as either dying, dead or, worse still, dinosaurs.

The popular British satire *The IT Crowd*'s famous parody, warning the consumer against stealing copyright, captured the mood of newspapers at the time. It's presented as a trailer to a movie and warns the paying customer that they wouldn't steal a handbag, nor a car, not even a baby, nor would they shoot a policeman and steal his helmet – only to use it as a toilet and send it back to his grieving widow! The message being you shouldn't steal movies, or music either. Work-shy Roy Trenneman (played by the brilliant Chris O'Dowd) chomps on popcorn and mutters 'these anti-piracy ads are getting really mean' to a wail of audience laughter.

Back then music may have been the laughing stock but soon the tables were turned. When Google released a beta version of Google News in September 2002 the seeds were sown. It shipped the official website in January 2006 and by 2011 was reaching a critical mass, having scanned 60-million newspaper pages and gained prominence in the search bar. As eyeballs were looking at Search, newspaper advertising revenue started to fall, and circulation fell with it. Like a vicious circle, they keep falling to this day. As Google, Facebook and a handful of others scooped up those ad-dollars from the newspapers, the US newspaper industry saw ad-spend collapse by 80 per cent from its peak in nominal terms and back to pre-Great Depression levels in real terms.*

Let's step back for a wee minute. The economics of music and news diverges when you think about snippets: if Google shares a snippet of a newspaper's headline this may be sufficient for your needs, eliminating any incentive to explore its original source. If Google shares a snippet of a song, it will probably encourage engagement (to hear it as a complete body of work). If intellectual property has a fulcrum, it is the careful balance between stimulation and satiation. Without a taste, few will bite; too many free tastes and few will need to.

The author Rick Webb, who we'll hear more from later, pointed out that as Google scooped up those newspaper ad-dollars, questions were raised over the role of advertising itself: is it still even a force for good? Webb points out that the early economic literature on advertising suggested it was a positive for the economy as it funded the mass distribution of news. Without ads, consumers would be less well informed. Now those ad-dollars no longer support journalism, Webb argues, it's not so clear-cut that advertising remains a 'net positive'.

* Benedict Evans, 'News by the ton: 75 years of US advertising', *Benedict Evans Essays*, June 2020.

Newspapers find themselves in sinking sand and trying to figure out how they get out begins with asking what they stand for: why do we even still call them newspapers? After all, for the majority of their current customer base, the touchpoint for engagement isn't paper; rather, it involves reading what's behind a piece of glass. What's more, the cost of physical distribution is prohibitive, as middle-man distributors will often demand an all-or-nothing bargain to send copies across the country rather than targeted regions or cities. Little wonder, then, that newspaper popularity has traditionally been measured by what was returned to the distribution warehouse, not what was sold on the newsstands!

Furthermore, we have to draw on Marshall McLuhan's observation – 'the medium is the message' – and ask which moves first. Do we choose to trust a specialist journalist (who just happens to write for a particular broadsheet title)? If so, would we follow them if a competitor title poached them into switching sides? Similarly, do we consume a particular theme such as finance or the arts and remain agnostic about who covers them, or place our trust in a broadsheet title and hope that we get served adequate portions of those themes?

Newspapers are one of many industries struggling to deal with Tarzan Economics and remain firmly attached to the old vine. There are of course many others who are in a similar predicament, such as shopping malls, universities, transportation and local government. In each, there is a 'means to an end' question to ask and we'll explore this shortly, when we tackle 'the theory of the firm'.

Can newspapers snap out of the downward spiral of circulation and ad-revenue by reframing who they are – be it journalists or broadsheet titles? Are they stand-alone entities that act in self-interest, or a collective of journalists and titles who act for the common good?

Classical economics assumes that we are all rational, and that we make decisions like make-or-buy based on the benefit that directly serves our self-interest. Tarzan Economics recognises that we're more complex than that.

Most importantly, we're social beings, and sometimes there is a greater motivation in making a decision that benefits the common good rather than just oneself. Whereas classical economics assumes that we make decisions by asking ourselves 'Is this going to make me better off?', Tarzan Economics takes a broader view. In the case of make-or-buy, the question is: when is it better to be in sole control of what you're selling, and when is it better to be part of a collective?

A key problem is that collectives sound too often like a relic from the Soviet-era, and the downfall of communism took their appeal down with it. Put more fashionably, then, when should you hold your cards close and fend off all possible competitors, and when should you put your cards on the table and collaborate with them instead?

Chapter 4 explained why digital disruption has given individual creators an incentive to retain control of what they create; now it's time to examine why joining hands to act in the interest of the common good and form collectives can be so beneficial, particularly when it comes to getting what they create to market. After all, more independence for artists means more fragmentation, which requires more co-ordination to solve more 'many-to-many' problems, where more individual creators want to trade with more individual consumers across more countries than ever before. Thus, we have a potential 'waterbed effect', where pressing down on the use of middlemen in creation (disintermediation – the removal of existing intermediaries) can push up the need to depend on collectives (reintermediation – the need for a new intermediary) to handle distribution.

This is why we need to understand what it takes to form collectives and why it pays to act in the common good of its members.

The cigar-smoking Julius Henry 'Groucho' Marx (1890–1977) gave the world many quick-witted idioms during his eighty-six years. My personal favourite: 'I must say I find television very educational. The minute somebody turns it on, I go to the library and read a good book.' Marx was a remarkable comic – he could run off endless one-line quips, each razor-sharp in its wit, yet somehow capturing the anomalies and complexities of life. It was Groucho (not the more famous Karl) Marx who opened my mind to the challenges that collectives face, at a time when the European Union was about to undertake the biggest challenge in its collective economic history.

At the turn of the millennium, I was studying economics in Glasgow and was obsessed with learning how a group of eleven European countries were making the unprecedented move to create the single European currency, the euro, which would replace each member's individual currency.

This was the biggest gamble in the fifty-year history of European economic integration. From an American perspective, this was a case of Europe playing catch-up. The United States began creating the dollar as the country's standard unit of money in 1785 and within seventy years it was a fully national currency. To capture this historical difference, you only had to look at the faces of American exchange students when you explained that by driving from Paris to Düsseldorf (about the distance from Baltimore to Boston), you might need four different currencies to ensure you could to pay for 'gas'.

The euro was, and still is, a remarkably ambitious project. It's one of the best examples of a collective – an organisation or business that is owned and controlled by the people who work in it. What bound the original members of this collective together was twofold: first, a political desire to forge an ever-closer union; second, an economic desire among the founding members (who were in rough economic shape) to import Germany's credibility in controlling inflation. (From as early as 1950, Germany was known for having sound fiscal policies, in contrast to many other applicants to this club.)

For those other European countries to rid themselves of their bad economic reputations, they needed to join a club whose membership could help them develop better habits. The euro would be that club, and its headquarters, unsurprisingly, would be in Frankfurt. For the euro to succeed, it would need to make a single interest rate work across many different countries, each with its own unique economic cycles of ups and downs. To bring the disparate performance of its members into line, the European Union needed to lay down some membership rules.

The solution was to design some criteria to force these disparate economies to get their books in order and demonstrate low inflation, stable budget deficits and debt-to-GDP ratios, and long-term exchange rate stability similar to the German Deutsche Mark. If you wanted to join this club, in other words, you needed to match Germany for its reputation of maintaining 'sound money'.

For strong and stable economies like the Netherlands this would be easy. For the weaker economies – such as Italy and Greece – it was much harder. These countries had a stock of debt that was worth more than their entire economies. This was compounded by their tendency to spend more than they received in tax revenue. And clouding it all was their inability to control inflation, which eroded their wealth. The Achilles heel of this was their tendency to resort to devaluation – reducing the value of their domestic currency in order to export their way out of economic malaise.

Devaluation was a quick fix that was politically convenient when re-election was on the horizon but it undermined the European Union project in the long term. It was impossible to form an economic collective among members competing with each other to devalue and gain export advantages over one another. Upon joining this new club, with its fixed exchange rates and shared currency, that 'get out of jail free' devaluation card would no longer be playable.

Financial markets were sceptical about the collective's ability to hold itself together. Could the poor-performing countries of southern Europe – especially Greece and Italy, whose economic reputation was (and still is) in tatters – seriously join a club that demanded German economic diligence and credibility? Even if they could, would they import German credibility for sound money, or might they instead end up exporting their own bad practices to other members? Would they play by the membership rules and carry out painful structural reforms to balance their books, or would they cheat their way into the club and take a free ride off its credibility?

A good example of a potentially infectious bad practice is the way the Greek government ran transportation. At the turn of the millennium, the Greek railway had more employees than passengers and was losing a billion euros a year. A former minister, Stefanos Manos, even said publicly that it would be cheaper to send everyone by taxi! Miranda Xafa, a Greek economist, explained how the authorities used a neat accounting trick to make the problem vanish: the railway company would issue shares that the government would buy. This was counted not as expenditure, but as a financial transaction (similar to how public sector redundancy payments are treated) so it did not appear on the government's budget balance sheet. Doing so ultimately enabled Greece to fulfil the EU's Maastricht criteria and sneak its way into the club.

If Greece was behaving badly, Italy was worse. Gustavo Piga, an economics professor at Italy's University of Macerata, reported that the Italian government used a high-risk trading strategy to sidestep the rules of the Maastricht Treaty and manipulate its entry into Europe's single currency. By playing with risky interest-rate swaps of Japanese yen-denominated debt, Italy was able to mislead European Union institutions, as well as its own citizens, about the size of its budget deficit. Both countries succeeded in joining a club that shouldn't have allowed them to become members. Their performance since justifies the cynicism.

When the first term of my 1999–2000 academic year came to a close, so too did a century that had seen huge turmoil in Europe but had ended with the hope of unprecedented unification. I asked my professor, Andrew Hughes-Hallett, if this gamble on a collective – a single European currency – could work. And if it couldn't or wouldn't, then what would be the forces that pulled it apart? An expert on the topic of the euro's prospects, he held the title Jean Monnet Professor of Economics, a tribute to the French diplomat who believed it was through economic integration that political integration would eventually be achieved. His answer was illuminating.

'The Groucho Marx Theorem tells you where this project is heading,' he replied.

Confused, and knowing my tutorial time was short, I asked, again, whether this collective would hold itself together. Would one size really be able to fit all?

'Haven't you studied that other Marx?' he joked – referring

to Groucho, as opposed to the more obvious Karl. I was embarrassed to say that I hadn't studied either; and I only had a vague recollection of black-and-white moving images of Groucho and his brothers from the 1930s and 1940s. He then quoted a Marxism that explained the inherent problem with collectives, one that favours self-interest over the common good: 'I don't care to belong to any club that will have me as a member.'

When applied to the euro, the Groucho Marx Theorem highlights that no country would – in its own self-interest – ever want to join a monetary union of other, less economically efficient countries that would clearly want them as a member. By the same token, any union of countries would want to try to persuade a more economically efficient country to join their union instead.

The key driver in the formation of the Eurozone was that high-inflationary countries wanted to join a club primarily to secure lower (German) inflation that they could not generate themselves. Groucho's own form of 'Marxism' highlights the risks of sacrificing self-interest for the common good. Parties may share the same task but have opposing goals (asymmetric incentives) and/or a party may benefit from a collective without participating in it (free riding).

Look at what happened to the European Union: over the subsequent twenty years it has grown to twenty-seven member states (adjusting for the departure of Britain by the time you read this), nineteen of which have adopted the euro. Yet with the exception of Finland, none of the high-performing Scandinavian economies have joined the euro club. Instead, the newest members of the club have mainly come from the poorer-performing southern region. During the bailouts of Italy and Greece at the height of the financial crisis, Finland was the most vocal opponent – just as Groucho would have predicted.

I was in Germany for New Year's Eve in 2001 and saw the new euro banknotes being delivered to the German bank machines, ready for their introduction on the 1 January 2002. Germany would go on to spend many of those euros on costly and embarrassing financial bailouts for the badly behaving members whose incentives were not aligned with their own. What if these members continued to ignore the economics behind Groucho's Theorem and the strain they put on the collective? How would this marriage of very different economies, draped in asymmetric incentives and free-rider problems, progress? Or, as Groucho observed: 'Marriage is a wonderful institution, but who wants to live in an institution?'

If Groucho Marx (and, with the benefit of hindsight, arguably Karl, too) tells us why collectives fall apart, a common desire to control costs and prevent fragmentation helps keep them together. To understand how that might work, we need to talk about 'transaction costs', which economists often add like a bookend to the end of their formulas. Transaction costs are broadly defined as any cost involved in making an economic transaction. There are three categories – search costs, bargaining costs and enforcement costs. Looking at the story of the euro, the unifying incentive of forming a collective with a uniform currency was that all three kinds of transaction costs would disappear. If you were inside the club, there was no need to find the right foreign exchange broker (search costs), no need to set up a contract (enforcement costs to ensure you get the exchange rate quoted at the fee agreed) and no need to pay fees for cross-currency transactions (bargaining costs). Should a member of the euro leave the collective, then these transaction costs would reappear, so members would be incentivised to stick around.

The origins of the concept of transaction costs are found in the beautiful and timeless 1937 paper 'The Nature of the Firm' written by the Nobel laureate Ronald Coase. For Hal Varian, now Chief Economist at Google, Coase's paper asked a deceptively simple question:*

> 'If the market is such a great tool for allocating resources, why isn't it used inside the firm or company? Why doesn't one worker on the assembly line negotiate with the worker next to him about the price at which he will supply the partly assembled product? . . . Instead of using markets, companies tend to be organized as hierarchies, using a chain of command and control rather than negotiation, markets and explicit contract . . . it all hinges on the costs of making transactions. What economists call firms, he [Coase] said, are essentially groups of activities for which it is more effective and less costly to use command-and-control than markets to have things done.'

Varian's succinct summary of Coase's timeless paper offers a lens to re-examine the nature of capitalism, and on close inspection, paradoxically, looks a lot like the central planning of communism. Think of it this way: would it be easier to get work done in a hierarchal organisation than a sea of independent consultants?

Follow the theory from its 1937 origins to the present, and one could easily argue that transaction costs have fallen. Searching online, for instance, is clearly a lot cheaper thanks to search engines like Google, but this can have the perverse

* Hal Varian, 'Economic Scene; If there was a new economy, why wasn't there a new economics?', *New York Times,* January 2002.

effect of increasing bargaining costs as there's more choice and more suppliers. Similarly, enforcement costs should fall thanks to the internet increasing transparency and reducing friction, but you'll find little evidence of lawyers getting any cheaper (or charging fewer hours).

When applying Tarzan Economics to the pros and cons of forming collectives, this catch-all term of transaction costs is problematic due to its vagueness. Economists are often guilty of sweeping under the carpet what they don't understand and hoping no one notices the practical shortcomings in their work. In transaction costs, what often goes unexamined is not what is being achieved but what's being prevented – and collectives help to prevent gridlock.

Gridlock occurs when the cost of solving co-ordination problems, such as working out who owns what, prevents trade from taking place. Let's revisit the 'tragedy of the commons' from our simple framework in chapter 1, where too many people share a single resource and tend to overuse it – for example overfishing the oceans or polluting the air. The quick fix for resolving the tragedy, or better still preventing it, is to assign ownership – as the property owners would benefit directly from conserving the resource. But ownership can cause new problems, too. Imagine if the skies above us were carved up and sold on to thousands of different countries or companies, or the oceans around us were privatised and put in the hands of individual owners around the world – each with their own terms and conditions. This would make trade in aviation or shipping virtually unworkable. Rather than have a tragedy of the commons, what could result is what Michael Heller, a law professor at Columbia Law School and author of 'The Gridlock Economy: How Too Much Ownership Wrecks Markets, Stops Innovation, and Costs Lives', calls an 'anti-commons' – where too much fragmentation leads to underuse of a good.

'Underuse' isn't an easy metric to measure, however, so it's tempting to ignore it. Our innate quantification bias, as we'll discuss in the final principle, favours the measurable over the immeasurable. If you can't measure what didn't get used, then don't expect it to get the attention of academics and policymakers. Underuse is an example of a zero – something that didn't happen – as opposed to a one, something that did.

According to Heller, one of the earliest-known examples of the anti-commons can be seen on a trip down the River Rhine. Before the emergence of Europe's railway network in the nineteenth century, and then motorways in the twentieth century, much trade had floated down the Rhine for over a thousand years. Or, at least, tried to.

If it were possible to fly over Europe in the thirteenth century and look down upon the landscape, you would have seen the 800-mile River Rhine working its way from its source in the Swiss Alps, passing through what are now six separate countries, and finally flowing into the North Sea at Rotterdam.

During the Middle Ages, the Rhine was an essential trade route, protected by the Holy Roman Empire. Merchant ships would pay a toll to cover the cost of the river's upkeep and safeguard their transit. The tolls were limited and assigned by a central authority – forming a collective of sorts. That all changed when Emperor Frederick III died in 1250 as he left behind a power vacuum. Not only was there no consensus over a successor, there was also no regulation. Robber barons spotted a gap in the market and started to exploit the market in the gap by collecting unauthorised taxes on the river. There was no co-ordination or regulation – simply profit-seeking by the barons. The castles the barons used to impose tolls were

**GRIDLOCK ON THE RIVER RHINE**

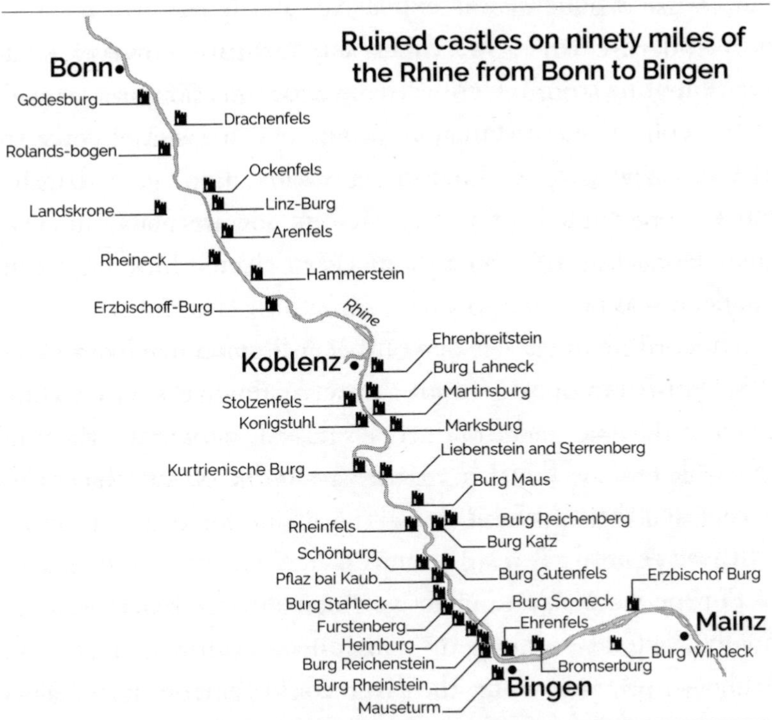


*Source: Adapted from Ludwig Schäfer-Grohe, in Walther Ottendor-Simrock's* Castles on the Rhine *(Chicago, Argonaut, 1967)*

bunched so tightly that one could argue they were within price-signalling distance of each other!

The river kept flowing, but the revenues did not. Due to the self-interest of the barons, trade along the Rhine became unworkable. Fragmentation of ownership led to an anti-commons – where financial gridlock led to underuse of the river. Too many tolls resulted in too little trade.

The merchants' response was to form a private collective, the Rhine League, to revive trade along the river. The Rhine League went to war with the barons, gathering a militia to attack the outposts of toll gatherers. Holding this collective together proved costly, though, as hiring the muscle to enforce the League's policies was expensive, and it was still hard to prevent free-riders – merchants and towns not paying dues yet benefiting from the collective. 'Groucho Marxism' tugged at the collective's sustainability and soon led to the collapse of the Rhine League. Free of regulation, the robber barons quickly reoccupied the power vacuum and were able to continue extracting tolls on an underused river for the next five hundred years.

Those five hundred more years of anti-commons had a massive opportunity cost. Count the zeros and think about what might have been, had the river developed a collective solution to enable trade to flourish, as opposed to the self-interest of the barons and their prohibitive tolls.

It wasn't until the 1815 Congress of Vienna that the leaders of Europe were able to effectively coordinate. Together, they finally started to remove the toll collectors that were causing gridlock, so trade along the river could flourish again. This wasn't just long overdue but, embarrassingly, would soon be exposed as being too little, too late – as a new and superior means of transportation was emerging just as the Rhine reopened for business. Railways were spreading throughout the region, removing the need to use the river to transport goods – further slackening the barons' half-millennium monopoly grip on the market for transportation.

Alas, this may sound depressingly familiar – especially if you've heard of the term 'regulatory fatigue' wherein badly behaving dominant firms move on to abuse their dominance in new markets before the lengthy regulatory process can catch them committing crimes in the old market.

For all their short-term profiteering, the barons may have left money on the table. Had they switched from self-interest to the common good and formed their own collective, then more merchants would have used the Rhine for trade. The more trade, the more opportunities for the collective's participants – merchants and barons alike.

But you can't expect thieving robber barons to sit down and shake hands on an amicable and sustainable collective model, and that's an important historical lesson – private firms struggle to form collectives. It will often take the might of a central government or international institution to spot an anti-commons scenario and shift the entrepreneurial activity of the self-interested barons away from extracting unworkable tolls that benefit the few towards a more productive collective that benefits the many.

This brief journey down the Rhine's history shows the value of collectives – where participants within a market act in the interests of the common good (a functioning river for all who need it) as opposed to the barons acting in their own self-interest (extracting as much money for private benefit). The Rhine League's response may have been short-lived, but it offers lessons of how to set up (patent or copyright or other rights) pools to assemble, or re-assemble, fragmented ownership rights.

The French lyricist and playwright Ernest Bourget (1814–64) may be little known today, but millions of creators around the world who are trying to make a living from their work should be grateful for his actions back in 1847. Without Bourget, there would not only be fewer musicians, but those who ply their trade would still be struggling to get paid for their work. The importance of Bourget's famous 'incident' can be heard every time you hear a song being performed – literally.

In 1847, the business of shows (what we now call 'show

business') was booming in Paris, although the 'businesses' were benefiting more than the 'show'. Paris was experiencing the growth of the Industrial Revolution and the new middle class, which had an appetite for live entertainment and cafe concerts. These 'Caf' Conç' were hugely popular thanks to the complementary nature of what was on offer – music, food and beverages – a winning formula that continues to this day. Cafe concerts would increase the price of the food and beverage inside their venue so that the music could be enjoyed for free. By doing so, they could not only pay for the performing musicians, but also generate a handsome profit for themselves.

Imagine we are sitting in one of these Parisian cafes back in 1847 and the composer Ernest Bourget walks through the door and takes a seat to enjoy the show. We are about to witness a pivotal moment in the history of intellectual property. Bourget has journeyed this evening to the Café Morel. As he sits at his table, a musical performance is reaching its climactic end. A large crowd of patrons are rapt, diverting their attention only to sip from their overpriced drinks and nibble on their expensive hors d'oeuvres. Bourget is gratified to observe that the song that has so captured the attention of the diners is one of his own compositions.

When the echoes on the final notes have died out, the crowd erupts in rapturous applause. Bourget gestures for a waiter and orders an *eau sucré* – essentially a glass of lightly flavoured sugar water. Bourget is shocked when the waiter refuses. In the name of increased profits Café Morel has a policy: after dark, guests may only order drinks which do not 'deceive the corkscrew', which is to say that after dark the cafe serves only wine, on which they make a better profit.

Bourget is furious. Here is the cafe entertaining its paying guests with Bourget's music and not only has he not been paid a penny for his work, but they won't even extend him the courtesy of serving him the drink he ordered.

The next day, Bourget sent a letter to the proprietor of the Café Morel, informing him that he 'would prohibit the representation of my *scènes comiques*, as well as my *chansonettes*; in short, the representation of all my repertoire for the singers at Café Morel. If you do not know the titles of my *scènes comiques* or songs, you'll find a few that I have listed at the bottom of this letter.' Bourget listed his compositions, making him the first composer to begin formation of what is now called a global repertoire database. When Café Morel failed to reply, Bourget escalated his case for compensation to the Tribunal de Commerce de la Seine and Cour d'Appel de Paris, which ordered Café Morel to pay Bourget a total of 800 francs.

With that decision, copyright licensing for the public performance of music was born. Regardless of whether it was orgeat syrup or a glass of *eau sucré* that Bourget asked for (ironically, historians still dispute the original order), the visit proved costly for the 'Caf' Conç's' showbusiness. Performing rights for authors were established and would be an ongoing concern for venue owners – even if the authors were not present.

Bourget's legal victory for composers was helped by the precedent that had already been set for literary authors. French law had granted the exclusive right of the literary author to public performances since 1793. A few years prior to the famous Bourget incident, the authors Victor Hugo and Honoré de Balzac lobbied to prohibit the reading of their books aloud in public squares as this would be deemed a public performance – a very early case of piracy.

The judge opined to Bourget that he needed 'good fortune' to impose the ruling. This meant that the performing rights needed to be enforced, and the monies generated needed to be collected; it wouldn't be feasible for Bourget to act in his own self-interest by trying to collect them himself. In the light of Coase's transaction costs, Bourget would have found that the search, bargaining and enforcement costs of acting alone overtook the monetary benefits of the tariff he had been awarded. The solution was to form a collective.

On 18 March 1850, roughly three years after the original incident, Bourget joined forces with fellow composers Victor Parizot and Paul Henrion, and publisher Jules Colombier, to form what would become La Société des Auteurs, Compositeurs et Éditeurs de Musique – the world's first music copyright collecting society.

By creating a one-stop shop for acquiring licences from the copyright holders, SACEM (as it would be renamed in 1851) drastically reduced the transaction costs for music licensing. The real benefit of Bourget's battle was the invention of the 'blanket licence'. As the name suggests, the blanket covered all of the bed, giving the buyer the right to use all of the world's copyrights in one seamless transaction and removing any liability – a 'one-stop shop' for an industry that would otherwise be stuck in gridlock. Paying for intellectual property couldn't be made any easier, meaning more composers got paid more money than would otherwise be the case.

Bourget's famous incident travelled across the Atlantic to the United States seventy years later. A rerun of the same arguments played out in the 'American Incident' between the American songwriter Victor Herbert and Shanley's Restaurant in New York City in 1917. The songwriter wanted the value his songs brought to the restaurant to be recognised, the business owner did not. Supreme Court Judge Oliver Wendell Holmes Jr. said, 'If music did not pay it would be given up. Whether it pays or not, the purpose of employing it is profit and that is enough.'

That's still how it works to this day. When a hair salon complains about having to pay a collecting society to play music in their commercial premises – often music they have already paid for in the form of a CD, download or monthly subscription to a streaming service – the music collecting society will counter by challenging the hair salon to run its business without music. The collecting society would point out that music is a benefit to the salon and refer to the same 'value chain' argument Bourget made in 1847 – that the performing right allows a fair share of that business to be passed on to the creators who wrote the music your customers are enjoying.

The way Bourget and his composer colleagues formed a collective to pool all their rights and centralise their administration enabled the market for compensating creators to not only function but also flourish. Today CISAC (the International Confederation of Societies of Authors and Composers) – the umbrella group that represents copyright collectives around the world – claims 232 member societies in 121 countries, and over 4 million creators across all geographic areas and artistic repertoires, from music and audio-visual, to drama, literature and visual arts.

But the real secret to the success of Bourget's 'expensive glass of water' is the creation of a 'one-stop shop' blanket licence. This is the transferable lesson which allows us to pivot through disruption – whether it's to use the entire length of the River Rhine or to perform the repertoire from the most obscure songwriters – eradicating the many-to-many problems of fragmented ownership and the risk of gridlock.

Blankets hold collectives together, as without them gridlock would cause the market to fall apart. It would be impractical (if not impossible) to find and negotiate with those 4 million songwriters around the world independently, yet a failure to secure a licence for all of their songs would create a risk of liability that makes trade unworkable. Having 99.9 per cent of all the songs isn't good enough – the value of the blanket is in the completeness of getting 100 per cent coverage – removing risk and increasing convenience.

Blanket licences are constructed in a way not dissimilar to the 'Caf' Conç' that Bourget would frequent to hear his works being performed: there would be a team of waiters serving tables and a group of chefs in the kitchen. Visually, these two professions couldn't appear more different. Chefs may be 'at each other's throats' in the kitchen, whereas the waiters need to be seen operating in a sea of tranquillity surrounding the tables of their guests. The rights holders who throw their hats in the collective ring are like chefs in the kitchen, privately arguing among themselves about who gets what share of a fixed pool of cash, whereas the blanket licence is served like a waiter offering a seamless way for the user of copyright to settle a bill for what in reality (underneath the blanket) is a deeply fragmented market.

The collective offers a frictionless transaction rather than the hassles of having to find every single owner/seller and is worth great value to the willing buyer. The buyer of the blanket licence is willing to pay more for the convenience (which is sometimes worth more than the good itself) and gives the collective wiggle-room to keep all of its members (or chefs in the kitchen) happy and solves the Groucho Marxism dilemma – where the most valuable member of a collective has the least incentive to join and the greatest incentive to leave.

If you are mathematically inclined, a model of Marxism maths is presented in the Annex at the end of this book so you can put Groucho back to work.

The collective model that Bourget's actions inspired is not without its shortcomings. As with anything in life, the closer you look, the more flaws can be found. Of all the flaws that emerge when entering a collective for the common good (and there are many), achieving a fair division of the earnings among members is the most prevalent and perennial. Bourget's creation of SACEM provided domestic protection for its members' works, with the introduction of (minimum) quotas for French music airing on French radio in 1994. That might produce a 'fair division' from a French perspective, but appears unfair when viewed from outside its borders.

Defining fairness, and more precisely fair division, is a problem that will never go away. The origins of fair division date back to the 1940s when Hugo Steinhaus and two Polish mathematician friends met in the Scottish Cafe in Lwów, Poland, and examined how to optimally split a cake between two parties. If one person cuts and the other chooses, then there is an inherent balance to the process, as it's in the cutter's best interests to use the knife as evenly as possible. Failure to slice the cake fairly will result in getting a smaller piece. The advantage of being the first mover – having control of the knife – is cleverly counterbalanced by the second mover who gets to choose between the two. This is known as the Divider/Chooser method.

Steinhaus and his colleagues went further, introducing a third person to the cake-cutting dilemma and solving for preference (when at least two of the three people want the same slice) and envy (ensuring all participants are happy with the slice they've got) and by doing so made 'fair division', a respected but arguably overlooked field of economics that is still taught at universities today.*

* Fair Division is even finding a new home in computer science. The start-up website Spliddit not only teaches us fair division, but allows us to apply it to solve everyday problems like splitting rent among a group of roommates.

The Scottish Cafe scenario invokes three broad questions about fair division amid disruptive markets:

Who controls the distribution?
Who controls the data?
Who decides how the value is split?

Making a market 'fair' relies on balancing these three roles. If one party plays multiple roles or can make it harder for others to play their role effectively, that can tip a market in their favour, making it less fair for others. This is where the theory of fair division has struggled to leave the academic corridors and enter real life. The inconvenient truth is that no matter how hard you try to make a division 'fair': it's always going to be susceptible to being gamed by those who have the power to do so.

I learned how fair division can be gamed by coming home drunk in the wee hours of the night and flopping out in front of the television. That's not something I condone, but appreciating that the complementary goods of economics and alcohol can reap the occasional reward.

In the summer of 2006, Britain was sweltering in a heatwave and the UK's main commercial television channel, ITV, had stumbled on some hot intellectual property – a way to make money without depending on commercial breaks. ITV had launched a quiz show called *The Mint* that would run from midnight to 4 a.m. from Monday to Thursday. It had a simple formula: two attractive and energetic hosts pose easy and provocative questions to the viewers, many of whom would be inebriated from earlier in the night, and the hosts would invite the audience to phone in with answers.

Thousands of bleary-eyed viewers paid for premium-rate

phone calls to enter *The Mint*, all of them blissfully ignorant of the odds they were up against in winning the prize on offer.

As its name suggests, the controversial format was profitable. ITV negotiated (with the phone company) for a big slice of the cash that came in from viewers' phone calls (which cost 75p from a BT landline, and even more from a pre-iPhone mobile). Commercial television typically balances the consumer's attention with advertising: too much of the former and the broadcaster won't be able to pay its bills, too much of the latter and the consumer will switch off.

*The Mint* tore up this formula. Every minute of the show was minting money thanks to the phone calls. In the first half of 2006, TV programmes like *The Mint* earned ITV's quiz-show channel ITV Play around £30m of revenues, and as it was all high-margin this would have made up around a tenth of the broadcasts' bottom line. Indeed, it was making so much money that it was hard to justify airing any commercials at all during these programmes.

Exploiting holes in the market like this can't go on forever, and *The Mint* came to an abrupt and controversial end. After receiving hundreds of complaints, the communications regulator considered reclassifying the entire show as an advert for premium-rate phone lines, leading to ITV removing it from the network (for breaching its licence). The investigation broadened with the Gambling Commission exploring if the controversial quiz-show format should be deemed a lottery, meaning a fifth of its profits would have to go to charity. Amid the controversy, ITV was defiant about its new business model, claiming that its aim was not to encourage people to run up huge phone bills but rather to profit from lots of people playing a little and often (instead of fostering binge-like addictive behaviour, of which it was accused).

ITV's management defended further its money-making show, pointing out that, of the people who contacted its shows,

86 per cent rang fewer than ten times a week. Among those callers at the upper boundary of this range who did make ten calls a week, not only would they have probably failed to secure any prizes but would have spent about three times the cost of the BBC's television licence fee over the course of the year.

*The Mint* wasn't just about the money. It was about music too. For bleary-eyed viewers with matchsticks holding up their eyelids, it was hard to ignore the music being played on a repetitive loop throughout the show. Even if you had dropped off to sleep on the sofa (perhaps while waiting to get through on those costly phone lines), you were still being serenaded by the music in the background. These weren't exactly beautiful compositions but rather classic quiz-show music: all filler and no killer. And it filled the entire broadcast of *The Mint* and that of its sister show, *Quizmania*.

ITV paid PRS, the music collecting society, a blanket licence to cover all of its music usage on all of its channels. PRS would then enact their fair distribution of this money to the composers and owners of the songs on a duration basis, treating all music the same regardless of the time of day and size of audience. As the collective was playing fair, so should its members.

Not so. This quiz-show filler music was essentially 'four bars on a loop' played continuously in the background, with no interruptions for commercial breaks. For the creator of these four bars, being played for twenty-five hours of a 168-hour broadcasting week meant a fair division of 15 per cent of the fees distributed by PRS for all ITV programmes. It gets worse (or better, if you're one of the lucky composers): not all of the other twenty hours in ITV's broadcast day had music playing under them, so *The Mint*'s effective share of the more narrowly defined music-broadcast-hours rose from 15 per cent to well over a fifth.

In an explosive article titled 'A License to "Mint" Money?', published in the songwriter magazine *Four-Four*, composer Dobs Vye suggested that ITV had paid around £14 million for its blanket licence to PRS, meaning the continuous music used in *The Mint* and *Quizmania* could have taken around £3 million out of this pot. Chris Smith of Barbershop Music, an award-winning composer and former PRS board member, went further and pointed out that the lucky composers who wrote these 'four bars on a loop' could have been earning more PRS money than Bono, Elton John or Paul McCartney. Thanks to fair division, a couple of the wealthiest PRS composers in the UK were not just unheard of but had hardly been heard by anyone awake enough to hear their work.

While the broadcast regulators were beginning to swarm around the show for breaching all sorts of rules governing gambling, the collective of PRS members was investigating how a couple of composers could walk away with their own jackpot for music that was neither rich in quality nor exposed to any significant audience. The suspicion was that a couple of members of the collective were acting in their own self-interest to deliberately game the system that was meant to produce a fair division of money among all of its members. Many other composers who produced higher-quality music and reached a wider audience were only seeing a fraction of what the composers of *The Mint* were making, because their work failed to eat up the clock – leaving less to be divided up.

The eventual solution was simple: the collective agreed to alter its distribution policy and no longer treat all music the same. PRS introduced different royalty rates for primetime, preventing *The Mint* from exploiting the wee hours to earn its own jackpot payout. Without this adjustment, the collective would fall apart due to members' dissatisfaction and so, too, would its blanket licence to broadcasters, who would no longer get the certainty of 100 per cent coverage in their licence. And without a blanket licence we would be back to the many-to-many gridlock of ITV having to negotiate with each composer individually, which would, as we've seen, invariably lead to gridlock – the underuse of all of their music.

Just when you thought this story of fair division had straightened itself out, it's about to get bent out of shape again. We know that ITV paid a reported £14 million to PRS to cover the cost of the blanket licence, and an estimated £3 million was paid to the lucky composer. But who was the jackpot winner? In his *Four-Four* article, composer Dobs Vye raised the concern that the publisher of this music may well have been ITV itself, meaning it was clawing back a substantial proportion of its blanket licence fee in a carousel of cash 'minted' by *The Mint*.

On reflection, it was not the fair division concepts of 'preference' (who gets to compose what music for what purpose) or envy (knowledge that another songwriter was earning more) that motivated Dobs Vye to speak out. Rather, it was: 'The business model of any production-cum-publishing house devising an overnight format which daily siphons off multiple hours from a channel's royalty fees was surely an abuse of the blanket license, especially when it was in cahoots with that channel.'

*The Mint* may have lasted only about a year before the regulatory pressure led to its closure, but it showed how a 'collective' model for bringing money in and getting money out will inevitably have to face perverse incentives to game a system that was designed to be fair to all yet turned out to be exploitable by one. Vye's view on fair division was that the balance between distribution, data and value was tilted by ITV, because they realised they had the power to do it. As a user of copyright, they were outside the collective, but by (cunningly) manipulating the distribution of their own money they had got inside and tipped 'fair division' in their favour.

That was then, this is now – and music streaming audiences have been offered an all-you-can-eat bundle of copyrighted music, and although some consume lots and others consume little, they all pay the same money into the collective pot. This presents a challenge in getting the money out fairly and efficiently to rights holders. As Jack Stratton from the US band Vulfpeck pointed out during the hype and hysteria surrounding Spotify's direct listing in April 2018: 'If Whole Foods came out with a ten-dollar-a-month subscription to food it would be a popular product as well [ . . . ] so everyone is betting on a [ . . . ] bizarre consumption model [ . . . ] the whole thing is jacked.'

Vulfpeck are, of course, no strangers to this debate. Indeed, their earlier (and now infamous) actions in 2014 feel eerily similar to that of *The Mint* in 2006, especially as they exploited the rules of fair division during the wee hours of the night. In March 2014 they released *Sleepify*, ten songs of silence that varied conveniently between 31 and 32 seconds – thus qualifying for a royalty as it passed the 30-second rule required before a song qualifies for monetisation.

The result was a five-minute album of silence that the band asked fans to stream on repeat while they slept. The aim was to generate enough royalties for the band to go on tour – promising free shows in return. According to a royalty statement shown to *Billboard* magazine by Stratton in April 2014, the band's Spotify earnings totalled $18,638. This figure could have grown bigger had Spotify not removed the album that same month. The pivotal lesson remains the same: a collective solution that needs to allocate a fixed pool of cash will always be open to abuse from its participants.

Vulfpeck's sneaky project shows us the dilemma we all face

if we are bundling an all-you-can-eat subscription to produce a fixed pool of cash that has to be divided up fairly. If this is going to be the future model of economic activity – how if we all act in the common good to sell convenience through a collective, some of us will resort to self-interest to maximise our return. In collectives it's all about displacement: one person's unfair gain results in pain to all the other fair players. You can trust all of the people some of the time but only some of the people all the time, as the incentive for those others to game the system cannot be erased.

*

Alison Wenham, the former chairman and CEO of the Association of Independent Music, stood on a stage at a CISAC conference in Brussels in 2007 and said: 'Collective licensing is best described as either capitalism with a touch of communism, or communism with a touch of capitalism.' She may have upset many in the audience for making this point but it's a profound observation. It often pays to act in the common good of a collective and not solely in one's self-interest.

Clubbing together into a collective may hark back to communism (with a touch of capitalism) but clearly it can be made sustainable. Conversely, extracting that added premium for the convenience of the blanket licence is capitalism, but it is only possible with a touch of communism that comes with the collective. For the many individuals, firms and institutions grappling with Tarzan Economics, I truly believe they will find solace in rebalancing communism with capitalism, or capitalism with communism.

Let's return to the woes facing the newspaper industry outlined earlier and consider how a touch of communism may help the fragilities of the traditional newspaper model. We know that some journalists are valued more than others, which can result in Groucho Marxism, and that paying per article would lead to gridlock when trying to access news. We also know that news, like music, wants to feel free – you don't know you're paying for music while drinking a glass of water in a cafe, and the fact you don't makes it more enjoyable – the collective has settled the bill backstage.

If news wants to be free but the journalist needs to be paid, revisiting collective solutions can help find a way out of the sinking sand that newspaper titles have found themselves in for the past decade. If the *Guardian* or the *New York Times* on the left of the political spectrum, or the *Telegraph* or the *Wall Street Journal* on the right, were to toss their respective hats into the collective ring, they could benefit from acting in the 'common good' – developing shared advertising platforms and exploring collective licensing and distribution of all their journalistic output.

Collectives may not make sense to the minority of consumers who currently pay for news, but they may chime with the majority who don't. A lost reader – someone who used to pay the cover price of a newspaper – may not be willing to pay for that same newspaper title behind a paywall but more than happy to pay a blanket fee for all. This poses a dilemma: the paper values its current realised value of its journalistic output, but that lost reader might have a higher actuarial value on the option to explore other forms of journalism. The Athletic website, a US-based collective of the world's best sports journalists plucked from the payroll of broadsheet newspapers, is already putting this into practice – forming a club that even Groucho would want to become a member of. Aggressive price-discounting, with monthly subscriptions now at £1 per month (a third of the cover price of just one edition of the *Sunday Times*) is matched with aggressive poaching of top writers, which creates its own network effect – the more poaching, the more audience-pulling power, the more pricing power.

This was the secret of Spotify's success; no listener really knows (or cares) if an artist or song is signed to Universal or Sony, so why should a reader care who a journalist is reporting for? What they want is the option to explore music (or news) on their own terms – be it a particular journalist, subject matter or editorial style. Newspaper proprietors might find the idea of throwing their hat into the collective ring absurd – consumers might as well visit Google News instead. (As you may have worked out, we've been here before, circa Napster 1999.)

The benefits of collectives permeate many industries facing disruption. Universities could give up on their unique brand identity to pool their expertise to further a specialist academic discipline collectively (prioritising progress over prestige); shopping malls could compete on shopfronts but form collectives to provide click-and-collect (reducing friction to fend off Amazon); local governments could form collectives with an aligned recycling policy across regional borders (as opposed to each having their own, at times, contradictory approach).

Whenever you look at businesses or institutions failing to cope with disruption, you have to ask yourself if it's the way they are organised which is leaving them clinging on to the old vine, and if they threw their hats into a collective ring would that then help them reach out to the new? However, forging a collective means forming a monopoly, and that isn't going to be easy; it would be foolish to ignore the anti-trust issues that this creates. Collectives may be a good idea, but monopolies are deemed a bad idea as they control supply and hike prices. At least that's how it continues to be taught in lecture halls around the world. Which is what we need to tackle next, and pivot our thinking to how today's monopolies work, expanding output and eliminating price, and ask if they are such a bad idea after all.

# 6

# PIVOTAL THINKING

My curiosity about economics started on a Scottish beach when I was eleven years old. My older brother Thomas had already taken an interest in the subject, and one day I overheard my father, a maths teacher, explaining some basic concepts to him. Sibling rivalry kicked in, and I wanted to catch up.

That summer, we spent six weeks in a remote Scottish seaside town – giving me plenty of time with my dad to get ahead of my brother. Sitting on the beach one day, I plucked up the courage to ask my father, 'What is economics?'

He clearly didn't want to be back to work as a teacher during his holidays, so he said, 'Let's talk another time, and enjoy the beach instead.' After all, it was a rare glorious sunny day in Scotland – a place that normally has just two seasons, winter and June.

But I persisted: 'Dad, you told Thomas what economics means, now please tell me!'

He sighed. Pointing towards all the families enjoying the North Sea (which was so cold it would turn your skin as blue as the Scottish flag), he said: 'Imagine you are the prime minister, and you've just been informed many children had tragically drowned last year swimming in the sea. Your challenge is to stand on the steps of 10 Downing Street and tell the grieving parents, angry politicians and a hostile press just what you are going to do to prevent it happening again.'

This was not the economics lesson I was expecting. Eleven-year-old me had never been asked to devise a governmental response to a national tragedy. I spoke from the gut. 'Well, Dad, why not make swimming lessons compulsory? No more children should drown; surely we need to ensure they can all swim?'

'That's politics. That's just making people who are upset feel like you're doing something. But let's apply some economics, which is about taking the time to understand and analyse the facts about what has actually happened.' Slightly arrogantly, I reminded him that drowned British children were a good reason to get upset, and that swimming lessons *would* save lives!

Adopting a more patient tone, he asked: 'Where were these children when they sadly died?' They were in the sea – obviously. 'Do people who can't swim usually go in the sea?' Of course they don't. 'So, then what do we know about the children who drowned?' Well, I guess they must have known how to swim . . .

Suddenly, the penny dropped. My father waited a little, seeing that I was perplexed by what had just hit me. 'So,' he finally said, 'would we have more or fewer children in the water as a result of your compulsory swimming lesson policy?'

As with those children in the water, I suddenly felt out of my depth. 'There would be more kids in the water, Dad.'

'And if a certain percentage of children swimming drown,' my father said, closing the loop on the problem I'd stumbled into, 'then increasing the number of kids in the water will increase the number of kids who drown.'

I asked my father, 'If you were prime minister, what would you have done?'

Looking out to the sea, he replied: 'Those kids who can swim would benefit from more information, such as which beaches are safe and when it is too dangerous to swim.'

I asked how this could be done.

'This beach could simply have a red-amber-green flag system that would alert the kids and their parents to when the water is too dangerous to swim.'

My first lesson in economics was a classic, albeit bizarre, supply-and-demand problem – if I demanded to make swimming compulsory, I would have supplied the British coastline with more kids swimming in its seas.

I still use that lesson when teaching economics – whether to high-school students or CEOs. And guess what? Regardless of age and experience, 'make swimming lessons compulsory' is the most popular response. Role-playing as the prime minister staring grieving parents in the face prompts an emotional, from-the-gut response similar to the one I came up with as an eleven-year-old. This is why my father used such a visceral and shocking scenario for his lesson – to show me that the context in which you find yourself making a decision can be just as important as the decision itself.

He wasn't just opening my eyes to what economics is, but also to the drivers behind it – politics, emotions, personal incentives – all ideas which are difficult (if not impossible) to reduce into numbers you can put into an equation. But that doesn't mean economics isn't approachable. Everyone can relate to incentives. They are where economics meets the real world.

Trying to make things better, and then learning that what you were proposing would have actually made things worse, was a 'penny dropping' moment for me. It got me hooked on economics. Knee-jerk reactions, which are so often the case in today's 'clickbait' culture, lack the necessary patience to abstract a situation and identify the correct symptoms and cures. Many years later I would learn of a similar lesson; this time it wasn't how best to prevent children from drowning but how to stop wartime planes from being shot out the sky.

Abraham Wald, a famous wartime statistician, noticed that when planes returned from their missions, mechanics were putting extra protection on the fleet based on the location of bullet holes. His pivotal thinking was that this wasn't the right solution, as these planes were successfully making it home despite being hit. The bullet holes that mattered were the ones that stopped planes from returning home. The air force needed to focus not on the positive signals, but the negatives. The zeroes, not the ones. Just like my father's lesson: don't focus on the people who couldn't swim, but those who could and were unaware of its risks – Wald taught us not to focus on the planes that came back but instead on those that didn't.

If the world's problems could be solved with purely rational thinking – by finding the right data and plugging it into the right equation – we would have done it by now. Yet we're still besieged by problems – social, economic and political – to which no purely rational solutions have emerged. In the real world, there simply are problems which no theoretical framework, no prescribed path from A to B to C, will solve. What is required is 'pivotal thinking'.

Pivotal thinking means looking beyond, over and around the obvious ways of thinking – swimming lessons, patching up the planes that come back – and finding ways to better understand the actual world where decisions need to be made. Why plot your way through the maze when you can walk around it?

The problem with rational thinking is that it can miss things.

**PIVOTAL THINKING**

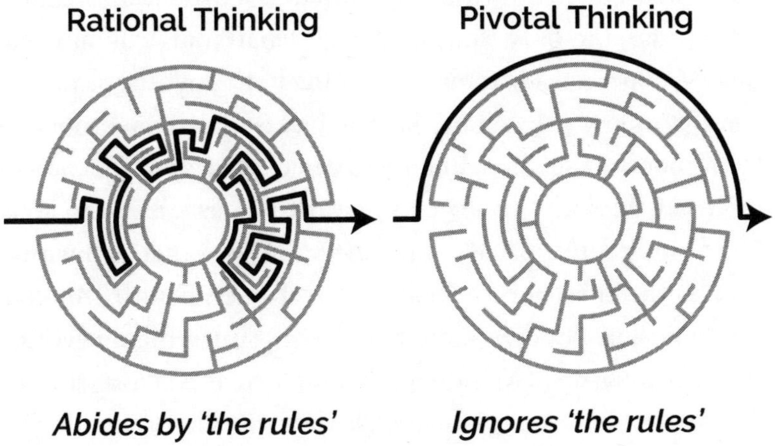


Source: Author and Rory Sutherland

My dad's insight about swimming lessons and Wald's about the bullet holes are simple examples. But examples of entrenched, 'rational' thinking missing the mark are everywhere, across the public and private sectors.

By contrast, pivotal thinking is about recognizing that 'the opposite of a good idea can also be a good idea'. This is the first of two 'Roryisms' we'll discuss in this book. 'Roryisms', for those who are not aware, are quips from the legendary ad-man Rory Sutherland, vice chairman of Ogilvy UK and author of *Alchemy: The Surprising Power of Ideas That Don't Make Sense*. This first Roryism tells us that we are not beholden to a set of prescribed rules and assumptions when trying to solve a problem. That it's okay to go outside the maze to get from where you are to where you need to go.

Let's look at three relatable examples. Take dining out at a restaurant. The linchpin of the restaurant experience is the menu. It is the customer's main source of information for deciding what they want to order.

Rational economic thinking would say that in assessing a dish's price, the only thing that really matters is the numeric value. An average customer is less likely to buy a high-priced item than a low-priced one. So, the higher the number next to the salmon, the fewer salmon you can expect to sell.

Pivotal thinking, though, reveals that there's more to consider. Beyond the price's numeric value, another influential factor is the currency symbol next to the number – the dollar or pound sign. Studies show that seeing that symbol reminds people of the pain of spending money. Change 'Salmon: £22' to 'Salmon: 22' and you can boost sales by around 8 per cent.* The gains may not be massive, but any failure to pivot to maximise revenue is leaving money on the table.

Next let's turn to the economics of giving, and look at how rational thinking can backfire when people are asked to dig into their pockets for good causes. In 1990, the UK government introduced the Gift Aid program to help citizens give to charity. If a UK taxpayer registers with the charity upon donating, the charity can claim 25p extra for every £1 donated. So, for example, if you donate £20, the charity can claim an extra £5 from the taxman, making your gift worth £25. It's not without its controversies, especially as the charity sector is awash with tax breaks. But rational thinking would argue the policy is a no-brainer, as people should theoretically give more in scenarios where others – namely the government – will match their gift.

That isn't always true. In some cases, highlighting the positive benefit of Gift Aid makes people less likely to donate. Why?

* Sybil S. Yang et al., '$ or Dollars: Effects of Menu-price Formats on Restaurant Checks', Center for Hospitality Research Publications, May 2009.

Because, for many donors, giving to charity is a social act – they give as an expression of their beliefs, or as an act of care. Gift Aid suddenly made it feel like a financial transaction, which puts some donors off. The 'Ogilvy Behavioural Science Annual 2018–2019' report found that the use of Gift Aid-branded envelopes as a fundraising strategy by charities significantly reduced return rates and total donations. Adding 25 per cent on 'for free' confused the relationship between the giver and the gift.

Pivotal thinking in this situation is about recognising the complex social and economic motives of giving, and not just maximising the financial outcome. The initial driver for people to give is because they care about the emotional and social benefits, more so than the cold-cut financial outlay. One could go further and argue that Gift Aid deprives the government of tax revenues which could help solve society's ills in other ways. Rational thinking doesn't take any of these elements of the Gift Aid strategy into account. Pivotal thinking does.

For our third example, let's go back to the beach and witness the seminal work of the American mathematician Harold Hotelling. If you've ever wondered why all radio stations sound the same, or why all the bestselling books have similar themes, you'll find the answer on Hotelling's beach.

Hotelling researched how sellers would choose locations along a linear market – for example, ice-cream stands along a beach. He assumed that if every seller was offering a similar product, customers would buy from the nearest seller, as this was the most efficient choice. Suppose we split the beach in half and put one ice-cream stand in the middle of each half. Assuming the sunbathers and swimmers are evenly distributed, each seller would capture one half of the beach's ice-cream market.

But Hotelling showed that this arrangement is not stable. If Seller A moved his stand closer to Seller B, he could capture

**ICE CREAM STALLS ON THE BEACH**

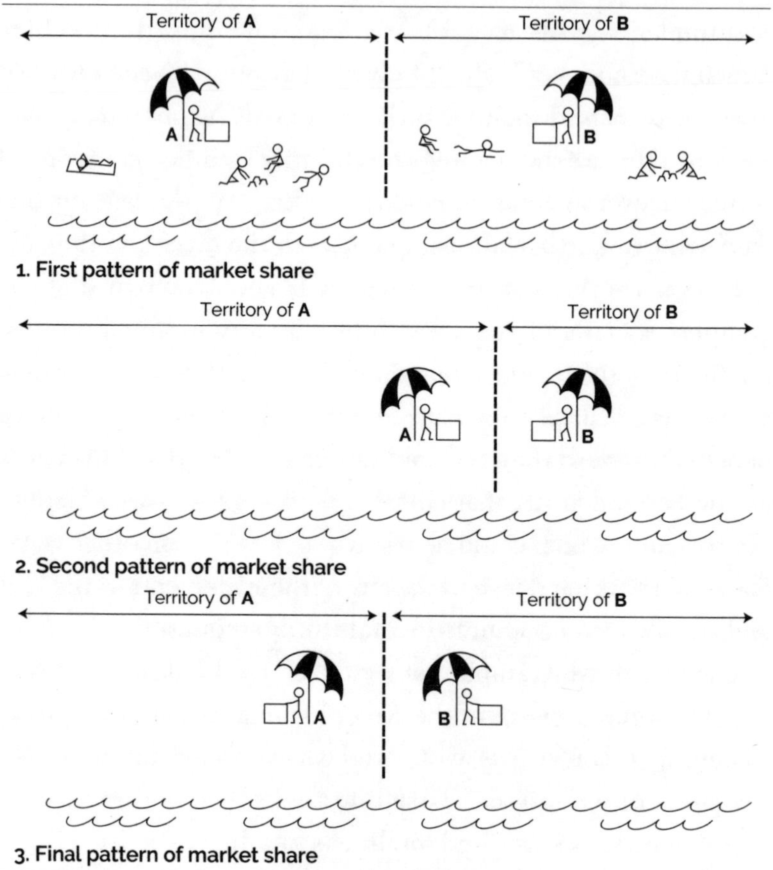


*Source: Author's adaptation of Hotelling's 'Stability in competition'* (Economic Journal, *1929)*

part of Seller B's territory. So, self-interest would drive Seller A to move closer to Seller B. In fact, Hotelling found, the most advantageous place for Seller A to be is *right next to* Seller B, which would allow him to capture three quarters of the ice-cream market. Likewise, Seller B would have an incentive to move toward Seller A. Eventually, the model shows, after some jockeying around for a locational advantage, both sellers will settle at the exact midpoint of the beach. As before, each gets one half of the market, but the difference now is that the swimmers, sunbathers and surfers occupying the edges of the beach have a longer walk to get their ice creams – an outcome that's less than ideal, especially as ice cream melts on its way back to the bathers' chosen spot.

If you ever wonder why things seem to converge toward sameness – whether it's the latest trends in music, the hottest sectors of the stock market or the tendency for consensus-based politics – it'll do you no harm to come back to Hotelling's beach.

But remember: the opposite of a good idea can also be a good idea. On the beach, ice-cream sellers can also uncover new opportunities by pivoting in their thinking and going out to the edges. In finance, for instance, the more customers tend toward index-tracker funds in the middle of the beach, the more a maverick fund manager can stand out at the edge. In politics, it seems the more societies converge toward middle-ground consensus, the more those with views on the edges are likely to seek populist alternatives. And when the beach itself changes, as it sometimes does, the ice-cream sellers have to change too. This is where Tarzan Economics comes in.

Take the UK's high street, where I am noticing a curious trend emerging: the same consumers are willing to shop at both Aldi (a low-cost, new-entrant German supermarket) and Marks & Spencer (an established, upmarket UK retailer). Who loses? Those supermarkets positioned in the middle, with Tesco (a mid-range supermarket) really struggling to compete. You get a thrill from a bargain and from extravagance – but you don't get a thrill from the middle road.

From the high street to the skies: up until the Covid-19 crisis hit, low-cost carriers like EasyJet had been winning market share but upmarket carriers like Singapore Airlines hadn't been losing it – meaning those in the middle, like British Airways (now the world's nineteenth favourite airline), had been losing out.

From the skies to the houses beneath them: you can pick up a vacuum cleaner on Amazon for around £20. Meanwhile, Dyson revolutionised the vacuum-cleaner market with a model that sucked up more than any other model could, and cost far more, too. If you want to get excited about something as mundane as a vacuum cleaner, it will have to cost you well into three figures.

From ice cream, airlines and vacuum cleaners, let's get back to music. We've learned how streaming took off at the flat price of £9.99 a month. That has remained unchanged since 2002, when label executives demanded that the earliest streaming entrant, Rhapsody, should mirror the cost of a Blockbuster rental card, making the cost of accessing all the world's music an increasing bargain with every year that passes. Yet we're also seeing £20 vinyl records continue a decade-long resurgence thirty years after records were declared dead. In the Mid-Year 2020 RIAA Revenue Statistics, the revenues generated by vinyl overtook that of cassettes, CDs and digital albums – the three 'ownership' formats that succeeded it.

Now the pivot point: MusicWatch, a consultancy, shows that almost half the people buying vinyl are also paying to stream music. People are paying a £10 ($10) monthly fee for the thrill of a bargain, and £20 ($25) per vinyl record for the thrill of luxury – but they are not willing to pay for what's in the middle: CDs and downloads. Rational thinking would never have predicted this, but pivotal thinking helps explain it.

This isn't a new idea. A fellow Scot, Adam Smith, made a similar observation a little over two hundred and sixty years ago in *The Theory of Moral Sentiments Part IV*:

> A watch, in the same manner, that falls behind above two minutes in a day, is despised by one curious in watches. He sells it perhaps for a couple of guineas, and purchases another at fifty, which will not lose above a minute in a fortnight. The sole use of watches, however, is to tell us what o'clock it is, and to hinder us from breaking any engagement, or suffering any other inconveniency by our ignorance in that particular point. But the person so nice with regard to this machine, will not always be found either more scrupulously punctual than other men, or more anxiously concerned upon any other account, to know precisely what time of day it is. What interests him is not so much the attainment of this piece of knowledge, as the perfection of the machine which serves to attain it.*

We all carry the precise time around with us on our smartphones, yet luxury watches continue to advertise with glossy double-page spreads in high-end publications – perhaps most ironically for the supposed rationally minded readers of *The Economist*. And it's working. Demand for Swiss watch exports reached 21.7 billion francs in 2019 (£17 billion), a 2.4 per cent increase on the prior year and twice the value at the turn of the millennium, despite the proliferation of smartphones. Rational thinking assumes that markets converge upon the middle. Adam Smith understood why people make choices at the edge. And so can you.

Fundamental to pivotal thinking is this idea of capturing the 'what might have been'. What we're not seeing. What we can't

* Adam Smith, *The Theory of Moral Sentiments: Part IV: Of the Effect of Utility upon the Sentiment of Approbation* (1759).

measure. My father's lesson about the risk posed by children who could swim, and not those who couldn't. Wald's realisation that the zeros were more important than the ones.

My earliest exposure to this was from a classic short novel by Joseph Conrad. *Typhoon* is the story of a steamship captain navigating his way through a terrible storm. Captain MacWhirr has a reputation of 'having just enough imagination to carry him through each successive day, and no more, and cannot fully believe any storm would be a match for his powerful ship.'

When the barometer hints at trouble ahead, MacWhirr remains untroubled and unwilling to change course to save time. His decision comes down to not being able to calculate the zeros – and demonstrate the 'what might have been':

> 'If the weather delays me – very well. There's your log-book to talk straight about the weather. But suppose I went swinging off my course and came in two days late, and they asked me: "Where have you been all that time, Captain?" What could I say to that? "Went around to dodge the bad weather," I would say. "It must've been dam' bad," they would say. "Don't know," I would have to say; "I've dodged clear of it." See that, Jukes? I have been thinking it all out this afternoon.'

Had Captain MacWhirr chosen to avoid the storm, he would not have been able to justify his delay due to the severity of the typhoon. The logbook would have recorded it as a zero as opposed to a one, like Abraham Wald's bullet holes. MacWhirr wouldn't have been able to calculate the opportunity cost – the 'what might have been' that affects all of our lives. Conrad's *Typhoon* taught me an early lesson in life: what we don't see – the zero – is often the number we need to measure most. Yet it often gets measured least.

Now let's turn to some much bigger problems than currency or charity, and explore how to pivot our thinking to be more aligned with the workings of the modern world.

Democracies will always produce outliers – political parties that resent converging on the middle and tend to drift out to the edges. Some parties campaign not to win elections but to educate or, at times, entertain the electorate. Between the years of 1963 and 1997, one of the most familiar TV images of democracy on election nights in the UK was an officer announcing the results of his constituency's election in front of the candidates. This often featured, alongside the soberly dressed men and women standing for the major parties, a man wearing a garishly coloured long coat, an oversized rosette and a tall top hat. His name was Screaming Lord Sutch. He, too, was on the ballot, representing the Official Monster Raving Loony Party.

David Edward Sutch was an entertainer who was ahead of his time. He started in the 1960s as a shock-rock musician, entering the stage from a black coffin dressed as Jack the Ripper, predating the theatrics that made Alice Cooper a household name. Despite his outrageous presentation, Sutch was a respectable musician. The White Stripes even covered one of his songs, possibly as a hat-tip to the fact that he occasionally performed with Jeff Beck and Jimmy Page – two of Jack White's biggest inspirations. Screaming Lord Sutch moved into politics in the early 1960s, standing for various youth parties before forming the Official Monster Raving Loony Party in 1983. In his first election representing the party, he won just 97 votes.

His political impact peaked in 1990, when he beat the Social Democratic Party (SDP) with 1.2 per cent of the vote – enough to embarrass the SDP into dissolving. Lord Sutch (un)successfully lost almost forty elections, a record for British politics.

For the UK electorate across the country, he was part of the furniture. He enjoyed being laughed at, because that meant people listened.

And bits of Lord Sutch's manifesto would sometimes become law, eventually. In the 1960s, he campaigned for lowering the voting age from twenty-one to eighteen. Votes for eighteen-year-olds were introduced in 1969. He campaigned to end the monopoly that the BBC held over radio in the UK by running his own station, Radio Sutch, from an army fort built on the River Thames; the first commercial radio licences were subsequently issued in 1972. The Official Monster Raving Loony Party campaigned for all-day opening of pubs in the 1980s, which became a reality in 1995.

Next to some of his notable hits, however, there were misses as well. Sutch's proposal to turn the European Commission's butter mountains (excess supply of dairy products caused by generous farming subsidies) into ski resorts failed to get on the slopes. He also argued for a new £20 note that wouldn't sink into a puddle should you accidentally drop it – claiming it would become a floating currency.

But even some of the failures bore the hallmark of pivotal thinking. In 1996, he proposed that traffic wardens should be tasked with the collecting and disposing of dog poo – reaching out to car drivers and pedestrian voters alike. On one hand, the pedestrians would welcome cleaner pavements. On the other hand, drivers would respect traffic wardens giving back to society and be more inclined to adhere to their parking regulations. What's more, this would be of little additional cost to traffic wardens as they walk the streets anyway, penalising drivers. Instead of being a cause of friction, under Sutch's loony logic, wardens would become a source of convenience.

And it was Screaming Lord Sutch who got us to our big idea

of pivotal thinking when he proactively asked, 'Why is there only one Monopolies Commission?' Sutch was arguing for two competition authorities. After all, he asked, why should the responsibility of fostering competition be given to one monopoly institution that has no competitor?

The current debate about tech monopolies suggests he had a point. Tech companies like Google, Facebook, Microsoft, Amazon and Apple dominate our lives – how we work and play. Questions about their growing power increasingly dominate headlines. In political circles, you hear cries of breaking them up because they are monopolies, but the cries are not followed by balanced evidence that they do more harm than good. It's more like a knee-jerk reaction that monopolies are bad and no further reasoning is required.

The idea of a monopoly affects so much of how economics is taught and practised. Ironically, although everyone in business wants to become a winner-takes-all monopolist, economics students are universally taught that monopolies are bad and should be broken up. This creates a dilemma: why would anyone want to commit investment to create and conquer a market if the prize will be taken away five years later?

It's a contradiction that I have always struggled with. Screaming Lord Sutch's adage about needing two competition authorities highlights that it is not monopolies, but our very framework for thinking about monopolies, that needs breaking up.

To understand why, consider how a monopolist competition authority affects our everyday lives. Think of something we all have to pay, like utility bills. In most Western markets that have pursued privatisation as an economic policy, bills for electricity, gas and water are paid to private, for-profit companies, regulated by a competition authority that makes sure consumers can easily switch suppliers if they're getting bad service.

A monopolist regulator of these household utilities would think that competition is working when they see more (not fewer) consumers exercising the choice that privatisation has awarded them and switching providers. Following that indicator might be a good idea, but the opposite holds, too – more consumers switching providers could be a negative signal that service standards are slipping. In which case, fewer people exercising their right to switch could be a sign that competition has worked, as households are happy with service standards across the market.

But economics – when examined properly – is rarely that simple. We also have to consider the cost to the consumer of switching – their time, labour and money – which will vary depending on the contract they have with their utility providers. Consumers who may want to switch for good (or bad) reasons may not be able to afford to do so because of the cost or hassle involved. Also, consumers who switch providers may decide to do so based on imperfect information. Price-comparison websites help correct for this problem but often fail to capture the detail behind it. For instance, you could have downward price competition in a market like home insurance (a good idea) accompanied by a parallel decline in what the insurance policy covers (not such a good idea). Lord Sutch, if he were still alive today, would argue that these examples highlight the risk of monopolising the institution that is tasked with preserving competition – because a sole institution naturally struggles to consider that the opposite of their good idea might also be a good idea.

We must rethink how monopolies work today, whether they should be regulated and, if so, how. Let's return to Adam Smith, who argued that monopolies develop via a three-step process: (i) businesses with a strong market position enforce barriers to entry from competitors, (ii) the limited competition confers the power to the monopolist to choose the quantity of the commodity in the market and (iii) the power to fix a price. In some sense, not a lot has changed since the late 1700s. Any rational business will still try to put up barriers to shore up its command of the market, control the level of supply and aim to fix prices to extract profits. A textbook example of a badly behaving monopolist is a property developer who refuses to build during a housing crisis for fear that if they build one too many houses, their grip on the property market will collapse.

But it never was that simple back then, and it's definitely not that straightforward now – especially when the monopolist competes for convenience, not inconvenience, as the textbooks teach us.

In the pre-digital era, say, before the 1990s, monopolies were thought to be terrible things for society. If there's only one business providing a service, the thinking goes, customers are disadvantaged because there's no competition driving innovation or keeping down prices. Anti-trust schemes went to great lengths to prevent such outcomes. In 1974, for example, the US Justice Department brought a case against AT&T, the owner of virtually all the country's communication technology. The resulting break-up of the Bell System several years later (similar to British Telecom in the UK) led to a surge of competition in the communications market, sparking a new wave of innovation and reducing prices for consumers.

The way a telco monopoly of the past was broken up tells us a lot about the way today's tech monopolies are created. Traditionally power used to be formed in the middle of a network and held among the few; now it can gather at the edge and be shared among the many.

The origins of this shift, from the monopolist in the middle to many monopolies gathering at the edge, can be found in the United States landmark Carterfone Case of 1968. The Carterfone allowed someone on the radio to talk to someone on the phone, a simple and appealing invention that challenged the notion that the consumer couldn't attach a device to the network as they would be in competition with the telephone companies who built the network. This landmark decision ruled in favour of Carterfone and allowed any lawful device to connect to the companies' network provided the device did not cause harm. The importance of Carterfone can be found in the modem, which was allowed to attach itself to the network and enable the internet to connect us all. Without the modem, there would be no internet.

The Carterfone may have been just a radio telephone you could put under your car dashboard in the late sixties, but the fact it was permitted as long as it did no harm to the network was transformative, liberating and empowering. It was the first in a long string of cases that chipped away at the telecom monopoly to actually succeed, scaling the castle's walls because the feudal landlord was screwing them. 'We pinned their ears back' reflected the phone's founder Thomas Carter in a 1982 interview in the *New York Times*. 'We made fools of them.'* Carterfone's success changed everything.

Carterfone took a can opener to the telecom industry in 1968, leading to the breakup of Bell systems sixteen years later on the first day of January 1984. As a result, power dispersed from the middle of the telecoms network and out towards the edge. This democratised the tools of technology. The Carterfone may have predated the modem by just two years, but this decision cleared the way for its growth and development; consumers with a computer and a telephone line

* Andrew Pollack, 'The Man Who Beat AT&T', *Special to the New York Times*, July 1982.

to access data services required no network alterations by the telephone company, no notice, no visit at all.

Technologist Jim Griffin, who coined the term Tarzan Economics, reflected on when he was first able to let go of the dependency of the Telco's old vine and reach out to the new vines of innovation found at the network's edge ten years after the breakup of Bell Systems. 'When our team at Geffen released online the first full-length commercial song – Aerosmith's 'Head First' in June 1994 – we did it because networking was self-organizing around Carterfone; people bought modems, attached them to voice telephone lines, and they joined networking services like America Online and CompuServe (two of the services that offered the Aerosmith track for free). Absent the new freedom to attach devices to networks, this would not, could not have happened.'

Carterfone changes went beyond technology itself and affected where it was deployed, as Richard Kramer, founder of Arete Research, points out: 'tech used to be locked up inside telecom operators; after Carterfone there was a way to break free from these monopolies'. Carterfone exposed a chink in the telco's armour that allowed firms to compete at the network's edge. IBM, then a centralised private network, used to be deemed a monopoly in the middle; they've since lost their primacy to Silicon Valley at the edge.

This brings us back to the purpose of this chapter – how we think is largely a result of how we are taught. And we need to teach ourselves to think differently. If we are taught that a traditional monopoly is a bad idea for reasons that have long since lost their relevance, then we need to think differently when faced with the oxymoron of today's tech monopolies (there's a lot more than one) who compete for convenience that didn't exist before. We need to ask: is that not a good idea? Demanding that all these monopolies are broken up is akin to the knee-jerk response I gave my father when I was on the beach, or to statisticians who analysed only the bullet holes they were able to measure. It may feel like we've solved the problem, yet such a reaction fails to understand the source of the problem: an inability to pivot our thinking.

This proliferation of tech monopolies at the edge of the network results in a dilemma that Screaming Lord Sutch would, if he were alive today, be well placed to solve – the irony that can be found in the plural form of the word when politicians cry out, 'We need to break up all these tech monopolies.' Sutch would have pondered this, while adding colour to the electoral podium awaiting another by-election defeat, and asked himself: 'How many tech monopolies do we need to have before we know we've not got a problem with competition?'

To understand how the motives of all these so-called tech monopolists on the edge of the network differ from that sole telco monopolist that used to occupy the middle, we need to find a way out of traditional economic thinking. We need to pivot from a world where the monopolist gain is the consumer's pain, to one where the motive for competition is convenience and the gains are shared.

To do this, let's consider the textbook concept of surplus. A consumer surplus is the difference between what a consumer is willing to pay and the price they actually paid. Producer surplus is the inverse: the difference between the price at which they sold a good and the lowest price at which they would have been willing to sell it. Put together, producer surplus and consumer surplus represent the total benefit to everyone participating in the production and trade of goods.

To put some hard numbers around this, let's work with a

subscription service we're now very familiar with, Spotify, and deploy some simple, hypothetical and round numbers to illustrate the point:

- Let's say the overall cost for Spotify in providing its service is £8 per subscriber.
- The price that Spotify charges is £10.
- There are ten consumers considering subscribing to Spotify, five of whom value the service at £13 or more and five who value the service between £10 and £12.

All these components that lie underneath the demand curve are plotted below, so we can follow what happens when price changes:

**SPOTIFY'S CONSUMER AND PRODUCER SURPLUS**

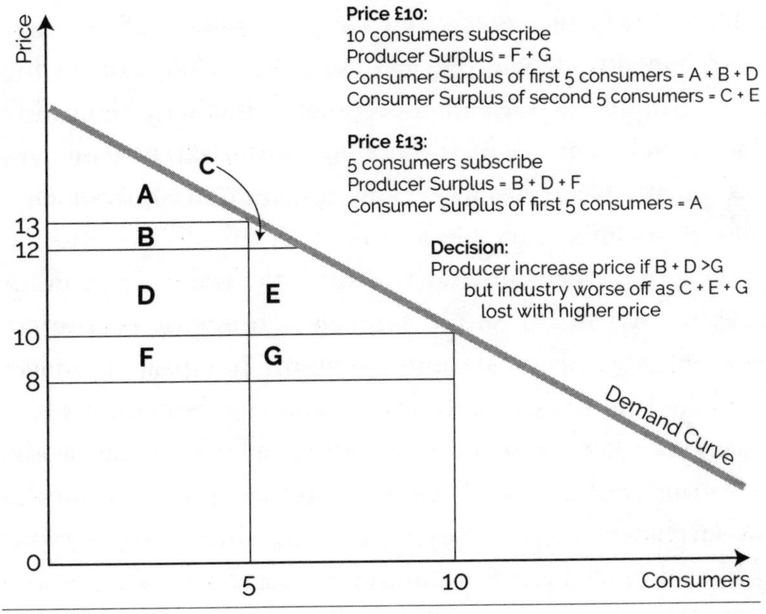
Price £10:
10 consumers subscribe
Producer Surplus = F + G
Consumer Surplus of first 5 consumers = A + B + D
Consumer Surplus of second 5 consumers = C + E
Price £13:
5 consumers subscribe
Producer Surplus = B + D + F
Consumer Surplus of first 5 consumers = A
Decision:
Producer increase price if B + D >G
but industry worse off as C + E + G
lost with higher price
Price
A
B
C
D
E
F
G
13
12
10
8
0
5
10
Consumers
Demand Curve

*Source: Author*

In this example, Spotify has a choice to make:

- At £10, all ten consumers subscribe as they value the service more than it costs them. This means that Spotify enjoys £2 of surplus per subscriber (£10 price – £8 cost), £20 overall.
- If Spotify increases the price to £13, then only 5 of the ten consumers subscribe, but Spotify enjoys £5 of surplus per subscriber (£13 – £8), £25 overall.

Spotify's choice looks simple: the producer surplus increases by £5 overall if they increase the price by £3 per consumer. Following the price hike, five consumers no longer subscribe and the five consumers that do, pay closer to the maximum they're willing to pay: the producer's gain is the consumer's pain. Crucially, there's lower overall surplus – consumers lose more than producers (C + E + G lost).

In this traditional textbook example of a trade-off, we have one side of a trade winning and the other losing – and in this case losing more. We can conceptualise this with the simple chart sketched on the page that follows overleaf, to show how this transfer of surplus used to work with traditional monopolies. A traditional monopoly would seek to shift the surplus away from the consumer and towards the producer by doing exactly what Adam Smith outlined – imposing barriers to entry, hiking prices and limiting output. To repeat, a producer's gain would be the consumer's pain – either in the form of paying more or foregoing use of the producer's good or service – and the purpose of regulation would be to shift some of the surplus back to the consumer.

But this model is antiquated. In contrast to the assumptions of traditional economics, digital platforms are not concerned with marginal cost; it doesn't cost them any more to serve 101 customers than it does to serve 100. And unlike most businesses in the past, digital platforms produce network effects, a virtuous cycle wherein the more consumers that use the platform, the better and more convenient it becomes for those that use it.

To understand why we need to follow Sutch's loony logic and ask why is there only one Monopoly Commission, we can 'flip' this simple chart re-sketch in the bottom-right to conceptualise what happens with innovative digital platforms that are not concerned with antiquated concepts like marginal costs and instead produce network effects – where more participation allows for more convenience.

**CONSUMER/PRODUCER SURPLUS**

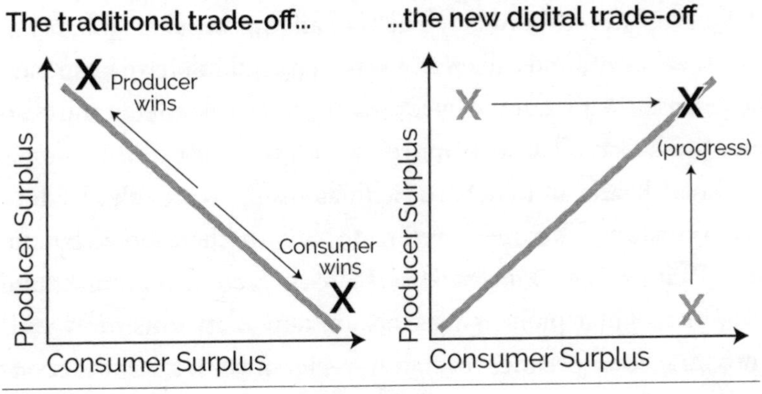


*Source: Author*

Network effects drown out everything else, as convenience is the new currency. The more consumers that use a platform, the more surplus they receive. And the bigger the platform, the more producer surplus grows. The more we adopt battery-operated cars, the more ubiquitous charging stations become, the lower the threshold of entry for more of us to drive battery-operated cars. Now the trade-off line flips, from traveling from south-west to north-east. No longer are we in a zero-sum gain where a producer's gain is the consumer's pain – in fact both sides of the market can benefit from the monopoly.

The evolution of digital platforms shows that a monopoly is not simply a 'bad idea' that controls supply and maximises prices. These innovative digital platforms are often called 'two-sided markets' because they are creating convenience for both the producer and the consumer. In our earlier example, Spotify connects more artists to more listeners than ever before, and the bigger it gets, the more each side grows. Facebook forms groups that previously did not exist, and the more groups that are formed, the more subgroups are spawned. YouTube global scale achieves more cross-border cultural exchanges than national domestic monopolies ever did – and the more it scales, the more cultures connect. They are all matchmakers that bring together buyers and sellers in a way that couldn't have happened otherwise – for example by leveraging network effects and zero marginal cost. That feels more like a 'good idea'.

David Evans and Richard Schmalensee, two of the leading economists in this field, refers to this in their book by the same name: *'The Matchmakers: The New Economics of Multisided Platforms'*. Their pioneering work on new platforms, now well into its second decade, teaches us an inconvenient truth: economists and economic theories are playing an embarrassing game of catch-up with the convenience of our digital realities. According to the traditional textbook, the price a producer sets should equal their marginal cost, as pricing above it attracts competition and pricing below it eliminates profit. In matchmaking markets, lowering the price on one side of the market drives adoption at higher prices on the other side, hence the overall size of the pie can be increased. Canny observers will note this is not new – nightclubs, for example, often let ladies in free so that men are willing to pay more to get inside.

Most of us have used Adobe at some point to open up a file. After all, the company offers us the option of downloading its Adobe Reader 'for free'. Should you want to create a file with Adobe, however, with access to all of its features, then you will need to pay an annual fee of close to £200. Creators pay, but readers don't.

This wasn't always the case. Adobe used to charge both sides to access its software. When it changed its pricing strategy, however, and made its Reader freely available, positive network effects increased demand on the creator side, who now had a big user base on the 'consumer' side. Adobe lost the revenue it had been generating by selling Acrobat to people who wanted to read PDFs (represented by the dark-grey segment on the left graph below), but it more than made up for it with

**ADOBE PRICES READERS AND CREATORS DIFFERENTLY**

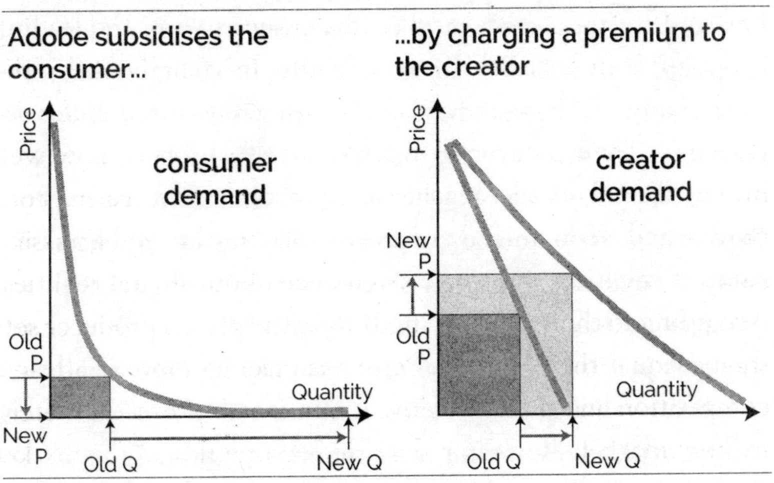


*Source: Author*

revenue from the increasing population of people willing to pay to create PDFs (represented by the light-grey segment on the right). As long as the light-grey block gained is bigger than the dark-grey block lost, price discrimination worked to the platform's advantage.

Adobe's success with this pricing strategy underscores the two most important concepts that define the economics of digital platforms: zero marginal costs and network effects. The traditional relationship between price (what you charge for something) and marginal cost (what each additional unit costs to create) has broken down. By leveraging this fact to exploit network effects – the more consumers, the more producers, and vice versa – companies create a 'flywheel' effect that allows for monopoly-like scale. But these aren't the monopolies of old. In fact, often the intention of such scale is to be able to lower prices even further. This divides opinion among economists and lawyers, who find themselves arguing that although what such a monopoly is doing might in theory be bad, the consumer's improved experience might suggest otherwise.

Flywheels completely transform the ordinary logic of a business as they capture the way convenience scales with adoption. We usually think of badly behaving monopolies in terms of the bigger they get, the more they can abuse the consumer. Businesses that incorporate flywheels effects often do the opposite – the bigger they get, the more convenience they can provide to the consumer. Businesses that have this flywheel dynamic build on themselves, getting stronger and stronger as they scale, just like a flywheel that builds up more speed as it spins faster. This dynamic has become a hallmark of Silicon Valley-style disruption. What makes flywheels work cannot typically be found in economics textbooks, as it's the sense of momentum that's inside the business model – once you get started it's easier to keep going than it is to stop. If you imagine a mouse on a treadmill, it's harder to get off than it is to keep going.

Amazon is perhaps the most famous of these flywheels. As Amazon provides a wider selection of products for its customers, growth comes from five forces interlinked with the broader selection: better customer experience, more traffic, more sellers – and the resulting decrease in costs and lower prices. A similar dynamic prevails across other digital marketplace businesses, like Airbnb and Uber. This effect has been responsible for billions of dollars of wealth-creation in the past few decades.

While the logic of flywheels is certainly more prevalent in digital businesses, it is not a new concept. In fact, Walt Disney had a deep understanding of the interconnected nature of media back when he was building Disney. Walt foresaw a digital media empire that spanned music, TV, merchandising and theme parks, with each one driving more traffic and brand awareness for the others. Mr Disney drew up a legendary diagram in 1957 (overleaf), showing how each piece of the Disney empire feeds the others. This resulted in arguably the most powerful media business of all time.

So far, we've assumed tech monopolies are rational actors. But if we're employing pivotal thinking here, it's worth stopping to question all our assumptions. Consider: along with the money users give to Amazon, they are also handing over massive amounts of their personal data. Is that a rational decision? Are users sufficiently informed about the data they're handing over to even call it a 'decision' in the first place? And if they are sufficiently informed but choose to hand over their data anyway in exchange for the convenience of shopping online, would we call that rational behaviour?

## WALT DISNEY FLY WHEEL

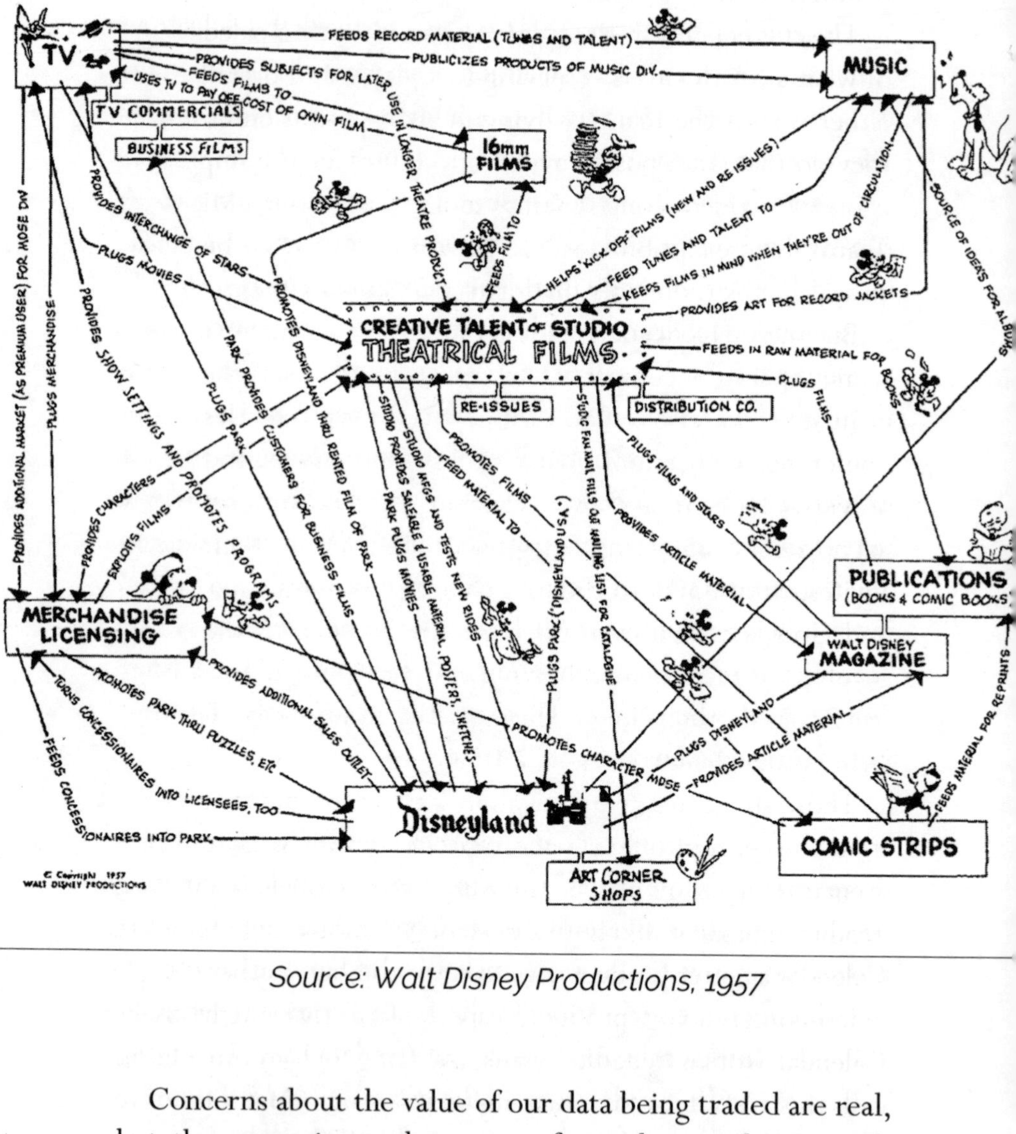


*Source: Walt Disney Productions, 1957*

Concerns about the value of our data being traded are real, but the convenience that comes from sharing data is real, too. One could argue that the use of data is an abuse, but this could be countered with this abuse producing benefits for the consumer that couldn't have been produced otherwise – another reason why we need Sutch's loony logic of having two competition authorities.

The current debate struggles to balance the two-sided nature of what a 'platform' is – serving the people and organisations either side of the market, living or dying based on how well they do that. In a post-Covid world, consider the impressive choice of video conferencing tools like Zoom, Microsoft Teams, Skype and BlueJeans. The reason they've all been able to scale is the monopoly platforms that support them.

But there is a deeper point about how these platform companies operate – competing for convenience means they often regulate themselves. If you think back to the relentless video conferencing that took place during the early period of the Covid-19 lockdown of 2020, you may recall how easy it was to set up a Zoom call using Google Calendar. Simply assemble the invites, drop down to the first choice of conferencing facility and Google would even populate the invite with the names involved. It may have gone unnoticed, but it was even easier to use Zoom through Google Calendar than it was to use Google's own product, Google Meet.

Think about that: why is Google pulling the rug from under its own feet and offering a competitor product more prominence than its own? The answer is that Google Calendar's product manager likely has a stronger motivation to make Calendar a better product than to help promote another Google video-conferencing product, especially if that might make Calendar worse. Benedict Evans, a leading tech commentator, calls this a 'strategy tax', making their own product inferior to cater to a higher-level corporate strategy. (Apple found this out when they had to notionally endorse Google Maps after their own failed launch of Apple Maps in 2012 – consumers didn't have time for an upgrade as they needed to get to where they were going, and Apple didn't want their brand to be blamed for them being late.)

Technology-driven monopolies are wary of charging themselves this strategy tax. Sometimes they may opt not to pay the tax, for example when Facebook cut off Twitter cards' access to Instagram in 2012, risking the appeal of its photo- and video-sharing social networking service. But more often than not, tech monopolies will often pay the tax themselves to compete on convenience – whether it be Google Calendar endorsing competitors' meeting apps, Amazon Prime promoting Netflix originals like *Narcos* on its homepage or Apple Watch supporting competitor music-streaming services. In each instance, convenience matters more than competition.

As antitrust concepts go, strategy tax is in its infancy – its legal definition is still a work in progress – but my own introduction to the topic came from a visit to Brussels, at a conference hosted by the European Commission's own 'trust-buster' Departement Generale Competition. The conference featured many seminal academics and policymakers poring over slides that tried to calculate Google's market share of search. I noted the debate was missing something that everyone in the room had in their pocket and would use once the conference dispersed – apps.

Apps offer a different means to the same end. Google's core business of search can be circumvented by the apps offered on its Android operating system, as the search queries with the most relevance and urgency (e.g. transport and weather) will happen in the more relevant app (e.g. Eurostar and BBC) and not the Google search bar. Yet the experts in that Brussels conference room didn't mention apps once during the whole seminar, nor did they factor it into defining the size of the search market. Yet when I asked about this omission, they acknowledged they would all be resorting to their apps to search for their next Eurostar train home (and checking the weather for when they arrive). The app store was biting off the 'search' hand that feeds it.

Strategy tax pivots our thinking as it puts us inside these tech monopolies and appreciates the process of innovation of new products (and the objectives of their product managers) is not revenue, but to make the underlying product more appealing. So, if a platform breaks the experience by blocking things your users want, they don't serve the underlying aim. In other words, these monopolies are incentivised to provide customers with convenience even if it costs them to do so.

Now step back and ask how much of this pivotal thinking about monopolies is being taught in business schools or applied by competition authorities today?

*

Pivotal thinking should hurt your neck – as you will be constantly looking behind to see how far back traditional concepts in economics have fallen in terms of their relevance. Today's tech monopolies are not focused on yesterday's framework of hiking prices and reducing output; they are focused on eliminating price, maximising output and taking friction out of the market. Conventional thinking, that monopolies are 'bad', needs to be challenged by the opposite idea: that monopolies that compete for convenience can also be a force for good.

When consumers don't behave like an economist's economic model would have predicted, they often blame the consumer for being irrational. But pivotal thinking calls time on such arrogance, and pulls back the curtain on why theory and reality have diverged. It is no longer acceptable to hold on to outdated frameworks of what is good and bad that simply no longer stack up.

Pivotal thinking involves 'learning by doing'; having the confidence to involve ourselves in the debate, rather than remain a bystander, and to actually affect the outcomes. Having the confidence to raise your hand and ask that 'dumb kid in the classroom' question that all others were frightened to ask. I learned to pivot my thinking back on that beach in Scotland when my father asked me to do the job of the prime minister and respond to a crisis. I wanted to make matters better, and learned how my actions would have made matters worse. An abrupt introduction to the 'what might have been' calculation of opportunity cost. Whether it's Abraham Wald's bullet holes, Captain MacWhirr's logbook or Lord Sutch's loony logic, the pivotal lesson is that they raised the importance of asking not just what might have been, but also 'what are we missing' – as the zeros you can't measure can add up to more than the ones that you can.

This is where we need to turn next, as many of the benefits that these technology monopolies have brought are free, and if nothing is paid for then the state will struggle to measure their monetary contribution to the economy. Consider Wikipedia. This free resource may have monopolised the market for encyclopaedias by becoming the sum of all the world's knowledge, but it does zero environmental damage and adds nothing to the economy. Now apply some pivotal thinking, as it's not hard to think about industries, like defence, which do not bring together all the world's knowledge, do horrific environmental damage and contribute a significant portion to the economy.

This raises questions about 'What does good look like?' A growing economy that damages the environment or a shrinking economy that doesn't? Do we really want to measure the post-Covid economic recovery by tracking how far off pollution levels are from their pre-Covid peak? And if we don't, why should we measure the economy using the same 'old vine' thinking as we did before the pandemic? We now need to carry that justified scepticism across to how we measure the economy itself. We need the confidence to be able to make a better judgement about the state we're in.

# 7

# JUDGING THE STATE WE'RE IN

When the ideas inside our heads are worth more than the roofs above them, it's a sign of the times. That is to say, investment in intellectual property – the business of ideas – is now worth more to the US economy than residential real estate – the business of bricks and mortar (see chart below). Only twenty years ago the tables were turned; residential real estate was not only worth more than intellectual property but poised to increase in value. But then the housing market collapsed, taking the world economy with it, kicking off a decade of convulsions that have brought us to where we are: a new normal where investment in the ideas inside us continues to outstrip the houses around us. Yet our ability to measure the contribution of our ideas remains worryingly limited.

Tarzan Economics requires confidence. One must let go of the old vine and grab on to the new. That's true whether you're talking about the music industry staring down the barrel of a gun called Napster in the summer of 1999 or governments surveying the wreckage of the mortgage market in 2009. Yet in order to be confident about when to make the switch, we must be confident in our understanding about where in our

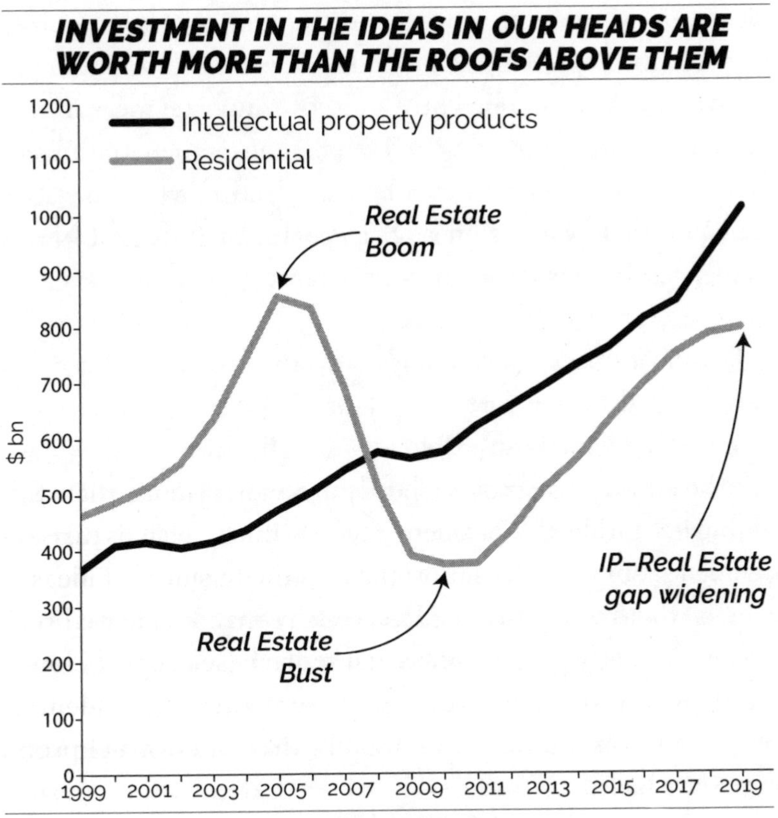


*Source: www.bea.gov*

swing we are. One might be forgiven for hanging on to the old vine and the familiarity that comes with years of things proceeding a certain way, rather than risk switching to a new one. But it's also true that the tools we use to determine the state we're in, based as they are on traditional economics, can make us more hesitant about reaching out to the new vine than we ought to be. Those old tools can alter our judgement about the state we're in.

In 1849, the Scottish writer Thomas Carlyle coined the term 'The Dismal Science', which may have followed on from Malthus's economic predictions about society's rising demands caused by population growth and the diminishing resources available to them. This dismal outlook continues to influence the way we (and, importantly, our governments) measure the state we're in, producing more pessimism than optimism, more focus on costs than on benefits, and more on negative scenarios than positive ones. The economist Andrew McAfee challenges this pessimism in considerable depth in his excellent book, aptly titled *More From Less*.

Pessimism pays, as it stands above the crowd. Mainstream news will always report sharp falls in the stock market, but rarely steady increases. Job losses will always make 'page one' headlines but reports of an uptick in net job creation will be buried inside the business pages. Court verdicts that are deemed shocking will capture the nation's imagination, but the tens of thousands of reasonable court verdicts handed down every day barely get a mention. The table below captures what I call the 'pessimism paradox', where the only way to stand above the noise and gather a crowd is to be pessimistic when times are bad.

**PESSIMISM PARADOX**

| | *During good times* | *During bad times* |
|---|---|---|
| *Economists Give a Positive Outlook …* | **No One Cares** | **People Hate You** |
| *Economists Give a Pessimistic Outlook …* | **No One Cares** | **People Love You** |

*Source: Author*

Such pessimism is fuelled by the judgements we make based on statistics we are told to trust. We are told that technology is destroying more jobs than it creates, and we believe it because the statistics support that conclusion. To pivot through disruption, we need to learn that these statistics are also based on judgements – we judge what we want to measure and what to discard, and we judge how to measure based on the measurement tools we have to hand, regardless of their imperfections. The way we judge employment statistics, for example, may have been suited to the stationary and tangible activity of manufacturing, but less suited to the non-stationary and intangible activity of technology. Consequently, technology may be destroying (some of) the jobs that are easy to measure but creating (even more) jobs that are hard to capture. Those imperfect statistics don't just affect governments, they affect the ability of all of us to see through the fog and grasp the value of the new vine.

Building the confidence to question these judgements really matters. There is an age-old (and regrettably sexist) expression that goes 'If a man wants to cause a recession, then he should marry his maid.' Why? Because governments judge that doing one's own household work doesn't add to the economy but doing it for someone else does. You need the confidence to question not just the politics of this situation, but the logic. Imagine a street with ten houses, all occupied by ten residents doing the same level of housework in their own respective homes. This would be judged as invisible to the radar of economic statistics. However, if each resident offered to do their neighbour's housework for the same fee – creating a carousel of cash changing hands – then the state judges that goods and services have been provided, thus expanding GDP. Nothing has actually changed – except that the government judges it has, with profound implications.

To begin this inquiry into the state we're in, let's return to our initial observation about the tangible business of real estate and look at how the houses we grew up in add value to the economy. Once you appreciate that even the oldest part of the economy – housing – and the statistics used to measure it are just judgements, you will have the confidence to judge them yourself.

Before entering rockonomics, I was a government economist, and coincidentally that's where I first developed a healthy cynicism for government statistics. Yet it wasn't inside the corridors of power that these clouds of doubt started to gather, but inside a dark and dingy nightclub in Edinburgh's old town. It was 2006, and the UK property market was booming with no slowdown in sight. The words 'credit crunch' were largely unknown, with the exception of a few of us who had bothered to read the work of Hyman Minsky – an American economist who coined the phrase 'stability is destabilising' and sadly died ten years before his ideas proved correct.

In the dark and dingy club, as the band were busy assembling their instruments onstage, queues were forming both outside the venue and at the bar. The organiser of the concert pulled me to the side and introduced me to his friend who had travelled up from Leeds. He had recently graduated with first-class honours in Law from Leeds University, the sort of degree that meant he didn't have to look for employment, but employers would look for him.

'Congratulations on your degree,' I said. 'I assume you must be busy working in the City now?' 'Yes, I'm busy,' he replied, 'but I'm not working for anyone. I'm buying and selling properties.' I was confused: 'But you're working, right? I mean, you recently got that top degree.' He looked dismissive and shook his head: 'No, working for the man doesn't cut it any more. I went straight into properties – buying, improving and then selling them on.'

Given my day job was understanding economic statistics, this was news to me. It was the summer of 2006, and this seemingly rational top graduate would rather play the property casino than enter full-time employment. I was intrigued that he said 'properties' in the plural. 'If you don't mind me asking, how many properties do you have at the moment?' He raised both hands so his fingers would do the talking. I counted six of them.

I was taken aback. 'Six!'

This wasn't the time or place to pry into his personal finances, but I needed to understand how a recent graduate – presumably loaded to the gills with student debt – could finance such a portfolio. I asked, 'How did you get the money to buy so many properties?' 'Easy, I got them all on self-certification. The banks didn't even ask for evidence of income.'

My jaw dropped. I started to do the mental maths on what I had just heard. Back in 2006, the UK property market was so hot that students could take out loans to buy their own flats, secure in the knowledge that the capital gain on the property would more than cover the cost of their education. Buying and selling property was so common, so fast-paced, so relentless, that most people had accidentally forgotten how to declare taxes associated with their sale. In my small home country of Scotland, our 'local' bank, the Royal Bank of Scotland, was well on its way to becoming the biggest financial institution in the world, largely by doing the same thing as our Leeds graduate, but on a much grander (and far more dangerous) scale.

Ten years later I saw the very same dialogue re-enacted in a memorable scene from the film based on Michael Lewis's book *The Big Short*. The difference: I was in a dingy night club in Scotland, and the scene from *The Big Short* takes place in a brightly lit lap-dancing club in Florida.

Steve Carell, playing the hedge-fund specialist Mark Baum, has decided to visit Florida to understand just how far (and how fast) the wheels had fallen off the US property market. Baum's work takes him – as analyses of complex financial instruments so often do – to the private booth of a lap-dancing club. As a dancer performs her routine, Carell ignores her bodily assets and focuses on her financial liabilities.

He learns that she lied on her mortgage application, and he explains to her how her monthly payments will jump 200 per cent when her 'teaser' mortgage rate expires. With loud music blaring across the conversation, she swings around the pole to express shock and asks what this could mean to all her 'loans'. Then, like me, he realises she used the plural of 'loan' and asks the dancer, 'What do you mean, all your "loans"?' While swinging out of her dance routine, she replies, 'I have five houses and a condo.'

Despite the different settings, our facial reactions were exactly the same. In 2006, it seemed that everyone everywhere was playing the property market. As the band in that dark dingy Edinburgh club started to perform, I recalled another infamous adage on why financial bubbles begin in the first place: 'When the music's playing, you know you've got to dance.'

Back at home after the show, I turned my attention to gauging the size of the problem. I wanted to know how many more property gamblers were out there, and, more importantly, how their gambling was being measured by the government. In my only (but by no means isolated) example, this recent graduate had taken out what were effectively unsecured loans to flip properties on a monthly basis, paying little attention to capital gains tax. I couldn't understand how my employer, the UK government, even measured how much money he was making, as the average capital gain on property transactions easily exceeded the median annual earnings for a full-time UK worker, of £23,000.

This is where my suspicion of government statistics first kicked in. I asked a statistician in the UK civil service for a coffee so I could try to understand if my concerns about the property-market casino not being captured were real. I wanted to know if any of this new activity was being measured, and if so, how? This is where he introduced me to the wacky idea of imputed rents.

'Imputed rent' is the way the government assigns value to owner-occupied and other rent-free properties. By assigning that value, properties that don't generate revenue – like homes that are privately owned by their occupants – can be included in a country's gross domestic product. Without imputed rent, economists would argue, GDP would be a flawed metric, one that ignored a huge section of the housing market. By inventing that metric, economists added about 10 per cent to the value of both the US and UK economies, without any real transactions taking place. Why, I wondered, should such a statistic be needed? Including things that do not exist in measures like gross domestic product seemed misleading at best and warped at worst.

Metrics like 'imputed rent' are a good example of statistics that make judging the state you're in more, not less, difficult. In 2006, the UK housing market had been on a steep upward curve for over a decade in the lead-up to the credit crunch, and it felt like our official statistical authority was both inventing and guessing at how steep this curve was. Firstly, it was inventing a payment that didn't exist (landlords do not pay themselves rent). Secondly, it was guessing the value they pay and adding it to GDP (repeat, they paid themselves nothing). Thirdly, their guesswork was based on a survey of actual rents, which was in itself prone to error. And to all of that we need to add a blunt fourth – most of the buy-to-let activity overheating the property market was undeclared anyway.

As the coffee break with my statistician friend reached its conclusion, I was torn. On the one hand, I now understood that the government's valuation of the housing market was based on fictional statistics. On the other hand, I was in a job that demanded a belief in those fictional statistics – the fictional statistics were necessary to calculate gross domestic product. In real life, the property casino was generating real money that translated into real economic activity, yet little of this activity was reaching the statistical radar of how our government measured our economy. We were believing stable and reliable statistics, while the truth was they were increasingly unstable and unreliable.

That day taught me to no longer feel intimidated by the history and tradition of official statistics. I'd asked a fairly simple question over coffee, and what I'd learned was akin to opening a can of worms. Clearly, there was something to be gained from having the confidence to challenge tradition with basic observations about how the world actually works. The lesson I learned during that coffee break was that over a tenth of what we call the UK and US economies was simply made up.

I left the government office that day determined to understand how widespread this problem of measuring the real economy was and scribbled three words on the back of a bus ticket: property, inheritance and e-commerce. I was sure these three ways of generating income were increasingly important to the real economic lives of people around me, and equally sure that none of them were being captured in GDP.

Property, I'd just learned, was largely a construct of statistical guesswork.

Inheritance, meanwhile, was a consequence of my concerns about property. As the UK (and US) has long since become a nation of homeowners, as people pass away, they pass those homes down to younger generations. The statistics might tell a simple story: a younger person inheriting a property worth £500,000 would become £500,000 richer. But the change of circumstances for that young person might have other, more complex effects that the statistics didn't capture. Maybe without the burden of having to pay rent or a mortgage, that young person might decide to work fewer hours at their job. That reduction in output would mean a net loss for the performance of the economy as a whole, even if the inherited house made that one person considerably better off.

And then there was e-commerce. I wanted to know more about how e-commerce, which was still in a fledgling state in 2006, showed up in GDP. Amazon's share price at the time was just under $42 – it is now closer to $3,000 – but it was already clearly stealing revenues from the high-street stores. Back then, my day job involved understanding retail statistics and the surveys that created them. Typically, this would involve domestic bricks-and-mortar retailers reporting their data to a national statistics authority. It wasn't clear to me how global online retailers were captured in GDP, nor how the income even appeared in the UK. If a consumer purchased a household appliance from the Amazon marketplace, who, if anyone, reported the trade – the platform or the seller or both? Where did the trade take place – the location of the buyer, the seller, or where the platform was registered for taxation?

My training told me that these three parts of everyday life had to be the exceptions to the rule, that the statistics that gave us a picture of the strength of the economy must be fundamentally sound. But my head told me otherwise – a significant slice of the population was now making money from property, inheriting wealth from their relations and spending it online. These were the rules, not the exceptions. The consumers had reached out to a new vine, while the statistics were holding on to the old. I wasn't alone in my suspicion either. Not long after, the US Vice President Dick Cheney famously remarked that you couldn't trust retail statistics, as they don't capture what's happening on eBay.

The British economist Diane Coyle has arguably done more than anyone not only to unpack what exactly GDP really means, but also to advocate for adopting something more meaningful in its place. In her wonderfully brief book *GDP: A Brief but Affectionate History* she unpicks the meaning of GDP – the anchor-like statistic for measuring the state we're in.

The origins of her doubts actually come from the person credited with inventing GDP in 1934, Simon Kuznets, who said, 'The welfare of a nation can therefore scarcely be inferred from a measurement of national income as defined [by GDP].' GDP, according to Kuznets, is a measure of production, not the overall well-being of the economy.

What makes Coyle's work on government statistics so illuminating is that she explains how those statistics are actually created. Take inflation. The headline measure of inflation is quoted in the media like it's the gospel truth, and even small changes in its rate are presented like they have a profound impact on our lives. But where does that 'inflation' statistic come from? Inflation is calculated based on the change in cost of a selected basket of 'typical' goods. But how do economists decide what qualifies as 'typical' goods? A digital camera and a smartphone might both be considered typical goods. But the latter can perform the task of the former. So, should statisticians remove the digital camera as it's no longer relevant? But if we simply remove it, the cost of the basket will go down, suggesting a decrease in inflation that hasn't taken place. So, it should be replaced, but with what?

Even without swapping items, you run into problems. When CDs were included in the inflation basket, they were judged to have a single average price point, but this was never really the case – the first-hand market included aggressive discounting strategies, and the second-hand market, especially on new digital stores like Amazon, was ripe with deflationary forces. Piracy, which had been mainstream for over a decade, also distorted the perceived price the customer was measuring as music had essentially become free.

CDs were part of the UK inflation basket up until March 2015. A judgement was made to remove the retail price of a CD from the basket and replace it with the monthly cost of subscribing to Spotify. CDs hadn't disappeared, but they were judged to be less important to the economy than Spotify. But in that case, we're swapping the occasional cost of owning ten songs with the recurring price of accessing 60 million more – arguably deflating the unit value of music and making choice more affordable. But CD prices had been in terminal decline for years, whereas the headline cost of streaming had remained unchanged at £9.99, making this swapping of goods in the basket net inflationary.

This, of course, has nothing to do with the increasing Average Revenue Per User (ARPU) explored in our first principle of Tarzan Economics, nor does it mean that CDs no longer exist – rather, the statistical authorities simply made a judgement about what should and shouldn't make up their basket of goods. And then it made a judgement about what should and shouldn't be taken into account when calculating the value of those goods. We need the confidence to question these judgements if we are going to let go of what we think we know and grab on to what we know we don't.

Tarzan Economics teaches us to look at government statistics like it looks at many things in life: with scepticism, curiosity and the confidence to challenge long-held beliefs. We've learned how headline statistics like inflation are predicated on arbitrary judgements, now we need to see how Tarzan Economics illuminates the way forward. The best illustration: the rise of 'cloud storage' – individuals, firms and governments are powering down their own local servers and adopting cloud services for their data-storage infrastructure. Tech giants such as Google, Microsoft and Amazon build hyperscale cloud utility services that make what was previously impossible with home-owned computing possible through massive scale.

In 2018, approximately 3.6 billion internet users used cloud computing services, up from 2.4 billion users in 2013.* Flexera's 2020 'State of the Cloud Report' estimated that 93 per cent of all cloud-based enterprises already have a multi-cloud strategy in place.† Adoption is now so widespread, it's not uncommon to find competing firms collaborating in the cloud: Amazon and Netflix will compete fiercely for eyeballs for their video-streaming services, yet Netflix is powered by Amazon's cloud infrastructure – similar to how ice-cream sellers would typically share the van to reduce the cost of distribution, yet

* 'Number of consumer cloud-based service users worldwide in 2013 and 2018', *Statistsa*, 2013.

† 'Flexera 2020 State of the Cloud Report', *Flexera*, 2020.

compete fiercely for customers once they had restocked their stalls on the beach.

Yet for all the mass adoption and productivity gains of cloud computing services, we have to raise concerns as to the ability of domestic government statistics to keep pace. The risk is that the more the economy moves into the cloud, the more it gets lost.

The first risk of cloud's impact being a blind spot for statisticians is pricing – capturing the presence of the cloud in national GDP statistics is one thing, tracking its price is another. The price of cloud storage has been dropping dramatically. Bezos's Law, named after Amazon founder Jeff Bezos, was coined by AppZero founder Greg O'Connor in 2014. The law stated that 'a unit of [cloud] computing power price is reduced by 50 per cent approximately every three years', and the cloud storage industry has more or less kept pace with that prediction.* † All of this crashing cost of data storage means the nominal spending by the firm will look far lower (and so the deflator needs to be more aggressive) even if firms are getting more for it.

Migration to the cloud has also created a second problem in accounting. The rise of on-demand digital infrastructure is causing firms to substitute fixed capital equipment (like servers) for cloud services. How do you reflect the shift from owning equipment to renting services on a balance sheet? Using the cloud is similar to leasing equipment owned by another firm, but the majority of businesses want to treat the cloud as capital expenditure. They're acting as though they own the digital infrastructure that they're paying for, and the most recent

* Bill Supernor, 'Why the cost of cloud computing is dropping dramatically', *App Developer Magazine*, January 2018.

† Greg O'Connor, 'Moore's law gives way to Bezos's law', *Gigaom*, April 2014.

rulebook, the International Financial Reporting Standard (IFRS16) is making it easier to do so. The risk is that, from the firm's perspective, capital expenditure is increasing, but from the government's perspective, it's decreasing – meaning firms are investing less capital yet achieving more output, which goes against conventional policy thinking.

The third risk is in locating the economic activity itself. It is not clear that the large US-based market leaders in cloud services are reporting their investment spending to authorities in their separate national markets. One can imagine a political game show of 'whose cloud is it anyway', where domestic countries all claim the activity of the cloud services within their own national borders, whereas the country of origin also puts in a duplicate claim. As these cloud services are often a subset of a much bigger organisation (Google's cloud platform is secondary to search, Amazon is retail, Microsoft is software), there is an incentive to book as much of the activity in the country that regulates you to maximise influence. The three main providers may want to 'shore up' their international cloud activity in their headquartered country of origin – and prevent leakage of their contribution to the other markets they serve. This does not eliminate the risk of double-counting as the other countries these companies serve may choose to measure the same cloud services in their own markets using their own methodologies.

The conundrum posed by the statistical measurement of the cloud offers a timely reminder of the Jevons Paradox – which suggests that if storage costs less, we'll use storage more. The paradox dates back to nineteenth-century English economist William Stanley Jevons and his book *The Coal Question*, in which he noted that new technologies that made burning coal more efficient weren't making Britons use any less coal. 'It is wholly a confusion of ideas to suppose,' he concluded, 'that the economical use of fuel is equivalent to a diminished consumption. The very contrary is the truth.' We can see the Jevons Paradox everywhere – in our kitchens, where refrigeration has become more energy-efficient so we buy bigger and bigger fridge-freezers to make more use of the more efficient refrigeration. Cars are more fuel-efficient, so we buy more of them and choose to live further from work, using their fuel more too. The cloud is similar: as it gets cheaper to store things on the cloud, more of us store things there. Build more lanes on a motorway and you invite more traffic. Build more space in the sky and you invite more clouds to gather.

GDP has had its cyclical ups and downs in what Diane Coyle calls its 'brief but affectionate history', but on this occasion it may finally have got lost in the cloud. The inertia in compiling government statistics, often using surveys based on recalling past events, means that government statisticians will struggle to factor in the impact of falling prices, accountancy treatment and multiple locations as companies adopt cloud services.

Worse still: even if done correctly and consistently in one country, other countries may purposefully choose to stick to the old ways. If a more accurate picture of the economy, based on new statistical methods, shows that the economy isn't as strong as the old methods suggested it was, then there is an incentive to stick to the old methods and the inflated valuation of the economy that they created. Governments have incentives to report on things that make them look good and not on things that don't – even if the people suffer for it.

As the real economy which we live in and experience every day grabs on to the new vine of the cloud, it has enabled firms to become more productive, yet the governments tasked with measuring them may be holding on to the old vine and misjudging the real state we're in as a result. The cloud is just one of many examples of why a misguided view about the state we're in creates a fear of letting go of what we know as we fail to measure what we don't.

GDP is based on what people pay for goods and services. If something is free, it is not counted in GDP. Facebook and Google are two of the largest companies in the world, and their flagship products – Facebook's social media platform and Google's search platform – cost zero. Free information goods like Facebook, Gmail and Wikipedia increasingly dominate our lives, yet they are not appearing in economic statistics. eMarketer, a research consultancy, reported the average time US consumers spend with media formats like Facebook and YouTube will rise by more than 1 hour per day in 2020 to 13 hours, 35 minutes, driven by the Covid-19 crisis and pre-pandemic trends.* Yet the share of the economy that can be contributed to the information sector today is around 4.7 per cent, exactly the same as it was in 1997, long before many of these media formats were invented. There may, then, be a massive part of the economy not reflected in GDP.

If the economy is underpriced, the best way to correct it is to revisit our concept of consumer surplus, the difference between the maximum a consumer would be willing to pay for a good or service and the asking price of that good or service. Let's recall our Discogs auction price example from our fourth principle, Make or Buy. If you would have spent as much as £91 for a deluxe box set of *In Rainbows*, for instance, but had to pay only £40, then you have a £51 consumer surplus. Consumer spending can be counted, but consumer surplus cannot.

* Mark Dolliver, 'US Time Spent with Media 2020: Gains in Consumer Usage During the Year of COVID-19 and Beyond', *eMarketer*, April 2020.

How do we work out how much users value free resources like Facebook? The simplest way to work out the consumer surplus of a free good is to ask users how much they would pay to stop the free good being taken away from them. The Massachusetts Institute of Technology (MIT) researchers Erik Brynjolfsson, Avinash Collis and Jae-Joon Lee have made giant steps to work this out as part of their 'Measuring the Economy Project'. In a write-up in *Harvard Business Review*, Brynjolfsson and Collins explain their process:*

> 'We start by asking participants to make choices. In some cases, we ask them to choose between various goods (for example, "Would you rather lose access to Wikipedia or to Facebook for one month?"). In others, they choose between keeping access to a digital good or giving it up in exchange for monetary compensation ("Would you give up Wikipedia for a month for $10?"). To make sure that people have revealed their true preferences, we follow up with experiments in which participants actually must give up a service before they can receive compensation.'

The spread of the surplus reported by the respondents was noticeable. A fifth of users surveyed were willing to give up Facebook for a month for just $1, but another fifth would not consider relinquishing use of the platform for anything under $1,000. Overall, the median price Facebook users agreed to in the survey was $48. Using this survey, and completing a follow-up experiment, the academics determined that US Facebook users derived $231 billion in value from the platform between

* Erik Brynjolfsson and Avinash Collins, 'How Should we Measure the Digital Economy?' *Harvard Business Review*, November–December 2019.

2004 and 2019 – that's $231 billion in value that's bypassing the transactional measure of the economy.

Critics of this consumer-surplus approach point to advertising revenues generated by the site as hard evidence that the value of Facebook is being captured in GDP. But the academics uncovered an annual consumer surplus of about $500 per person in the United States that was much higher than the average revenue per user, which is only around $140 per year, indicating the revenue generated by Facebook from advertising was less than the value they were providing their users. Advertising is not a substitute for consumer surplus.

The MIT team has ambitiously suggested a new measure of the economy that captures this surplus, with a new acronym: GDP-B (the B standing for Benefits). The thinking is that this would supplement the traditional GDP measure by quantifying the value consumers get from free goods. By considering these benefits, lawmakers would not only be in a better place to make evidence-based decisions about policy but also avoid the pitfalls of policy-based evidence-making by misjudging the state we're in.

Large-scale choice experiments have their limitations. First, a full range of goods needs to be included, and that involves a long tail of items that will be hard to even identify, let alone measure. Second, free goods produce costs as well as benefits, such as their impact on our greatly reduced attention spans, as we explored in our earlier chapter on paying attention. Third, free goods can also be viewed as a means to an end – loss leaders encouraging more purchasing of paid goods. The reported difference between the consumer surplus for Facebook and its advertising revenues could perhaps be counted through our additional spending on products that were advertised on the platform. Finally, it must be acknowledged that it's easier for users to say they'd pay for a free good than it is for the user to actually cough up the cash.

Still, to reflexively dismiss new ideas like GDP-B is to demonstrate a fear of letting go of what you know. Sure, it's easy to underline its limitations, dismiss it as fuzzy maths and stick with the old vine of traditional economic statistics. But it's getting harder and harder to deny that the old vine is not fit for purpose. As we learned from the examples of imputed rents, inflation and increased adoption of the cloud, there is already a lot of fuzzy maths in the current methodology for GDP. Instead, GDP-B asks you to grab on to a new vine and judge for yourself your own personal value on goods and services that you don't pay for yet but are fast becoming a priceless part of your everyday life.

In addition to the GDP-B, which captures what free goods we value but don't measure, we also need to consider the merits of the 'GDP-of-now' – understanding of our current 'welfare' as Kuznets put it back in 1934, not a misplaced measure of the count of transactions that took place in the past.

In the prologue we learned that music has set itself apart by embracing that model already – using newly available data tools to understand consumption of music right now as opposed the sales of music last quarter. We saw how this could apply to health (belonging to a gym doesn't mean that you went to the gym today), transport (car sales last month do not tell you how many cars are on the road) and houses (knowing how people are living is more valuable than what property was sold). Trying to hack together a measure of the 'GDP-of-now' means working with data that might be less granular than what official statistics would adopt but timelier. That's a trade-off worth making as technology is accelerating change and statistics have been left lagging far behind.

The way I learned to think about the 'GDP-of-now' came from a most unusual source, following the most unpredictable set of events.

Much of my time across the many time zones at Spotify was spent helping Public Relations mop up the mess of the latest media crisis. Spotify has been attacked by everyone from Taylor Swift ('I'm not willing to contribute my life's work to an experiment') to Neil Young ('I don't need my music to be devalued by the worst quality in the history of broadcasting or any other form of distribution'). Even in the London office, the downstairs neighbours were criticising Spotify for having concerts in the canteen area – which would have been understandable had the downstairs neighbour not been Live Nation!

As I made my way to my desk on that spring morning in April 2018, I heard that Spotify was now taking shots from privacy groups. It seemed the chief economist of the Bank of England, Andy Haldane, had given a speech at King's College Business School where he'd suggested that the central bank of the United Kingdom was using Spotify listeners' data to gauge what he called 'people's sentiment'.

The *Guardian* led with 'Spotify trends could help us gauge the public mood – Bank of England' and countless other newspapers followed. The *Financial Times* followed with 'Spotify offers a window into our souls – and wallets'. Critics were up in arms about the idea that a tech company was trading the private data of its customers with a central bank which could affect the cost of the nation's mortgages.

Wrong on all counts: Spotify wasn't trading data, nor was the bank expecting it to – but if there's one lesson I've learned about public relations, it's that bad news stories are akin to a turd that won't flush. Perhaps contrite for the firestorm he'd caused, Haldane himself offered to visit Spotify's offices in the heart of Soho (a distinctly different environment to Sir John Soane's famous Portland-stone-clad Bank of England) to explain himself. This was a first for Spotify; it regularly has bands like Coldplay perform but had never had a rock-star member of the Bank of England's Monetary Policy Committee.

After realising the PR shit-storm he had created, Haldane apologised profusely, and then proceeded to explain the logic of his argument.

> As it stands, we have to set interest rates later this week with a three-month-old manufacturing survey from Solihull to help inform us. My view is that there's only so much you can tell from an out-of-date survey of factory orders in Solihull. What's more, what it tells you isn't what you need to know – which is sentiment. How do people feel right now, not how many cars were produced last quarter?

On hearing this, all the Spotifyers in the room leaned in. He continued:

> If you think about the ongoing negotiations with Brexit, I believe people are very anxious and anxiety might have a far bigger role in their response to interest rates than last quarter's manufacturing orders in Solihull. I want to look everywhere and anywhere for real-time signals of sentiment to help set policy and that's why I referred to Spotify.

Anxiety! It felt clear to me that many people in Britain were anxious about the outcome of what was then a very uncertain Brexit process (not least the millions of Europeans living in Britain who didn't get to vote on it) but there is no economic statistic to capture anxiety. It may be that all the economic metrics are doing just fine but a slight move in interest rates could tip anxiety levels over the edge and cause a radical change in consumer behaviour.

Haldane's remarkable vision made me revisit my mental trade-off of timeliness versus granularity – you can use more granular data later or less granular data now. The most robust manufacturing surveys in the country could neither encourage us to ask, nor answer, what he really needed to know: how people are feeling now. His view was that Spotify captured real-time data and that might reveal real-time sentiments. Are the people living in Britain suffering from anxiety due to Brexit, and, if so, how would an increase in interest rates affect them? Emotions matter far more than manufacturing metrics. The GDP of the last quarter does not even attempt to answer this question but exploring the 'GDP-of-now' might.

Haldane's lesson in Tarzan Economics is that the fear of the unknown is self-made – as we haven't really tried to find out what's behind those fears: a real-time understanding of how we are feeling in the present, not a production-line measure of what we produced the past.

Saying we need to embrace a completely different way of judging the state we're in is one thing; doing it is another. The way the state calculates our economy in the past gave it a false sense of certainty and that has become ingrained to the point where it exaggerates the risks of an unknown alternative. We've been conditioned to accept a simple headline of GDP but none of us wants to know the 'black box' tricks involved in making sure the income, output and expenditure measures all add up. Next time an economic commentator is rolled out on the evening news to refer to small decimal-point movements in GDP with expressions like 'we should all feel a little better off', ask yourself if you should go to bed with an assurance that that's actually how we all feel.

Covid-19 made this even more apparent. To listen to apparent-experts-in-unprecedented-events discuss how the economy would recover after the lockdown was eased by dumbing it down to a discussion about letters of the alphabet – be it a V-shaped recovery (presumably a short and sharp recession) or a U-shaped recovery (perhaps a more u-bend shaped recession). It made me think about Chauncey Gardiner, the main character in Jerzy Kosinski's classic novel, *Being There*.

For those who are unfamiliar with either the book or the rib-hurtlingly hilarious 1979 movie starring Peter Sellers, *Being There* is an allegory about a simple-minded man – Chance, the gardener – whose world is defined by what he has seen in the garden and on TV. Through various twists of fate, Chance the gardener becomes Chauncey Gardiner, and is catapulted to the upper echelons of society, business and government. To the backdrop of Eumir Deodato's funk cover of 'Also Sprach Zarathustra' (*2001: A Space Odyssey*) Chauncey walks straight into the White House. His advice is sought by the president and his circle of economic advisers, who interpret Chauncey's simple statements about the garden as metaphors for macroeconomics. President 'Bobby', gullible and misguided as he is, is so taken by the gardener's approach to gardening that he announces to the nation that things may not be as bad as they seem:

> 'I found Mr Gardiner to have a feeling for this country that we need more of. To quote Mr Gardiner, a most intuitive man, "As long as the roots of industry remain firmly planted in the national soil, the economic prospects are undoubtedly sunny." [ . . . ] So I'm gonna rethink my position and find

> another solution. [ . . . ] For once, gentlemen, let us not fear the inevitable chill and storms of autumn and winter. Instead, let us anticipate the rapid growth of springtime. Let us await the rewards of summer. As in a garden of the earth, let us learn to accept and appreciate the times when the trees are bare as well as the times when we pick the fruit.'

It should be stressed that, while Chauncey was a satirical and fictious character, any resemblance to actual persons, living or dead, or actual events, is purely coincidental. Nevertheless, his horticultural references were there to mock the level of economic debate at the time, just as we need to have the confidence to ask if the current references to letters of the alphabet like 'V' and 'U' in 2021 really represent an improvement?

What is needed to let go of the old vine is an appreciation of what differentiates risk from uncertainty. In *Radical Uncertainty: Decision-making for an Unknowable Future*, the authors John Kay and Mervyn King (a former governor of the Bank of England) argue that economics used to be defined by trying to understand uncertainty and the mysteries it produces. But now economics is more concerned with probabilistic puzzles and the methods and techniques it uses to solve for a calculable risk. As a result, there is an addiction to precision – to the stationary, easily quantifiable puzzles – that often results in the government ignoring any data it can't easily measure.

Puzzles like the rise and fall of manufacturing numbers are clearly defined and will produce broad agreement when solved, whereas uncertainties like the level of public anxiety will often fail to produce a consensus. Policymakers may like a clearly defined problem that produces broad agreement in its solving – such as 'Yes we are in recession because two consecutive quarters of statistical data tell us so' – but that shouldn't negate the need to solve mysteries that may prove to be far less conclusive but far more relevant to help us move forward.

If we go back to our Haldane example from the spring of 2018, having lots of granular data about manufacturing from a few months back might provide a well-defined dataset, from which mathematicians can calculate risk for the central bank to set interest rates. But it won't actually give you a useful picture of life in anxiety-ridden Brexit-era Britain. For that, we need to evaluate more mysterious uncertainties of our time, elements of life that aren't easily reducible to numbers. Elements like anxiety. As we'll learn in the next chapter, we need more 'thick data', even if that data is less measurable.

We've learned that the new normal is a world where the ideas in our heads matter more than the roofs above them; we've learned that there is little chance of those ideas being captured in GDP. The economy continues to move into a borderless cloud despite national borders determining its domestic performance. GDP-B and the GDP-of-now offer two signposts to help us get back to dealing with the uncertainty of mysteries that are not easily quantifiable rather than obsessing about probabilistic puzzles. Recall our lesson from the earlier chapter on the need for pivotal thinking: if the challenges of measuring the state we're in could be solved with purely rational thinking – by finding the right data and plugging it into the right equation – we would have done it by now.

*

Becoming a better judge of the state we're in gives more confidence about our direction of travel and less fear about what we're leaving behind. Fears about what technology is doing to our lives are over-reported partly because the benefits that disruptive technology brings go under-reported. Imagine if Wikipedia's contribution to the economy was captured in the same way as the manufacturing of military weapons. Yardstick metrics like GDP were never built to answer questions we are currently asking; even the man who invented it said as much back before the war. Once we collectively know when it's time to let go of GDP, we really are in a brave new world – a blank sheet of paper to begin judging the state we're in.

Covid-19 eradicated any remaining excuses for holding on. When the economy went into a tailspin, any attempt to measure it became futile. The income measure of public education would have remained stable as no one got fired, but the output measure would have fallen off a cliff as few kids were in class – so try marrying up those disparate figures for the purpose of measuring GDP accurately! While the experts talked of (yet) another Great Depression, illustrating my pessimism paradox, the stock market rallied like it's never had it so good. The system is broke.

We're in a world where what matters most is often what is measured least, yet what matters least will be measured most. The contribution to the US economy from the creation of the smartphone is minimal, as the 'value added' part is allocated to its manufacturing base in Taiwan or South Korea despite it transforming the lives of quarter of a billion American citizens. At the other extreme, the contribution to the economy of having a car crash has a positive multiplier effect as you have used the measurable output of emergency services, insurance markets and (even) the production and consumption of a replacement car. Again, the system is broke.

In my favourite film of all time, *All the President's Men*, there is a memorable scene where the journalist Bob Woodward meets his secret source, 'Deep Throat', in a dark car park. His investigative journalism is taking him closer to the White House and fears he may be in too deep. Deep Throat calms his nerves by remarking: 'Forget the myths the media created about the White House. The truth is, these aren't very bright guys, and things got out of hand.' That's how I want you to feel when apparent experts talk about the economy using antiquated statistics – the truth is their claims are not very bright and the statistics got whacked out of shape.

To propel ourselves forward we need to know when we can smell a rat in the statistics we're presented with and perform the mental acrobatics to construct something more trustworthy to judge the state we're in. This is inevitably going to involve data, lots of big data, but we can never forget our second, and most famous, of Roryisms, which is to remind us of where all big data comes from in the first place – the past.

# 8

# BIG DATA, BIG MISTAKES

'The term "Big Data," which spans economics, statistics and computer science, probably originated in lunch-table conversations at Silicon Graphics Inc. (SGI) in the mid 1990s, in which John Mashey figured prominently', writes University of Pennsylvania economist Francis Diebold.* Amazon reveals over 9,000 book titles with the words 'big data' included. Some titles suggest big data exists on Excel; others argue that to qualify it should be too big to fit inside a spreadsheet. Some even conflate big data with 'big pharma', a reference not to the actual data being used but, rather, the size of the companies that are using it.

I take a different stance. For data to be considered big, it needs to be big enough to be capable of causing a big problem – quantification bias. This is a term popularised by Tricia Wang, who we'll be hearing from later. Quantification bias favours the measurable over the immeasurable, and disregards what can't be measured as unimportant (or, worse, non-existent). Quantification bias affects the way we work, what we are directed to work on and – more importantly – the way we

* Francis Diebold, 'On the Origin(s) and Development of "Big Data": The Phenomenon, the Term, and the Discipline', Working Paper, 2019.

are appraised for our work. Quantification bias can even affect whether we get a job in the first place – AI software is increasingly being used by HR departments in their hiring processes, despite evidence that it leads to worryingly biased decisions.

Quantification bias is a problem because it prioritises actions that generate data as these are considered more valuable than ones that do not. Consider two workers in an organisation, one whose job is to make something good happen, and one whose job is to stop something bad from happening. If your job is about achieving things, then your success will generate lots of positive data points – ones rather than zeroes. But if your job is about preventing things, then your work is generating no measurable data – zeroes rather than ones. Quantification bias puts the second worker at a disadvantage, as they might only get noticed when their work fails.

A perennial example of this disadvantage happens in firms' PR and communications departments. Within these teams, there are typically two core functions. Some workers are responsible for creating positive headlines that can be measured against sales or performance statistics. Big data is their friend – the more headlines they create, the more exposure for the company's brand and products or services, the more data there is to measure.

At the other extreme are workers dedicated to preventing bad headlines. They will spend much of their day glued to their phone preventing a potentially damaging story from being written. If they succeed, there will be no measurable results – just the absence of an undesirable outcome. They've turned a negative one into a safer zero – but those valuable zeros don't add up to much.

Quantification bias favours the measurable achievements over the immeasurable preventions. We measure performances based only on boxes we can tick, not counterfactuals we cannot. When going for promotion, you will be asked what you have achieved, and rarely will you be given time to explain what you prevented. These imbalances can affect not just employee morale, but organisational strategy.

We are in what feels like a golden age of big data: hiring more data scientists and using or developing tools to work with bigger and bigger data sets. That's generally a good thing, and countless books and blogs celebrate this progress. But to avoid big data causing big mistakes requires taking a step back and spotting the problems that this explosion of big data can bring. Nobody is questioning the big progress of big data, but we need to reduce the risk of ignoring the big mistakes that have been left behind.

The Discover Weekly playlist feature represented a paradigm shift for Spotify and media in general. For a long time, Spotify had boasted about its ability to curate music at scale, but hadn't done much to prove if and how that would work. In the early-summer of 2015, Spotify was closing in on 100 million monthly active users, each with their own unique taste – how do you curate playlists for each and every one of them? The 20th of July 2015 (the third Monday of that month) was the day that the world found out the answer to that question.

Discover Weekly didn't introduce me just to new music (though it did that), but to a much bigger development in how media is distributed – the shift from a 'one to many' model to 'many one-to-ones'. With the launch of Discover Weekly, every Spotify user began the week with a gift of thirty songs, curated just for them. No one else had the same playlist. No one else knew what you had received. Then, every Sunday night, those thirty songs would be removed and replenished with a new thirty-song playlist. Within its first year of launch, Spotify was reporting that Discover Weekly had reached 40 million users and had over 5 billion tracks streamed.*

The secret sauce behind Discover Weekly's success had two ingredients. First, Spotify built a model of all the music it had in its libraries, powered by data generated every time a user listened to a song or added one to a playlist. Second, Spotify developed technology to analyse that data to identify patterns in each user's music taste. Every Monday morning, Spotify performed some clever filtering and delivered music that other users had been playlisting but would be brand new to you – a unique playlist for the unique tastes of every user.

Personalised curation at scale had become a reality. Discover Weekly made an immediate impact on music demand, democratising access to content away from traditional record-label promotion. Record labels had two responses: 1) 'Discover Weekly is amazing!' and 2) 'How do we influence it?' But Discover Weekly was amazing because no record label or other external signals could influence it. And, if they could, it would stop being so amazing.

Discover Weekly was the brainchild of Matthew Ogle, who had previously worked with Hannah Donovan on a start-up music-scraping service called 'This Is My Jam'. This simple site allowed users to choose one song a week as their 'jam', share it on their social networks and listen to a playlist of all their friends' selections. Donovan coined the term 'notable data' rather than big data to explain the appeal of the site, as it focused on asking for one important bit of data – the song that you really wanted to share each day – rather than trying to subtly capture every piece of data it could.

* Ben Popper, 'Spotify's Discover Weekly reaches 40 million users and 5 billion tracks streamed: What started as an in-house hack has become one of the company's most successful products', *The Verge*, May 2016.

Ogle's first day at Spotify was 15 January 2015, and his squad was able to ship Discover Weekly to market on Monday 20 July 2015 – just half a year later. Forget the countless conferences and PowerPoints on what 'agile' means; my definition is simple: when an individual can ship a game-changing product that leads to the democratisation of music, for ever – all within six months of getting his feet under his desk at Spotify – that, for me, epitomises agility.

As it happens, Discover Weekly wasn't the only new feature that became available to music lovers in July 2015: Discover Weekly landed on users' smartphones less than a month after the launch of Apple Music. The financial press portrayed Spotify as David and Apple as Goliath – a fair comparison, as the Cupertino giant was well on its way to becoming the world's first trillion-dollar company.

In the summer of 2015, *Billboard* magazine's Glenn Peoples offered a helpful visualisation of just how big Apple had become, and how Apple Music, even if it were as big as Spotify, was still only a tiny part of its empire:

> 'Consider Apple's enormous size. Analysts predict Apple's revenue at $232 billion this fiscal year, according to the *Financial Times*. If Apple had Spotify's 20 million subscribers, revenue per 12 months would be just $1.92 billion, or 0.8 per cent of Apple's annual revenue. To put that in comparison, if Apple weighed 195 pounds – the average weight of an American male – Apple Music would weigh just 1.6 pounds, or about the same weight as the original iPad.'*

* Glenn Peoples, 'Apple Music's Goal: Some Subscribers Now, Lots of Hardware Sales Later', *Billboard Magazine,* June 2015.

The expectation was that Goliath's entrance into music streaming would crush the incumbent David, yet the launch of Discover Weekly – and its unexpected success – would create a moat to protect Spotify's castle. Big data was pouring out of Discover Weekly like never before. Spotify data scientists dived in, studying signals including dwell-time (duration spent continuously listening), skips (songs that failed to get played for 30 seconds, therefore not earning a royalty) and saves (songs users saved to their own personal playlist). As the avalanche of data grew, analysts grew more sensitive to data that had previously not seemed significant, such as time of day: the data told us that 4 p.m. on a Monday was the optimal time for users to listen to Discover Weekly, and that 8 p.m. on a Sunday was the time when they went back and saved tracks from the playlist before a new one was generated.

Despite the abundance of data (and data scientists examining it), we still couldn't answer the most important question: Why did Discover Weekly take off when so many other playlist initiatives had failed? The question was uncomfortable for many. Discover Weekly reached critical mass despite having no significant marketing support. There had previously been many big marketing initiatives from Spotify, but none that came close to this level of impact. And there was a still more confusing detail to this question – if word of mouth was driving its success, why were people recommending something to their social network that is so personalised to each user? Why was Discover Weekly such a viral success when there was nothing specific to share?

We had all the quantifiable metrics about Discover Weekly, and we needed to produce answers – and quick. The looming threat of Apple Music was creating fear, especially as it was now flexing its muscles with commercials during peak-time programming like live sports – something Spotify couldn't afford. Apple was also experimenting with exclusives, ponying up large cash advances to artists to release their new albums on their platform only – again, something that Spotify couldn't afford. Apple was also experimenting with hardware integration like Siri – hardware Spotify didn't have. Spotify may have an abundance of quantifiable metrics, but those metrics weren't answering the questions swirling around Discover Weekly. For that, we'd need to embrace the mystery and ask some qualitative questions about the world where Discover Weekly users actually lived.

As discussed in chapter 3, analysing hits that happened without specific intent can often teach us more than studying those that were intended – those which were heavily promoted and backed with a marketing budget.

**THE FOG OF DATA**

To further explore quantification bias, let's move from the music-streaming wars to actual wars. For full disclosure, I am a US political junkie, having read countless books and watched all available documentaries on US presidents. For me, the most impactful of this genre is *The Fog of War*, a masterful, haunting interview with Robert McNamara, the US secretary of defence from 1961 to 1968. McNamara pioneered the application of statistics in war but, as he reflected on Vietnam twenty-five years later, he noted how the availability of only a selection of statistics could distort one's ability to assess a situation. The film's title is a phrase McNamara references in the interview – 'fog' refers to the unavoidable fact that in the chaos of warfare, the intelligence gathered is always incomplete, thereby making any strategic decisions foggy. In the documentary, McNamara offers eleven lessons to help overcome the fog of war, the most important of which is to 'be prepared to re-examine your reasoning'.

It may have taken McNamara twenty-five years to re-examine his reasoning, but around the time that the United States was beginning to leave Vietnam, a little-known book was already doing just that. Daniel Yankelovich's 1972 *Corporate Priorities: A Continuing Study of the New Demands on Business* sets out four steps to committing what he termed the Quantification Fallacy:

> The first step is to measure whatever can be easily measured. This is okay as far as it goes. The second step is to disregard that which can't be easily measured, or to give it an arbitrary quantitative value. This is artificial and misleading. The third step is to presume that what can't be measured easily really isn't important. This is blindness. The fourth step is to say that what can't be easily measured really doesn't exist. This is suicide.*

* Daniel Yankelovich, 'Corporate Priorities: A Continuing Study of the New Demands on Business', Stanford, CT: Yankelovich Inc., 1972.

McNamara's fog of war descended upon our experience at Spotify as we struggled to explain the success of Discover Weekly despite an abundance of data. Were we committing the same mistake as McNamara, seeing what we wanted to believe, and failing to examine our reasoning? Had we fallen foul of the quantification fallacy and disregarded anything we couldn't measure?

My search to explain the success of Discover Weekly in light of so many other marketing initiatives that had failed took me to the University of Chicago in a freezing-cold winter. This university has an economics division that is literally divided. On one side of the street is the famous economics department committed to the belief that economic agents have perfect information that allows them to make rational decisions. On the other side of the street was the office of Nobel Prize-winner Richard Thaler, who had built up an army of behavioural economists who took a different stance – namely, that people didn't have perfect information, nor were they predisposed to making rational choices. The division between the two reminded me of that famous Steve McQueen line in the film *Bullit*: 'You believe what you want. You work your side of the street, and I'll work mine.' Thaler had combined microeconomics with psychology to look for new ideas, and I had an inkling that he might lead me to some answers for why Spotify users were recommending a uniquely personal experience to their networks. Had the brand (Discover Weekly) become bigger than the band(s)?

At my first meeting with Thaler he prompted me to ask if consumers even understood that the playlist was unique to them. Perhaps they were still wedded to the idea of a one-to-many broadcast like radio, which had produced decades of water-cooler moments for listeners to share their experiences. Because all of us at Spotify were immersed in the data generated by the platform, we assumed that users understood how unique and personalised their experience was. The 'curse of knowledge', as he put it, had made us see what we wanted to believe – that users were recommending Discover Weekly because they appreciated the cleverness of the personalisation algorithm. They didn't. Consumers had no interest in the intricacies of the algorithm; they simply pressed a piece of glass, put it in their pocket and discovered new music.

The 'curse of knowledge', as he persistently reminded me, is the misplaced assumption that the people around us share the same knowledge in an area where we have developed our expertise. Spotify didn't need to look far to see an example of this 'curse', as Thaler would hold up his smartphone to show this was glaringly obvious to everyone when they opened the app. The oversized shuffle-play button took up the lion's share of the screen, with the actual play button found being tucked away in the bottom corner. The misplaced assumption being that consumers would always want to randomize their musical experience, even when listening to an album or playlist that had been designed to be played in a particular order. Coders mistakenly thought that anyone who wanted to do that would easily figure out how to do so, because it was obvious to them. As Thaler repeatedly pointed out: 'After all, they had written the code!' This curse of knowledge was not something that would easily appear in Big Data.

Skips were another bit of data that we were misinterpreting. If a consumer skipped a song from their Discover Weekly playlist, that skip would produce a quantifiable metric, which we interpreted as a negative signal – the song that was skipped must be a bad match for that individual's unique taste. But what if they already knew and loved that song and they skipped it because they went to Discover Weekly to find new songs – in other words, what if the song had been skipped because it was *too good* a match? That would mean the skip wasn't a negative signal, but rather that the right song was in the wrong setting – they liked the song but didn't want to hear it on Discover Weekly. The data told us a lot about what users were listening to in the present, but they couldn't tell us about music they liked before they started using Spotify – and every one of Spotify's (then) 100 million users had fallen in love with music long before Spotify existed. (This is why Facebook's timeline is such a valuable feature, populating your life before the platform existed.)

Thaler made me realise that the further I stepped back from what was being easily measured, the more I could see that what wasn't being measured mattered more. Thaler and I embarked on a project with six of his students to learn more about the behavioural economics of Discover Weekly. After six months of testing consumers' understanding and experience of the service, it was time to sit down with the prof and analyse the results. They were, unfortunately, murky. We stumbled on some evidence suggesting that consumers were unaware that their playlist lasted only for seven days and that their music had effectively become 'perishable' – a digital game-changer if true – but not enough to substantiate any serious claim. Similarly, there were tentative signals that consumers were unaware that the playlist was unique to them, but nothing conclusive given streaming's fledgling state. I was gutted. I told the professor I was stuck, and the investigation had run dry. I had literally nothing to show for my work. We had scraped and scrutinised all the data and tested the consumer yet still come up blank.

Thaler told me to stop looking at data and start looking at counterfactuals. Discover Weekly was a surprising success, but was there anything we could learn by looking at the products that failed? He encouraged me to learn by counting the zeroes, given that we weren't getting anywhere by counting the ones.

Sitting in his office on a cold Chicago afternoon, surrounded by his books and many more from his mentors Daniel Kahneman and Amos Tversky, Thaler placed his hands on the armrest of his chair and leaned back. 'So, you're telling me you tried 'Throwback Thursday' playlists and that failed?'

I replied defensively: 'Well, failure is harsh on our curation team, but it certainly didn't take off.'

He seemed to sense that there might be a pattern: 'Okay, then you told me about some sort of 'Feel-Good Fridays' playlist which also bombed and never went anywhere?'

'Yes,' I replied, 'that one simply didn't get traction.'

Now Thaler leant in: 'But you are telling me you launched Discover Weekly on a Monday and you've had this unprecedented success with 40 million people listening to 40 million uniquely curated playlists?'

I nodded.

'And you still don't know why?' he asked.

Frustrated, I replied, 'No. We've monitored, measured and tested every quantifiable metric that the playlist has produced, and I still can't see the source of the success. We're at a dead end.'

He smiled the sort of smile that reminds you who is the professor and who is the student. He reached for a handful of academic papers from his shelf. 'It's because,' he said, 'you launched it on Monday! There's ample research from Katherine Milkman and her colleagues at Wharton on the Fresh Start effect, to show that mental accounting periods like the start of the week, month or semester make it easier to engage in aspirational behaviour.'*

My mind jolted back several time zones to my home in North London and that start-of-the-week journey on the London Underground. Approaching the Underground stations, it's always on a Monday when volunteers in bright jackets are handing out flyers for gym memberships or yoga classes. Thaler had reminded me that these bright jackets and these flyers don't emerge on any other day of the week.

The answer had been staring me in the face all along. Monday is the day when people are receptive to new things, whether a gym membership, free newspapers – or new Discover Weekly playlists. Thaler cleared the fog of data that was keeping me from seeing the solution. I had committed the quantification fallacy and disregarded what couldn't be measured, such as the importance of the day of the week, as irrelevant. That was my big mistake. The answer I'd been looking for was something as simple as the first day of the working week – and not the deluge of big data that was pouring out of this weekly randomised trial with millions of participants. I reflected on a different 'big decision' that the global recorded-music industry had made around the same time – to move the global release date for new songs from Tuesday to Friday – and wondered if that, too, had been a big mistake.

Like the red herrings in a good crime story, data can send us in one direction, while the real clues slip past unnoticed. While

* Hengchen Dai, Katherine L. Milkman, Jason Riis, 'The Fresh Start Effect: Temporal Landmarks Motivate Aspirational Behavior', *Management Science*, 2014.

many of my economist peers were evangelising the potential of big data, I was starting to become an outsider, looking for other clues and evidence that they had missed. I had embraced a healthy scepticism of the value of big data.

To avoid succumbing to the temptation of quantification bias, we need to employ a kind of thinking that is often missing in economics – common sense. Take the perennial challenge of correlation and causation, a fundamental part of data science. It's very easy to use big data to capture correlation when the data appears to show a relationship between two variables. Causation (what actually caused a connection between two variables) is a lot more difficult to determine. Just because you can spot a correlation between two variables doesn't mean that they actually influence each other.

Tyler Vigen's Spurious Correlations site (and now a 'ridiculous' book) is a hilarious illustration of this fallacy, using charts to show a correlation between US statistics that common sense tells us obviously have no relationship at all.* Two of my favourite graphs show a strong correlation between the number of people who drowned by falling into a pool and the number of Nicholas Cage films per year. There is also apparently a strong correlation between the number of divorces in the state of Maine and per capita consumption of margarine.

Preston McAfee was one of the first chief economists in technology, becoming the chief economist of Yahoo! in 2007, before going on to lead economic teams at Microsoft and Google. A mentor to me, his career path as one of the very first economists to apply the discipline to the technology giants gave me the confidence to pursue mine as the first economist in music.

* Tyler Vigen, *Spurious Correlations,* Hachette Books, 2015.

One of the reasons he's succeeded is that he has the right balance of technical skills and common sense to avoid making big mistakes with big data.

In an interview with the Federal Reserve Bank of Richmond, McAfee recalls wrestling with correlation and causation during his time at Microsoft: 'Like most computer firms,' he said,

> Microsoft runs sales on its Surface computers during back-to-school and the December holidays, which are also the periods when demand is highest. As a result, it is challenging to disentangle the effects of any price changes from the seasonal effects, since the two are so closely correlated.*

McAfee's observation illustrates the danger of assuming that correlation implies causation when dealing with a simple spike in sales – was it the discounted price that drove an increase in demand, or was it just seasonal buying patterns? And why is Microsoft slashing prices when demand is at its highest?

McAfee's team at Microsoft went on to develop machine-learning technology to help explore causality, and he points to the microeconomics teams at companies like Amazon who are also answering questions that the companies were previously unable to understand. Demand for big data within the tech giants, in other words, is now on the rise. The challenge is that, for every economist within a firm, there will typically be hundreds of people in the marketing department – and these people will be paid (and get bonuses) if they can show that their marketing spend is not only correlated with increased sales, but that it was the marketing campaign that actually caused them.

If you've worked either in or alongside an advertising or

* https://www.richmondfed.org/publications/research/econ_focus/2018/q4/interview

marketing department for any amount of time, you've probably heard, 'Half the money I spend on advertising is wasted. The trouble is I just don't know which half.' The quote belongs to John Wanamaker (1838–1922), who founded one of the first department stores in the US and championed marketing. Advocates of big data have long argued that it can answer Wanamaker's question by tracking the advertising that works and eradicating the ads that don't. But a hundred years after his passing, it's evident that the rise of big data has the potential to make Wanamaker's confusion worse, not better.

Traditional broadcast advertising had a causation problem: you could get close to knowing how many viewers had seen a particular ad, but it was impossible to know what ad actually caused the viewer to go out and buy a product. Big data was supposed to solve that problem by directly measuring click-throughs – it could count how many people saw an ad, clicked on it, and made a purchase. Yet over the past several decades, while digital advertising may have taken huge chunks out of the budget for print advertising, it has failed to land a meaningful blow on television and radio.

According to Statista, TV advertising revenue in the United States will grow from $71 billion in 2018 to $72 billion in 2023. Likewise, global TV ad revenue is projected to increase from $173 billion to $192 billion between 2018 and 2022.* A similar story is reported for radio, with ad spending in the United States predicted to grow from $17.9 billion in 2019 to $18.4 billion in 2023. (Note: All these predictions will require revisiting as a result of the Covid-19 crisis.)† If 'linear broadcast media is dead', as many non-linear tech companies have

* TV advertising revenue in the United States in 2018, 2019 and 2023, *Statista*, 2020.

† Radio advertising spending in the United States in 2019 and 2023, *Statistsa*, 2020.

proclaimed over the past two decades, then these modest north-easterly forecasts of ad revenue suggest there is a lot more life after death.

Author and entrepreneur Rick Webb, whose essay on the website Medium is suitably titled 'Which Half is Wasted?', makes an insightful observation about why the advocates of big data in advertising have made a big mistake. Citing both the English economist Joan Robinson and Harvard economist Edward Hastings Chamberlin, who studied this almost a century ago, Webb points out that companies advertise in two ways: through direct advertising, and through brand advertising. Direct advertising is aimed at the point just before you decide to buy something, perhaps by offering a direct discount. Brand-building adverts try to create positive associations in the audience's mind with a specific type of product – e.g. Nike's 'Just Do It' campaign, or L'Oréal's 'Because You're Worth It' – so that when you later have to make a purchase choice, you might gravitate towards a particular brand.

Webb argues that the internet has won the battle for direct marketing but failed to make a dent in brand-building. The incredibly sophisticated, large-scale data-driven targeting platforms that Facebook and Google have built are perfect for delivering an incentive to purchase at a given moment. When we like something on Facebook, or search for it on Google, we are showing intent to buy, and an ad with a direct offer may convert us. Brand marketing has slower and more complex goals than a single purchase. Brand marketing tries to change attitudes or behaviours – to make you feel like you can be an athlete if you wear Nike shoes, or that you will be more attractive if you use a particular cosmetics product. It's in this area of hopes and dreams, rather than direct sales, where traditional formats like television and radio still reign supreme. They can reach many people at once, compounding its subtle message, as opposed to a lot of people individually, where that overarching message gets lost. There is also a level of legacy prestige offered by seeing a product advertised on TV and then seeing an ad in the context of a show that you like that is intended to create a link between the product and your positive feelings about the show.

Finally, in a 'winner takes all' media market, where consumers might go to see just one blockbuster movie during the summer season, owning the billboard presence up and down the country can ensure that one blockbuster is your own. A Hollywood executive once told me that the marketing budget for a Will Smith movie was set to ensure one in three Americans knew it existed: 'Spend whatever it takes to get to that one-in-three level of saturation and you'll have a blockbuster on your hands, fail to hit the tipping point and the movie will flop.'

One economist who used badly needed common sense to examine the impact of advertising was Steve Tadelis, a University of California, Berkeley professor who – like Preston McAfee – pivoted from academia to tech and led a team of economists at eBay between 2011 and 2013. Back then, Tadelis questioned whether buying ads on Google for eBay's own brand was effective.* So, his team stopped purchasing ads on Google in some markets and took a look at the effect on their sales. They found that for the most part, paid advertisements didn't yield a significant increase (or any effect at all) in sales. Even in the case of a related increase, the ad spend exceeded whatever increased sales were brought in. People were finding their way

* Steve Tadelis, Tom Blake and Chris Nosko, 'Returns to Consumer Search: Evidence from eBay', 17th ACM Conference on Electronic Commerce (EC 2016), 2016, pp. 531–45.

to the site anyway, either by clicking on 'natural listings' that were prioritised by the search query (Googling 'vintage clothing on eBay' is going to take you to eBay regardless), or by going directly to eBay's site (or, increasingly, using the eBay app) and circumventing search engines entirely.

Advertising eBay to their own established customer base (or preaching to the converted) was having little net effect. Tadelis's work at eBay suggests that all companies should look carefully at the return on investment of their search-marketing spend. It also underlines the importance of common sense in questioning conventional wisdom when claiming both correlation and causation based solely on those isolated and measurable clicks.

Common sense is particularly important when we look at metrics for the number of clicks, sales and downloads that ads generate. In their article 'The new dot com bubble is here: it's called online advertising', Jesse Frederik and Maurits Martijn argue that, more often than not, these quantifiable metrics fail to distinguish between two distinct effects. First, there is the 'selection effect' (clicks, purchases and downloads that are happening anyway); and then the advertising effect (clicks, purchases and downloads that would not have happened without ads).*

The risk of conflating selection and advertising effects is magnified by the advertisers' algorithms' tendency to increase selection effects. Consider the following: if Nike buys ads from Facebook and Google, the advertising platforms' algorithms will target users who have shown an interest in Nike's products. And who is most likely to click on Nike ads? Nike's existing

* Jesse Frederik and Maurits Martijn, 'The new dot com bubble is here: it's called online advertising' *The Correspondent*, November 2019.

customers. Thus, the algorithms are generating attention, but not necessarily the kind of attention Nike wants to attract with its advertising. Big data was effective at driving existing customers back to the brands, but it was a big mistake to think it was just as effective at acquiring new customers.

In the nineteenth century, American entrepreneur Clark Stanley promoted his proprietary brand of snake oil. Claiming it was produced by collecting the fat from a boiled pot of rattlesnakes, Stanley peddled his product as a cure-all for a wide variety of ailments. Stanley's 'invention' went viral at the 1893 World's Exposition in Chicago, during which he sliced open a live rattlesnake to make his snake oil on the spot (one can only wonder how that would travel on Instagram today).

Stanley's sales pitch came undone in dramatic fashion, however, when researchers questioned not only his claims, but also the contents of the product. Not only was Stanley's rattlesnake oil not very effective, it didn't actually contain any snake oil. Clark Stanley was fined just $20 (about $429 in today's dollars) for violating the food and drug act and for fraudulently misrepresenting his product.

Big data and artificial intelligence have a snake oil problem too, according to Arvind Narayanan, an associate professor of Computer Science at Princeton University. In his presentation titled 'How to recognize AI snake oil', he explains that AI has become an umbrella term for a range of related technologies. Some of these have made remarkable progress, which has given the term 'AI' a marketing value that other, less innovative companies can use to sell inferior products. Hundreds of millions of dollars have been invested, for example, in companies that claim their AI can screen new-employee applicants better than human HR departments, but there is little evidence that those technologies work; in fact, they can perpetuate biases and prejudice.

Narayanan draws an important distinction between these 'general' AI systems and a 'narrow' application like AlphaGo, the computer program developed by DeepMind Technologies that dominates the board game Go.* Narayanan says that 'AlphaGo is a remarkable intellectual accomplishment that deserves to be celebrated. Ten years ago, most experts would not have thought it possible. But it has nothing in common with a tool that claims to predict job performance.' He concludes that when an AI label is 'slapped' onto software predicting job performance, it is nothing more than an elaborate random-number generator.

'AI Bias' is essentially the niece (or nephew) of quantification bias. What we tend to call 'AI' is generally more accurately described as 'machine learning', in which a computer analyses a huge amount of data in order to be able to make decisions or predictions about other data. So, the theory goes: you feed a machine-learning algorithm a massive amount of hiring data, and the machine can 'learn' how to make good hiring decisions. Benedict Evans argues the key issue is that any decision a machine makes is based on the data you feed it. If you feed the machine incomplete, insufficient or biased data, the machine makes faulty decisions. He points to a company that claimed to recognise shoplifting from security videos, but whose data set was created by paying a dozen actors to spend a day pretending to be shoplifters on CCTV. That's nowhere near enough data, and even if it was, it would only recognise bad actors, not actual shoplifters.

Gary Marcus, co-author of *Rebooting AI* with Ernest Davis,

* Arvind Narayanan, 'How to recognize AI snake oil', *Arthur Miller lecture on science and ethics, Massachusetts Institute of Technology*, November 2019.

astutely raises an even bigger risk in big data, and AI especially, in his 2019 article 'An Epidemic of AI Misinformation'. That risk is overpromising. Marcus frames this risk as a version of our tragedy of the commons, in which all the fishermen overfish a particular set of waters in self-interest until the entire population of fish crashes, and everybody suffers. So many companies, he argues, have exploited the marketing potential of the AI label that an unrealistic expectation of the abilities of artificial intelligence has begun to take hold. When a certain number of those companies fail to deliver on the AI miracles they're offering, public sentiment about AI could shift, which could risk slowing development of AI programs that do work, that could change the world. 'If and when the public, governments, and investment community recognize that they have been sold an unrealistic picture of AI's strengths and weaknesses that doesn't match the reality,' the author wrote, 'a new AI winter may commence.' The disappointment in AI's under-delivering thus threatens to throw the proverbial baby out with the bathwater.

Marcus cites *The Economist* 'World in 2020' magazine, which ran a story titled 'An artificial intelligence predicts the future: What would an artificial intelligence think about the year ahead?'* In the article, *The Economist* claimed that they trained an AI system on a database of *Economist* articles, and it then generated a series of uncannily human-sounding predictions. Marcus pointed out that *The Economist* was guilty of peddling snake oil in the article, as it misleadingly said that the AI's predictions were 'unedited', when in reality each prediction they published was selected from among five options, filtered for coherence and humour. On Twitter, an

* Gary Marcus, 'An Epidemic of AI Misinformation', *The Gradient*, November 2019.

expert in this subject field tweeted he was impressed with big data's achievement and that 'the answers are more coherent than those of many humans'. The big mistake stemmed from swathes of human writing that the system was able to draw from and the intervention of human journalists who filtered for coherence. Marcus noticed that retweets of the original hyperbolic headline outnumbered tweets of his correction by about 75:1 – a metric that shows another kind of bias – news about big data travels faster than news about it making big mistakes.

From dealing with big numbers associated with machine learning to interpreting just one number in survey responses, the risk of big mistakes is pervasive. In December 2003, a *Harvard Business Review* article by Frederick F. Reichheld proposed a new metric by which to measure performance.* The Net Promoter Score (NPS) latched on to business leaders' minds thanks to its simplicity, as Reichheld proclaimed: 'This number is the one number you need to grow. It's that simple and that profound.' Big data was being bolstered by a blunt number that could allegedly be scaled across entire organisations.

The timing is intriguing: less than ten months later, *Wired* magazine published Chris Anderson's famous 'Long Tail' blog, which claimed the future of business was selling less of more. It remains a coincidence that two influential articles came out so close to each other and a decade-and-a-half later continue to influence how we perform and measure our performance. We've already learned how the long tail theory got turned on its head as some choice is better than none (but more is not

* Frederick F. Reichheld, 'The One Number You Need to Grow', *Harvard Business Review*, December 2003.

necessarily better than some); now let's address Reichheld's 'One Number' – as it, too, can lead to big mistakes.

As a frustrated economist, I've been chewing people's ears off about the flaws that are inherent in the dreaded NPS survey every time I'm asked to fill one out. And as the survey is so ubiquitous, so frequent, so repetitive, that's a lot of ear-chewing – a real problem for those who wear glasses!

So, imagine my reaction when I realised there was someone else out there who felt exactly the same, and could articulate it better too. Jared M. Spool, a design and user-experience expert, 'hit a bingo' with his seminal 2017 article 'Net Promoter Score Considered Harmful (and What UX Professionals Can Do About It)'. Spool, like myself, calls time on this one number – apparently the only number – we need to know.

The NPS score ticks all the boxes of a 'grab and go' business metric, as it's easy to measure and even easier to grasp at a glance, which makes it very useful when you're looking to bolster egos and play that other three-letter acronym game (CYA, cover your ass) that's common in hierarchal organisational turf wars. By this point, though, you shouldn't be surprised to learn that a single number that claims to accurately represent the health of an organisation is going to cause more problems than it solves. Yet NPS fosters the same quantification fallacy of encouraging leaders to ask no further questions, which risks casualties.

To measure NPS, survey respondents were asked one question: 'How likely are you to recommend a company to a friend or colleague?' – and offered an eleven-point scale to form their answer, from 'Not at all likely' to 'Extremely likely'. The NPS's 'scale', however, has a twist – not all numbers are treated the same. You might assume that NPS was just an average of respondent scores, a portrait of how likely, on average, a customer was to recommend a company. But that would be wrong. Instead, the NPS segments the scores into three components:

9s or 10s are considered Promoters.
7s or 8s are considered Passive respondents.
any score below 6 is considered a Detractor.

To derive the NPS score, you take the percentage of Promoter respondents (those who rated a 9 or above) and subtract the percentage of Detractors (who rated a 6 or below). In Spool's simple example, let's assume we have 10 respondents' scores: 0, 0, 1, 4, 5, 6, 7, 8, 9 and 10. A simple average of these 10 numbers is 5. But the NPS is –40: 20 per cent (the two people who scored 9 and 10) minus 60 per cent (those six people between 0 and 6). The logic of the NPS is to outweigh the extremes. If a consumer is very enthusiastic about your company, they will recommend it, and so they should be counted in the NPS. If they are very unenthusiastic about your company, they'll tell other people not to use it, so their effect should also be captured in the NPS. But if they're lukewarm – unlikely to either promote or detract from your company's brand – they don't really matter and are left out of the NPS equation.

Respondents aren't aware of any of this weird scoring, or at least they are not supposed to be. But as NPS is now so widespread (as it is apparently the only number we all need to know), any prior knowledge of the methodology by the respondent would lead to strategically selective scoring – such as scoring a 9 or 10 when a 7 was merited – and undermine the results. The Keynesian Beauty Contest raises its head again as we won't score on what we believe but how we think the judges will interpret.

It's a simple idea that produces a simple number, and it's not hard to see why it caught on. But with the NPS, you see evidence of a lot of the fallacies previously discussed. It depends on survey data, which is never particularly strong. Surveys require that users identify their own behaviour with no outside check that their self-evaluation lines up with reality. Plus, survey sample sizes are always abysmally small, making them less useful in extrapolating trends out to the wider world. Think of Abraham Wald observing the aeroplane mechanics fixing the bullet holes in the wings of Second World War fighter planes: they knew where the last bullets hit, but that didn't tell them where the next ones would hit. In the same way, you can only know what the people who responded to the survey said, but that doesn't give you a full picture of how the rest of the world feels.

Further, NPS evaluates customers narrowly: whether they think they would recommend your company. It attempts to capture a huge range of human psychology and behaviour in one number.

And a new problem: the NPS is a perpetrator of what UX expert Kate Rutter refers to as 'analytics theatre' – part of the allure of the NPS is that it creates dramatic swings in numbers. It exaggerates volatility but hides magnitude, which can be good for headlines (or for ass-covering) but bad for making products or services better. Macroeconomics has similar theatrics with its addiction to PMI surveys, which ignores the respondents who see no change in the outlook and reports only the net difference between those who are up and down, making it possible to have a headline that 97 per cent of survey respondents (3 up, 2 down and 95 no-changers) disagree with.

We can return to Spool's article to see how this 'one number' can adversely affect our performance and, more importantly, our morale. Spool asks us to imagine we've been tasked with turning around a failing department and our baseline NPS is –100: everyone scored the service a zero. One year into the role, you've successfully increased all ten of those scores from zero to six, an incredible turnaround that surely merits bonuses, additional resources and any other wind that can be put in your department's sails. But the NPS wouldn't budge as those sixes are still a detractor. Imagine the damage to morale when you've achieved so much but scored so little.

Next, assume that you quit the department (that you've successfully turned around) owing to the lack of due recognition, and a new executive joins the company to pick up the great work you've left behind. If she raises the average respondent's score by just 3 measly points to a 9, she'll hit the NPS jackpot. In 'analytical theatre' terms, the performer who moved NPS from 0 to 6 got booed off the stage whereas the performer who raised it just three notches further to a 9 received a standing ovation and was called back for an encore.

Brushed under the carpet of this one number we're all supposed to use are the many caveats that affect how you're supposed to use it – especially the response rates. These are typically horrific, making it hard to extrapolate that non-responders (who probably quitted due to a negative experience) would respond similarly to those who did. That makes any NPS data highly suspicious. From experience, my own mobile-operator network relies on this one number and doesn't have any other method to learn what's actually happening with my experience. As my experiences are usually bad, I resent being surveyed at the end – meaning they probably are drawing incorrect inferences. What's more, as they've drunk the Kool-Aid by trusting this one number, they haven't bothered to ask any more questions.

For example, they've never asked me if I've ever recommended WhatsApp to a friend. Have they ever asked you?

The sheer size of the datasets we now have to evaluate can give a sense of completeness; the temptation is to present a model as a contained environment, taking into account every variable. But in real life no system is so neatly contained. In response, we have a tendency to add more and more data, to try to reach a comprehensive dataset. But we need to keep that impulse in check – the quantification bias favours measurable activity over the immeasurable absence of activity.

The pendulum needs to swing back a bit from big data and towards something more human, and we'll call this 'thick data', a term coined by tech-ethnographer Tricia Wang of Sudden Compass, a consultancy that puts customer obsession into practice, who argues that people are the data and not the metrics they produce. 'Thick data' is at the opposite end of the spectrum and aims to capture the most direct, unmediated data from humans and the full context of their emotions and stories by – wait for it – meeting them. This is such a wonderful phrase to counter the hype around 'big data'. On one side, we've got snake oil merchants selling promises based on millions of points of data; on the other side we've got deep, patient observations of real humans, listening and talking to each other. Wang openly acknowledges how it sits on the shoulders of other terminology that came before it, like ethnography, qualitative data or just sensible thinking. In a recent interview, she explained:

> I've heard it called so many things. Being open to the unknown means you will embrace data that is thick. Ostensibly it is data that has yet to be quantified, it's data

> that you may not even know that you need to collect and you don't know it until you're in the moment being open to it, and open to the invitation of the unknown in receiving it.*

This means rescuing precious data like human emotions, personal circumstances and cultural traits that cannot be quantified; rescuing the human context that big data can't collect. Wang argues that big data will often result in dashboards that create an abstracted picture of events, but it is thick data that helps us look out of the windscreen to see what is actually happening, what's coming towards us, and, crucially, what might happen next.

When I witnessed Tricia Wang onstage at the Nudgestock 2019 festival, the premier gathering of behavioural geeks at the cliff edge of Folkestone's UKIP Riviera, the gusto with which she delivered her argument grabbed me by the lapels and shook seven shades of brown stuff out. It reminded me of many instances at Spotify where we trusted what we could measure (the metrics people produced) and ignored what we couldn't (the people themselves).

Let's go back to our success story of Discover Weekly, which launched in the summer of 2015. Less than a year afterwards, Spotify shipped another popular product, 'Family Plan', which matched Apple Music's generous offering of six sub-account holders' access to Spotify Premium for the cost of £14.99. I recall going to the customer support offices, which were located in Cambridge, around the same time, as that's where you get the feedback that matters most. That's where you get the edge.

Discover Weekly was producing one column of data, Family

* Carrie Neill, 'People Are Your Data', Dscout, May 2018.

Plan was producing another column of data, but the concept of speaking to the families to read across those columns hadn't been explored, up until then. One of the most frequent queries from those families I was overhearing went something like this: 'Why's the song "Let It Go" from the film *Frozen* in my Discover Weekly?' Spotify customer support would ask if they had children? 'Yes, two daughters.' Clearly their children were interfering with their algorithm and they wanted it to stop – making the offer of Family Plan ever more appealing. By listening to people, not plotting the data they produce, it was clear that customisation was driving commerce, and commerce was driving customisation.

I realised that big data was missing the big picture. Take the data-led decision to stop building Spotify for the earliest models of the iPhone. At some point someone will need to wield the axe based on usage data and operating-system upgrade cycles and say that Spotify is no longer available on an out-of-date smartphone. Yet when I spoke to families, I learned that parents will typically hand down their old iPhones to their children. And as the proposition of subscribing to Family Plan becomes more attractive if more of your family can use it, the act of handing down an old iPhone is a catalyst to subscribing. Spotify was shooting itself in the foot, selling Family Plan on the one hand yet removing the ability of (members of) the family to use it on the other.

There are countless more examples I could draw upon where only through human engagement can one spot what big data cannot. It's not difficult to achieve, either – rather than sit within your own commercial teams where 'group think' can foster, sit within the customer support teams and listen in on the issues they're dealing with. And if you find yourselves wondering where the customer support teams within your organisation are located, then that should tell you a lot about what you don't already know.

*

It does no harm to inject a healthy dose of scepticism into the state of economics, be it the robustness of government data or the reliability of big data. Both chapters have instilled you with the confidence to know when to raise your hand and ask the 'dumb kid in the classroom' question that everyone else was too nervous to ask. To challenge the authoritative view of the macroeconomist or the persuasive predictions of the data scientist and point out what doesn't make sense. To spot snake oil when it's being sold. To seek out a more meaningful understanding of the people who produced the data points and not just the data points themselves.

The call to action is to rebalance the scales – for every data scientist being deployed to make sense of what they can (only) measure, ask how much resource is being deployed to ethnography, cultural awareness or simply engaging the consumer. If the inequality feels explicit, do something about it. Pull the pendulum back from the measurable to making sense of the immeasurable and insert some common sense into the correlation–causation debate. Sit within your customer service teams; better still, talk to the actual customers and stop reducing them to data points.

Where we risk going with this matters. If we don't curb our enthusiasm for big data, then artificial intelligence risks becoming more artificial than intelligent. If machine learning observes that both car prices have gone up and the volume of cars has also gone up, it will conclude that price elasticity is positive – you need to raise your hand and point out that both the quality of the cars and the wealth of the customers will have had a role to play. Worse still, if machine learning observes that people display a tendency to gather around a tragic car accident in a city centre observing those who are injured, it will simply assume that people like standing around in a semicircle looking at injured people in a car accident. You need to raise your hand and point out that this is patently not the case.

In advertising, there's an expression which goes, 'If you can't sell yourself, what can you sell?', and those who can smell the persuasiveness of big data know how to oversell it. This was best explained to me by a colleague who worked in finance for a tech start-up; she'd spent a long day trying (and failing) to close a quarter's accounts due to the claims of her advertising department failing to be found in her columns of P&L data, and planned to spend a longer night drinking Argentinian Malbec wine to put it behind her. In between sips, I asked her what it's like trying to separate the 'wheat from the chaff' when it comes to the 'big data' claims of advertising and marketing people. Her response was the sort of advice that can only be hard-earned over years of on-the-job training: 'The people who work in advertising aren't all that bad, because at least when they talk to you, you know they're lying. It's the folks in marketing you have to be wary of – they're near-scientific about lying.'

Don't be caught up in herd-like mentality when it comes to data, as you should never forget that most famous of Roryisms – it all comes from the same place: the past. You can't put a price on what's priceless, and common sense may well be falling into that category. Ironically, we are being urged to reach for the new vine of big data, but, sometimes, the old vine – common sense, talking to people who created that data and listening to what they say – is what works best. Tarzan, in this instance, doesn't always swing to the next tree as we've learned that the danger with big data is that people assume it to be always true, when, in fact, unless it's understood properly, data proves to be a more compelling liar than even the most gifted of thieves.

# CONCLUSION

## Builders and Farmers

For someone who has never smoked cigarettes, nor developed a taste for coffee, I owe these two addictive substances a lot. The copious amounts of time I've spent with smokers and coffee-drinkers inspired much of this book. This is, of course, good economics – I get the hit without the expensive addiction or side effects.

It was thanks to coffee and cigarettes that I came up with an expression that takes the ideas in this book and makes them practical for you, the reader. I'd go further and say that this expression will prove more addictive than the substances being consumed across the table when I first coined it.

Back in 2017, Spotify was preparing for an Initial Public Offering (IPO) on the New York Stock Exchange. Stakes were high, as Spotify was no normal start-up, and this was no normal IPO. Traditional IPOs involve a lot of fanfare and complicated financial skulduggery, but Spotify took a different route, opting for a direct listing, simply rolling onto the stock market overnight. This was just as the competitive landscape was heating up: Apple was beginning to give Spotify its first true taste of competition in the streaming arena. Things were getting spicy.

I was fortunate enough to be on good personal terms with one of Spotify's early investors. We met semi-regularly, but not in Spotify's posh Soho offices. He preferred to meet in the street *in front* of the offices, so that he could more easily indulge both of his two vices: coffee and cigarettes. These were not languid, sprawling meetings. Between sips and drags, I would be pressed for a warts-and-all description of what was happening inside this big green Swedish streaming machine. Preferably one that he could grasp before he stubbed out his cigarette.

Several months before the direct listing, I found myself once again on the street, shivering in an early-winter London morning, with the aroma of Italian roast and nicotine wafting around. I listened to him intently as he rifled off questions about the turbulent times in tech – the sell-offs and buy-backs, the hiring and firing, and the mergers and spin-offs. With the prospect of going public on the horizon, he wanted me to cut through the fog and summarise whether the turbulence had arrived at Spotify. He knew how things were being portrayed in the press, but he needed a reality check, and he needed it – as he seemed to need everything – fast.

'Well,' I replied hastily, 'the builders are leaving, and the farmers are moving in.'

It was as succinct a summary as I could muster to capture the state of affairs of a ten-year-old tech start-up that had redefined a recording industry that was then valued at $16 billion on the eve of its most aggressive financial move to date.

He took one last draw on his cigarette and, unusually, asked me to elaborate.

'Well,' I said, 'the people who built Spotify are leaving, and the people who will run Spotify are taking over. The builders value flexibility, creativity and agility – those are the attributes they used to build the company, to make Spotify out of nothing.'

He nodded.

'But the people who are taking over as we prepare to go public are more like farmers. They want to reap the benefits of Spotify for years to come. So, they're obsessed with process, predictability and frameworks.'

He nodded again. I waited for another volley of questions. But after a moment, he simply muttered 'Thank you', stubbed out his cigarette, threw his coffee cup in a recycling bin, and walked off.

I'd had these types of meetings many times, but this felt different. By the next time we would meet, 'SPOT' would be on the ticker of the New York Stock Exchange (NYSE). For a company that started to build out in 2006 with just six people, this was the time for some serious stocktaking before the stock became a tradable good.

For everyone involved in the company, the April 2018 IPO was a monumental event. It seemed to mark the conclusion to the music industry's 'first to suffer, first to recover' journey through disruption. For Sweden, Spotify's success was a badge of honour, a Stockholm-based company with a capitalisation that towered over that of Volvo – back then one of Sweden's biggest companies. It was so unusual, in fact, that the NYSE mixed up the country of origin and flew Swiss flags outside their building by mistake. (Their apology pointed out that Switzerland did make great chocolates!)

Several months after the direct listing, with 'SPOT' sliding from right to left across stock tickers on trading screens the world over, I once again found myself taking the lift down to street level for another meeting with our investor. Change is a fact of life in such a disruptive industry as digital music. Even so, I was unprepared for what greeted me when I exited the doors of the building: my investor friend had quit smoking.

Not that that slowed down the pace of our conversation at all.

'That expression you used last time we met,' he remarked, 'it's really caught on – people are using it a lot.'

'Which expression was that?' I asked. I had no recollection of what I'd said.

'Your reference to builders and farmers – it neatly captures the life cycle of a tech company. You can be one or the other, but you can't be both. The key is for the builders to know when it's time to move on and let the farmers take over. It's about knowing where you belong in the life span of a technology company – because you don't belong for ever.'

Though I'd forgotten having said any of that, hearing it parroted back to me, I thought it made some sense.

If this 'builders and farmers' expression was to have real value, it needed to be put to the test, so I asked my investor friend how he saw himself. It felt awkward, as my binary description didn't seem to fit his role in Spotify's success. After all, he had come on board before any significant building had even started. After some contemplation, he replied abruptly: 'I'm more like a surveyor: I climbed up a mountain (with Spotify's co-founder, Daniel Ek), saw land on the other side, and came to the conclusion you could build there. Once I knew that land had value, I raised the capital and got out of the way so the builders could move in.'

Builders, farmers and surveyors – we're on an occupational roll! Who else can we cast in this metaphor? Venture capitalists are the land developers; regulators the planning authorities; and, arguably the most important – the offensive tackle, in National Football League terminology – are the people who know how to get around the authorities: the lobbyists. The list is as intriguing as it is endless. In any company, you have to know when to let go of the vine of builders and grab for the farmers; equally, as individuals, we need to know when we move from one to the other.

Ernesto Guevara de la Serna, better known as Che Guevara, was an Argentine-born Cuban revolutionary leader who became an icon thanks to the famous *Guerrillero Heroico* photograph of him by Alberto Korda in 1960 – arguably one of the most iconic photographs of all time. Ironically, this Marxist revolutionary made private T-shirt sellers a lot of money. It didn't make the photographer a penny, however, as Alberto Korda was a devoted communist and never tried to assert any economic rights to the work – although he did assert his moral rights once, when Smirnoff tried to use it!*

Guevara travelled to Mexico in 1954, where he met Cuban revolutionary leader Fidel Castro the following year, and played a key role in the eventual success of the guerrilla war against Cuban dictator Fulgencio Batista. In 1959. Castro took power of Cuba, appointing Guevara to run the National Bank of Cuba, and the Ministry of Industry. At home, Che quickly put in place plans for land redistribution and industrial nationalisation, much to the ire of the Americans who were watching this unfold from just 90 miles away. Abroad, Che became a globe-trotting Cuban ambassador, advocating a Marxist revolution wherever he went.

Castro, meanwhile, played a cunning game of bait-and-switch, swearing to the Americans he was a 'Fidelista', not a 'Communista', while quickly nationalising the country – much to the ire of his original US financiers. An infamously botched attempt by the Americans to invade Cuba had the unintended

* Matt Wells, 'After 40 years and millions of posters, Che's photographer sues for copyright', *Guardian*, August 2000.

consequence of moving Castro closer to the USSR, a relationship from which Guevara sought to distance himself. As the Cuban economy faltered, at least in part due to American trade sanctions, Guevara began to fall out with the other Cuban leaders.

On the face of it, Fidel and Che appeared united in their revolutionary struggle, but their priorities were very different. Castro wanted power; Guevara wanted revolution. Castro wanted to govern; Guevara wanted to change the world. Castro was a cunning political operative who could change course to keep control, whereas Guevara was an ideologue obsessed with justice. After a while, these differences proved irreconcilable, and Guevara took his revolutionary ambitions elsewhere. He died fighting a hopeless war in Bolivia in 1967, while Castro ruled Cuba for five more decades.

Guevara had the energy for overturning the existing order in order to create a new Cuba, but he didn't have the patience to actually run the country. Meanwhile Castro didn't have the urge to constantly remake the world but did possess a skill for politics and for governance. In other words, Guevara was a builder and Castro was a farmer. Together they demonstrate how builders and farmers may complement each other temporarily but will inevitably be driven apart.

The obvious question, then: when should the builders move out, and the farmers move in? For the HR department, this is paramount – if the builders stay too long, they can become agitated, scattered and unfocused. And if farmers arrive too early, the company can become rigid, risk-averse and slow to pivot. In a nutshell, builders create what farmers can't, and farmers can scale what builders can't. The challenge is not just knowing whether you need builders and when you need farmers in your organisation but working out when the time has come to hire one or the other. There are three moments when it's most likely time to 'ring the bell' for the builders to move out and the farmers to move in:

(i) when the company becomes profitable
(ii) after an IPO
(iii) after the effects of government regulation

In theory, these moments can occur separately, but in practice they often happen all at once.

Let's tackle profitability first. A typical disruptor loses money on each sale during the formative years, before reaching a tipping point where it makes money instead. Andrew Bud, a serial entrepreneur and founder of the identity verification company iProov, once explained to me that 'It's easy to confuse a fantasy business model for true disruption – until the capital subsidising the appearance of disruption runs out.' Builders are better suited to this risky 'cash burn' environment, whereas farmers have a preference for the more sustainable period, where marginal revenue exceeds marginal cost and the business is a going concern that can be reliably harvested.

**LET INVESTORS PAY TO DELIVER YOU THAT MEAL**

A wise friend once told me that I should make the most of the array of food delivery apps on my phone while they were still 'going concerns'; every time I used them, their Venture Capital (VC) backers or public market investors would be picking up part of the bill.

It was a shrewd observation, as these companies were burning cash on each transaction in order to reach scale – they were businesses being run by builders. As these businesses went public, the builders moved out and the farmers moved in, as the scrutiny that comes with being a publicly traded business demands not only growth in users, but also rising incremental cash flow margins.

Once exposed to the scrutiny of capital markets, the tipping point between builders and farmers can create turbulence, but it needn't be binary – a 'core' business can be handed over to farmers to find operational efficiencies, generating cash (if not profits), which can be used by builders to enter new lanes of activity.

The first majorly successful ride-hailing taxi app, Uber, offers a great example: it went public in May 2019, with the vast majority of sales coming from its original 'ride-sharing' business (now over a decade old) with the bolt-on food delivery business, Uber Eats. Farmers, therefore, seek to find efficiencies in delivering passengers while builders work out a sustainable delivery system for meals.

Arete, a fiercely independent boutique equity research provider, delved into Uber's financial statements to establish the unit economics for both an average ride in an Uber and the average cost of its food delivery service (ignoring the company's central corporate overhead costs, which would wipe out profits in both areas).

The chart overleaf shows that each Uber ride recovers its costs and then some – a business with profits that can be harvested by farmers. Uber Eats is still in its infancy by comparison and loses money on each delivery, as it competes for market share to reach scale. This side of the business suits builders, especially as many of its competitors will also be burning cash on each order.

Remember, it's Uber Eats and not the restaurant that takes the hit: the unit costs being illustrated are in distribution, not production. If a meal cost a family £40 and the total cost of Uber Eats including delivery came to £45 – the restaurant got paid its £40 minus a commission from Uber, but not one large enough that, when combined with the delivery fee, it covers both delivery and operation costs, forcing Uber to subsidise around £2. Uber calls these extra fees 'excess driver incentives'. The simple translation: 'We couldn't get a driver to deliver the order for less than the £5 delivery fee charged to the consumer, so we had to pay them more.' So, my wise friend was right! Using Uber Eats made sense as the investors are picking up part of your bill. And you should do so before they run out of cash!

The second tipping point is the one I discussed earlier: when a company goes public. To recall our two-wheeled analogy, in the early stage a tech company is akin to a bicycle – if it doesn't move forward it'll fall over. Before going public, the frequent

**UBER RIDES AND UBER EATS: FARMERS DELIVER YOU, BUILDERS DELIVER YOUR FOOD**

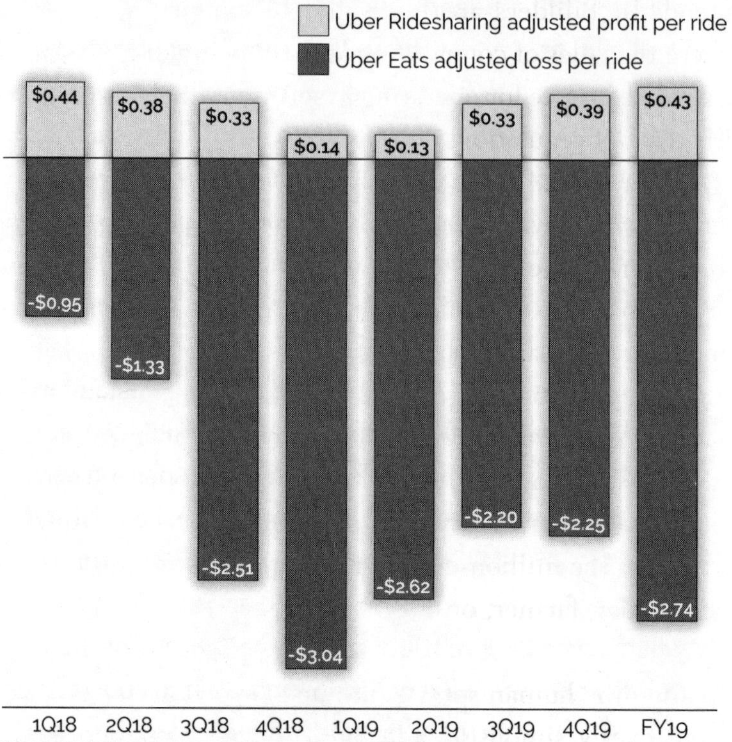


*Source: Arete Research*

and volatile swings in the fortunes and foul-ups mean a company needs builders. Once publicly traded on stock markets, however, it not only needs to become compliant with the rules of the market, but also needs to sustain the momentum to ensure that the bicycle keeps moving forward at a steady and predictable pace during good times and bad. This is when the farmers should move in.

The third and final tipping point is government regulation. Intuition suggests that builders enter a gap in the market to build a monopoly, whereas farmers only come in to harvest the profits that the monopoly has sown (dismal economist pun intended). Builders are motivated to explore new territory where the rules of competition are still being drafted; farmers have a preference for operating in settings which have an established set of regulations.

As mentioned, these three tipping points may happen independently or may converge into one big event, either by accident or design. For example, the introduction of regulation may force a company to reduce its cash-burn and accelerate its IPO ambitions. Similarly, the intention to list on public markets may invite the attention of regulators and force a company to shift plans from growth tomorrow to achieve profitability today.

So, if we know the three tipping points that signal when you need builders and when you need farmers, we now need to turn to the million-dollar question – who do you think you are: builder, farmer, or both?

Dividing the human species into just two character types may sound overly simplistic. Yet there is plenty of precedent. In February 1920, Robert Bencley told *Vanity Fair*, 'There may be said to be two classes of people in the world: those who constantly divide the people of the world into two classes, and those who do not.' American writer Damon Runyon fell into the former group, as when he classified our species into 'those who love delis, and those you shouldn't associate with.' Organisational psychologist Adam Grant made things a bit more complex with his three groups of people: givers, takers and matchers. Just as Grant brilliantly sought to help people find their identity, so too is my taxonomy of builders and farmers meant to help you determine where in the lifespan of a tech company you belong.

Imagine a simple bell curve. On one end are the pure builders, people who can only perform builder functions and no farmer functions. On the other end: pure farmers, people who can only perform farmer functions and no builder functions. Some people will find themselves at the extremes, others are somewhere in the thickest part of the curve, possessing some builder traits and some farmer traits. It is the extremes, or what psychologists call 'dark traits', on this bell curve where we need to place our focus, as these are people who excel at who they are but can't and shouldn't pretend to be who they're not – even if the HR department has designed a career development framework that incentivises them to try.

Professor Adrian Furnham of the Norwegian Business School is widely recognised as a leading organisational psychologist, with 95 books and 1,200 peer-reviewed academic journals to his name. His approach to identifying the 'dark side traits' – the extremes on this bell curve – is to look for early signs of whether an individual skews toward an extreme, enabling signals of both builders and farmers to surface. This can be asking simple and intuitive questions about people's past, like 'Did you accumulate money at university, or did you accumulate debt?' They can also be more abstract questions, such as how they would approach design challenges. A builder might ask, 'How would you decorate this room?', whereas a farmer might ask, 'How much carpeting do you need?' Similarly, the choice of educational paths can reveal a lot about convergent and divergent thinking; those who study the arts will have a tendency to diverge, whereas those who study the sciences will converge. Finally, self-selection on where individuals chose to work after graduation might tell us about their attitudes to responsibility – builders have a preference for small firms with higher accountability, while farmers have a preference for larger firms with lower accountability.

These street-smart observations help us tee-up a core tool for occupational psychologists. More than two decades ago, psychologists Robert and Joyce Hogan created a framework for evaluating these 'dark side' traits – eleven qualities that, when taken to the extreme, resemble the most common personality disorders. These traits can be classified into three simple clusters: moving towards, moving against and moving away from other people. What makes the Hogan Development Survey (HDS) work distinct, and has led to its successful widespread adoption, is its focus on failure as much as success – that is, identifying the traits that lead to leadership derailment. After all, isn't learning from failure the most important criteria for success, as 'what doesn't kill you makes you stronger'?

Traits don't define us. They are flexible. They can appear in different forms in different contexts. But what they give us is a language, clear and replicable, that we can use to translate the world around us into a clear and simplified model. Hogan's model gave the world a new language with which to view occupational psychology. My model, though slightly less ambitious, wants to give you a language for looking at the people you work with, your friends, your family, through the language of builders and farmers: on which side do you sit?

Getting to grips with your 'dark side' traits helps to tease out who you are – a builder or a farmer – and whether you find yourself at the extreme, where you cannot and should not attempt to be both. If you find yourself frustrated in your working life because you feel you lack a framework for career development, you may well be a farmer in a builder's role. If you are unable to develop a new business idea due to the operational red tape of the company, you may be a builder in a farmer's role. Remember the lesson that Spotify's early investor taught me: the key to this is knowing 'when' – when in the

## *WHO DO YOU THINK YOU ARE?*

| *Traits* | *What makes Builders and Farmers distinct* |
|---|---|
| *Tolerance for Ambiguity* | **Builders** have a high tolerance of ambiguity and low tolerance of a process<br>**Farmers** have a low tolerance of ambiguity and high tolerance of process |
| *Risk Preference* | **Builders** like the risk of designing planes once they're in flight (or figuring out a business after launch)<br>**Farmers** prefer the assurance of knowing how that plane needs to land |
| *Goal Achievement* | **Builders** prefer the excitement of the journey and not the destination<br>**Farmers** are motivated by the destination more than the journey |
| *Opportunism* | **Builders** are motivated by identifying gaps in the market<br>**Farmers** are more cautious and prefer to question if there is a market in the gap |
| *Scepticism* | **Builders** push back on scepticism as if they don't go somewhere, they end up nowhere<br>**Farmers** deploy scepticism to garner both power and longevity |
| *Fear of Failure* | **Builders** welcome failure as a means of discovering success<br>**Farmers** avoid failure to demonstrate success |
| *Idea Application* | **Builders** measure themselves in terms of the quality of their ideas<br>**Farmers** measure themselves in the delivery of those ideas |
| *Known Unknowns* | **Builders** prefer applying an unknown discipline to a known marketplace<br>**Farmers** prefer to apply a known discipline to an unknown marketplace |
| *Granularity* | **Builders** skip over details to win an audience<br>**Farmers** demand detail before addressing an audience |

*Source: Author's own adaptation of the Hogan Development Survey (HDS)*

lifespan of a company it's time for the builders to move out and when the farmers need to move in.

Regardless of who you think you are, getting this occupational balancing act right when dealing with disruption is never going to be easy. It may feel like builders are the ones in the best position to navigate disruption – the heroes of change. We're prone to idolising innovators, and it's easy to think of farmers as the kindergarten teachers trying to constrain the innovations of the builders in the interest of minimising uncertainty. It's more exciting to think about an invention than it is to think about its distribution.

But the world needs farmers. They know how to industrialise. They know how to scale. They know how to take a message and find the bottle that will help it to travel. Builders may build, but it's farmers who spread.

Given that you've been able to swing into action with Tarzan Economics, thanks to ploughing through the eight principles for pivoting through disruption, you now have a better idea of a knowing who you are with respect to builders and farmers. So, let's go back, way back, and revisit each of those eight principles to show how their application differs depending on who you think you are.

And here's why. There is no 'one rule that will change all our lives', as so many business books proclaim. If you want to take that clickbait, then you are likely to lose as there are many rules for many schools and we're all different. Headlines like that might grab your attention in airport bookshops but won't help you pivot through disruption in a hotly contested market for attention. Rather, you now have eight truly transferable principles that need be tailored to only two personality types, so you have the confidence to know when to let go of what we know and reach out to what we don't.

## BUILD AND THEY WILL COME

Chapter 1 recounted music's 'first to suffer, first to recover' experience with Tarzan Economics. The past two decades resemble two halves. The first half saw the industry resist change with a defensive legal strategy of suing customers, websites and internet service providers – akin to an actual (as opposed to theoretical) farmer resorting to pesticides to preserve crops rather than tilling the land. The music industry's pesticides did more harm than good; it spent millions and lost billions.

The second half saw the industry establish the macro- and microeconomic evidence it needed to reach out and grab the new vine of streaming. The industry's ongoing recovery is now the envy of all those experiencing their own Napster moment today.

Builders viewed the problem of rampant music piracy as one of monetisation: consumers were consuming more music than ever before, and the industry just needed to make a better platform to monetise that consumption. This was the original vision of Spotify – build and they will come. Farmers, on the other hand, saw the problem in a black-and-white legal mindset: consumers were stealing instead of buying, and if the thieves could be stopped, the industry would recover. Builders got the business to the place where it could recover. Yet, here's the twist in the tale that my investor friend reminded me about over coffee and cigarettes: now it's up to the farmers to move back in, stabilise the industry's recovery and ensure the long-term growth of the industry.

*Distilling it down*: Builders prefer to solve fewer, bigger problems; farmers like to solve more, smaller problems.

### SPECIALISING OR OPTIMISING

Chapter 2 took us away from music and towards something that's ubiquitous in all our lives: attention. The first fork in the road that you face when navigating the path ahead is the economics of attention. It can appear binary – you have it or you don't – but it's also stackable: many distractions can tug on our attention at once. The contestability of attention reminds us of how the battle plays out – how one attention merchant's gain is another's pain. Building upon our framework in Chapter 1, we're witnessing a 'tragedy of the commons' where these attention merchants all want more of our time, and we all have increasingly less to give. Monopolising attention is not solely about getting 'attention in', but increasingly it is in being able to 'screen distractions out'.

If Netflix can win over fifty hours of our precious time by enticing us to binge-watch five seasons of *Narcos*, then that's fifty hours that no one else can claim. Not only does Netflix win, but the long list of losers is left with even less attention to go around – making contestability even more crucial to understand.

Builders specialise in monopolising attention, with an all-or-nothing bargain; farmers are more suited to optimising it, where stacking sources of attention means different distractions can complement each other. Builders are more suited to the Netflix model, where there is a pure-play offer of attention in one form; farmers are better able to juggle bigger and more diverse bundles, like Apple One, an all-in-one subscription that bundles up to six Apple services, where different attention-seeking properties need to be catered for.

*Distilling it down*: In contesting for attention, builders specialise; farmers optimise.

## QUALITY OR QUANTITY

Chapter 3 showed us how two old rules of drawing a crowd remain relevant to our new schools of thinking. The most important lesson we learned from Tupperware was how Brownie Wise developed a bottom-up viral network in response to the failure of top-down marketing; Tupperware parties leveraged social networks and social pressure to sell more Tupperware than conventional advertising ever did.

Similarly, Russ Solomon's Tower Records showed us that some choice is better than none, but more isn't necessarily better than some. Solomon's bricks-and-mortar stores stocked a tiny percentage of the music available on a modern streaming service, and yet that relatively small stock of discs would have accounted for about 90 per cent of the streaming business today. You don't need all the content on earth to draw a crowd, you only need the right content.

Builders will be more agnostic to which crowds they draw and are motivated to 'gun it' for scale at all costs; farmers will know that some crowds are worth more than others. Builders will have little time for such nuanced lessons in scale, focusing instead on headline metrics like 'active users' and asking how big a crowd is. Farmers want to know how active those users are.

*Distilling it down*: Builders scale the quantity of crowds; farmers harvest the quality of crowds.

## HAVING THE GUTS TO GO IT ALONE

Chapter 4 told the story of Radiohead's famous *In Rainbows* experiment, when the band decided to break from its record label and release an album themselves. The band made more money thanks to their 'ballsy move' than they did on their previous records, but they also had more freedom to experiment and learn about their fans. Radiohead's experiment explored new territory in the decision to make or buy – to go it alone or bring in the services of others to get there – and left a map that many have followed since.

Platforms like Patreon and Kickstarter have put new tools in the hands of those willing to go it alone. Meanwhile, the role of the traditional 'audience-makers' has changed – even a creator who is ready to cede control to an audience-maker will find that same audience-maker expects the artist to build their own audience. So, increasingly, the builders – the creators looking to forge new paths to success independent of traditional gatekeepers – are empowered to go it alone. And the farmers – the traditional intermediaries – are having to justify their relevance in the value chain.

A chasm, then, is opening up between the builders and the farmers. Builders instinctively see the educational value in 'making it themselves' and developing an audience directly. Should they need to buy in intermediaries, then they will be on better terms to do so and needn't let go of the direct relationship with the fans they've made along the way.

Farmers need to pivot to remain relevant and adapt to these new terms of trade, leaving behind a world that was akin to a Keynesian Beauty Contest, in which we compete to win over the judges, and moving towards a world where we communicate directly with the consumer.

*Distilling it down*: Builders win over consumers; farmers win over judges.

## 'COMMUNISM WITH A TOUCH OF CAPITALISM'

Chapter 5 taught us that as creators seek more independence by making (as opposed to buying), they become more dependent on collectives to distribute and monetise what they've made. Throwing hats into the collective ring, as opposed to selling our hats separately, makes sense. Without this collective solution, these fragmented markets would be unable to function due to the risk of anti-commons – where it becomes so complicated to deal with the many players in a fragmented market that the entire market ends up underused. Yet it is the revelation of 'Groucho Marxism' that reminds us what makes this balancing act so delicate: the most valuable member will have the least incentive to join (and the greatest incentive to leave).

Collectives are either 'capitalism with a touch of communism' or 'communism with a touch of capitalism'. It's a balancing act, and a delicate one at that. Builders tend to have a narrower focus and prioritise 'looking after number one' and are less motivated to spend time and energy forging and maintaining collectives. Farmers will be more attuned to the delicate diplomacy of keeping all the collective hats in the ring and beating off the Marxist temptation for the most valuable of those hats to leave.

*Distilling it down*: Builders lack the patience to form collectives; farmers possess the patience to keep them from falling apart.

## WHY WE NEED TWO COMPETITION AUTHORITIES

Chapter 6 introduced us to 'pivotal thinking', drawing on the late great Screaming Lord Sutch of the Official Monster Raving Loony Party's famous policy proposal of having 'more than one competition authority'.

After all, how can we assign the role of upholding competition to a monopoly? This is especially true when you look under the bonnet of how economics is being taught today, where core concepts, especially that of 'monopoly', are neither taught correctly at universities nor applied effectively by policymakers. Rather than reducing output and hiking prices, as the textbooks would have you believe, today's tech monopolies want to expand output and reduce (or even eliminate) price. Today's monopolies are oblivious to the concept of marginal cost and compete for convenience instead.

Defining the market is what distinguishes builders from farmers. If there is no defined market, then one cannot derive a market share. If builders are building something that has never been built before then, intuitively, market share isn't on the radar. Farmers find themselves on the other side of the fence, preferring markets that are well defined – where precedent has already been set. There is a simple test to ascertain whether it's builders or farmers who should prevail within your current environment: just ask 'What is the market share?' If the response is a bemused 'Market share of what?', then the farmers should move out and the builders should move in.

*Distilling it down*: Builders will circumvent theory to exploit gaps in the market, whereas farmers will seek to apply theory to understand the market in the gap.

### WHAT MATTERS MOST IS BEING MEASURED LEAST

The seventh principle was to assess the state we're in, lifting the lid on the worrying shortcomings in how the state measures the economy that surrounds us. At the highest level, making money on real estate, inheriting money from relatives and spending money on e-commerce has become a social norm for many in society, yet it's not clear how any of this is accurately captured by government statistics. Look a little closer at how the economy is moving into the cloud and you see an even bigger divergence between what we do and what the state measures. Look closer still and there's the increased popularity of free goods – Wikipedia, Facebook – none of which are adequately reflected in the state's numbers. To paraphrase Robert Solow: The digital economy is everywhere except in government statistics.

A desire to close the gap between what you can and cannot measure is what separates builders and farmers. Farmers are more content with the status quo – data that's been compiled over the years and the trends they produce – whereas builders are wary of this inertia and are more willing to start afresh. They'll be willing to look elsewhere for real-time signals of hiring (and firing) in professions that traditional surveys haven't yet categorised, like the impressive work of the LinkedIn economists who are capturing categories of employment that the official survey leaves behind, like AI. Herein lies a tension: farmers would feel threatened by this new approach of displacing the legacy of what's been built up over the years.

*Distilling it down*: Farmers frame policy answers around what they can measure; builders ask policy questions about what they can't measure.

## CONJECTURES AND REFUTATIONS

Chapter 8 builds on the sceptical view of government statistics and jumps off that most important form of transportation, 'the bandwagon' of big data, arguing that it risks us making big mistakes.

We've leaned too far in the direction of big data and need to rebalance with 'thick data': understanding the people and not the quantifiable data points they produce. The temptation to use and abuse big data, to link correlations with causation, has clouded out common sense and risks falling foul of the quantification fallacy – disregarding anything that can't easily be measured as irrelevant. Nowhere is this more needed than in a thorough re-examination of the NPS score – one number that claims to tell us so much but actually tells us so little.

To distinguish between our two personality types, we need to lean on the work of the influential philosopher Karl Popper and his theory of conjectures and refutations – everything we say needs to be challenged (or refuted) to prove that it's true. Builders have a vested interest in making bold big data conjectures bolder to maintain funding for a start-up or academic institute, whereas farmers are more able to challenge the quantification bias, contest these claims with refutations as well as seek out better explanations. Builders will rush to market their big-data predictions for the future, but farmers will remind us that all data comes from the same place: the past.

*Distilling it down*: Builders make conjectures from the big data they're able to measure; farmers provide refutations by drawing meaning from what can't be measured.

Knowing who you are will not only give you the confidence to deftly utilise Tarzan Economics but will help you apply these eight principles to better pivot through disruption. We all have different strengths and weaknesses, and we all possess our own unique motivations, values and preferences. We are all different horses, suited to different courses. There is ample reading on the 'how' and 'why' of dealing with disruption, but knowing who you are helps you understand the 'when' – when, in the course of disruption, can you add the most value and when should you step aside?

Asking and answering 'Who do you think you are?' helps you, the reader, learn how and when to pivot in the face of disruption. But you would be forgiven, as we reach the conclusion of this book, to flip it back to me, the author preaching all these principles in pivoting, and ask 'who am I?' Where on some spectrum of motivations, values and preferences would I put myself and other like-minded souls? To get the answer, I want to pivot from builders and farmers to a much older analogy and, in doing so, complete my own hat-trick and – for the third time – draw on a passage from Adam Smith's influential work *The Theory of Moral Sentiments Part IV*, where he explored the differences between mathematicians and poets.

Smith observed that: 'The morals of those different classes of men of letters are, perhaps, sometimes somewhat affected by this very great difference in their situation with regard to the public.' He goes on to say,

> Mathematicians [ . . . ] have little temptation to form themselves into factions and cabals, either for the support of their own reputation, or for the depression of that of their rivals. [They] are pleased when their works are approved of, without being either much vexed or very angry when they are neglected.*

* Adam Smith, 'Part III, Chapter II: Of the love of Praise, and of that of Praise-worthiness; and of the dread of Blame, and of that of Blame-worthiness', *The Theory of Moral Sentiments*, Anthony Finley, 1817.

Smith recognises that mathematicians can have great influence, but they do not themselves seek to be influencers. If social media existed in the late 1700s, the mathematicians Smith is writing about would be unlikely participants. Likes and retweets would have had little resonance with this community during Georgian times.

At the other end of the spectrum are poets, who according to Smith,

> are very apt to divide themselves into a sort of literary factions; each cabal being often avowedly, and almost always secretly, the mortal enemy of the reputation of every other, and employing all the mean arts of intrigue and solicitation to preoccupy the public opinion in favour of the works of its own members, and against those of its enemies and rivals.

Poets would be the Georgian equivalent of click-baiters, doing what they can to grab attention and sway public opinion, forming Facebook groups that champion those inside and trolling on Twitter everyone outside with views they oppose.

Unashamedly, be it nature or nurture, economists like me are drawn to the middle, in between the mathematician and the poet – pivoting between the desire for truth and the need for recognition. It may not just be the dismal science that finds itself stuck in the middle. Recall how we described the process of drawing crowds, where the room has become increasingly crowded, making it harder and harder to recognise those at the back. Those professions who previously didn't feel the need to stand out from the crowd have found themselves getting lost within it – meaning if you don't pivot and push yourself to the front of the room, the relentless rising tide of digitisation will leave your discipline (and its relevance) languishing at the back.

It's this pivot which takes us to the purpose of this book: everyone everywhere is experiencing disruption in their lives – arguably more than anything we've experienced ever before in such a short period – as a result of Covid-19. We're all staring at our Napster moment. We all need to do something about it. This book, and these eight principles, can be thought of as your alarm clock as disruption doesn't always give you the required eight hours of sleep. If you've been caught napping, then these eight principles will help you wake up with the urgency needed to catch up. Take a moment to consider the old vine you're holding on to. Is it slipping through your fingers? Is it time to take the leap and reach out for the new branch?

This book has been my chance to transfer all I've seen and understood about music's journey through disruption, helping you avoid the mistakes the industry made during the first half of its twenty-year journey and learn from the success it achieved in the second. Disruption requires us all to stare into the darkness, and the eight principles taught by Tarzan Economics assure us that there is light at the end of the tunnel. Once you know that there is light at the end, you can pivot through with more confidence.

Above all else, confidence is critical in applying these eight principles: the confidence to adapt from moments to movements, from working with borders to a borderless world, from communicating top-down to the consumer to a bottom-up world where customers have become the new broadcasters; confidence in drawing your own crowd as no one else is going to invest until you do; confidence in giving up short-termism of self-interest to collaborate for a better future for the common good; confidence in realising the opposite of a good idea can also be a good idea; confidence in counting zeros as we know that what matters most is often being measured least; confidence in knowing that quantification bias can send us in the wrong direction, and how to correct ourselves with the people who produced the data in the first place and steer a better course.

As we all find ourselves staring at our Napster moment, we need to embrace Tarzan Economics in order to address life's challenges sooner rather than later, as delay only means the problems get bigger and harder to solve. Where you go next after reading this book is your decision, but you can now pivot faster and more effectively than any individual, organisation or institution that you choose to help. So, if there's one final lesson I can share to help you navigate the path ahead it is this:

Don't wait for your perfect job description,
create your job description instead.

ANNEX

# Groucho Marxism Maths

To make our sixth principle, 'Self-Interest vs. the Common Good', a truly transferable lesson, it helps if we do some maths – Marxism maths. We need to return to Groucho Marxism and face up to the inconvenient truth that always has, and always will, undermine collectives – that their most valuable participant has the greatest incentive to leave. Marxism teaches us about the imbalance that collectives bring.

To win the argument for the common good of collectives, we need a simple model to demonstrate how the reduced transaction costs and increased value of the blanket licence can tip the scales in favour of the collective yet solve for the perverse incentives of Groucho Marxism; meaning that if you are in, you are now suitably looked after to no longer want to be out, and if you're out you now have a sufficient incentive to want to be in.

To do this, we'll sketch out a very simple model to capture the dynamics of what holds a collective together. Here's how we will visualise this. The buyer (or rights user) negotiates with the collective management organisation (CMO), which represents all the rights holders, who are backstage and removed from the negotiation – all they see is their fair division. By forming a collective the CMO can offer 'blanket coverage' for a premium – and it's this premium that glues the collective together.

Going back to our Bourget restaurant story, this is like a customer at the restaurant negotiating with the waiter for a blanket licence fee for an all-you-can-eat access to the menu. The waiter then needs to go into the kitchen and ensure all their chefs (or rights holders) are on board. The blanket must cover all of the bed – or all of the menu. Having 99 per cent coverage isn't good enough – it's either all or nothing. Should one of those menu offerings not be available then the all-you-can-eat premium is no longer worth paying.

**MARXISM MATH MODEL**

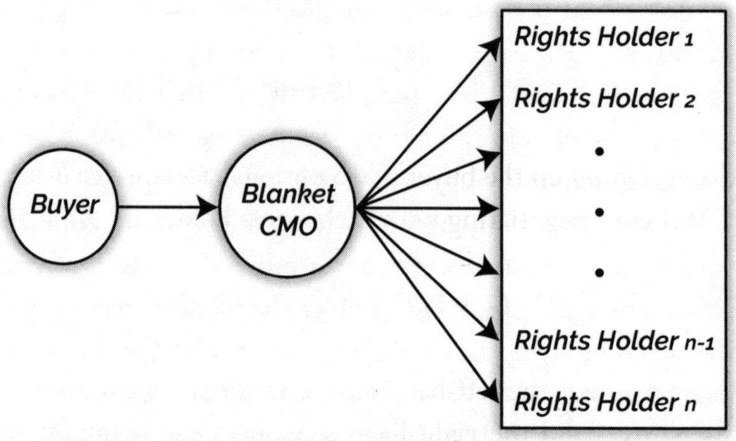


Source: Author

In this model, the rights user (buyer) negotiates with the CMO and transfers a cheque which has three components: firstly, the total fee distributed to rights holders ($L_B$); second is the premium paid for receiving the blanket ($P_B$); and third is the transaction cost ($t$). We'll express this as:

$$L_B + P_B + t$$

The alternative for the buyer is that they negotiate with each rights holder individually and directly (number of rights holders $= n$), facing a payment to each rights holder ($L_i$) and a transaction cost not with just one agent (like with the CMO, $t$) but with numerous rightsholders ($nt$). To add some whizzy maths, we add $\Sigma_{i=1}^{n}$, which simply captures the assumption that the total sum distributed is the total that all the rights holders would have received individually. In other words, the CMO distributes to the rights holders what the rights holders could have achieved individually with the buyer – only that the CMO retains a premium for the blanket and faces zero transaction costs. The total cost of the buyer making a deal with rights holders is:

$$\sum_{i=1}^{n} L_i + nt$$

So, weighing up the buyer's two options, they prefer using the CMO over negotiating with each rights holder if:

$$L_B + P_B + t < \sum_{i=1}^{n} L_i + nt$$

As explained, the left-hand side is what the buyer would pay the CMO, and the right-hand side the total payments to all rights holders. The difference between both options can be simplified to:

$$P_B < (n-1)t$$

Don't worry if this equation looks confusing. Put simply, buyers will pay a premium for a one-stop shop if it's worth more than the hassle of having to deal with lots of people individually. Amazon's Prime subscription works on a very similar concept.

Now, let's leave the restaurant and go to the kitchen and imagine removing the assumption that all money is distributed on a pro rata share to all members. Now the CMO has some wiggle room and can choose to distribute a higher or lower amount to rights holders than the rights holders would have achieved on their own. This allows us to now solve 'Groucho Marxism'.

If we ignore transaction costs to simplify things, then the rights holder wants in on the CMO deal if $L_B$ (what rights holder gets from CMO) $- L_i$ (what rights holder would get by negotiating on own) $> 0$. This can be expressed as:

> If $\frac{L_B}{n} - L_i \geq 0$, rights holder wants in.
>
> If $L_B - L_i < 0$, then we have Groucho Marxism to deal with as these rights holders want out as they could get more by negotiating with the buyer themselves.
>
> If $\frac{L_B}{n} - L_i < 0$, the rights holder wants out.

Depending on the number of Grouchos that are inside the kitchen, or the size of value that they bring, it may be necessary for the CMO to use its blanket premium war chest, $P_B$. For example, it can distribute some of $P_B$ to any Groucho rights holders who either have a credible threat of leaving the blanket licence or are lacking an incentive to join. Essentially,

> Think of $P_B$ as the glue that holds the whole collective together.

This model captures what makes the common good of a collective work – the value of universality achieved at less cost has to be worth more than the most valuable participant acting in self-interest and going it alone. Collectives have to treat all members the same, but the premium from the blanket licence gives CMOs wiggle room to ensure the most valuable members are accommodated. After all, without this premium, why would anyone want to join the club that would have them as a member?

### SKYSCANNER APPLIES MARXISM MATHS TO SCAN ALL OF THE SKIES

Marxism maths comes to life on the many travel-tech platforms that we use to find the best flight. The Edinburgh-based Skyscanner, whose unique selling point is that it scans all the sky, not just some of it, provides us with the perfect example.

Network effects are at the heart of Skyscanner's success. The more consumers on its platform, the more airlines want to list their flights, the more it is able to become a price-maker (as opposed to a price-taker). In November 2016, Trip.com Group, the largest travel firm in China, bought Skyscanner for $1.75 billion.

Back in the company's early days, however, there was one pesky hold-out airline seeking to exploit the Marxism maths outlined above: Ryanair, which offered the lowest-cost no-frills service available. Without Ryanair, Skyscanner couldn't claim to scan the entire skies – just like a blanket licence can't charge a premium if it doesn't cover all of the bed.

Ryanair played hardball, arguing they provided the value and Skyscanner provided none. Skyscanner was convinced that its value depended on a comprehensive view of the skies and Ryanair knew it too. Exploiting its 'last mover advantage', Ryanair ended up getting Skyscanner to pay it to carry its fleet. It was only going to join a club that had to have them as a member.

The value of comprehensive scanning of the skies proved to be a win-win for Skyscanner, Ryanair and, thanks to the network effects, many smaller airlines, who often appeared atop the search results. Gareth Williams, co-founder and then-CEO of Skyscanner, reflected on what its blanket coverage did for the wider industry:

> The network effects were found in completeness of coverage, not frequency, as consumers discovered airlines they didn't know existed – even in their home markets. Even large airlines benefited from increased awareness of destinations outside of their hubs. I think our competition underestimated the value of this blanket coverage of the skies.

Skyscanner's success exemplifies how a collective supports the common good. The value of universality achieved at less cost has to be worth more than the most valuable participant acting in self-interest and going it alone. A quick search on Skyscanner today will tell you that London to Frankfurt costs half as much on Ryanair as on Lufthansa and saves you the hassle of having to visit two sites acting in their self-interest. Sure, collectives have to treat all members the same, but the value a blanket licence provides – and captures – tends to give the wiggle room needed to ensure the most valuable members stick around. 'Communism with a touch of capitalism', as one wise woman once said.

# BIBLIOGRAPHY


Albinsson, Staffan, 'A Costly Glass of Water: The Bourget v. Morel Case in Parisian Courts 1847–1849' (Swedish Journal of Music Research, 2014)

Anderson, Chris, *The Long Tail: Why the Future of Business is Selling Less of More* (Random House, 2006)

Bazalgette, Peter, *The Empathy Instinct: How to Create a More Civil Society* (John Murray Press, 2017)

Burrough, Bryan and John Helyar, *Barbarians At The Gate: The Fall of RJR Nabsico* (Vintage, 1990)

Conrad, Joseph, *Typhoon*, revised edition (OUP Oxford, 2008)

Coyle, Diane, *GDP: A Brief but Affectionate History* (Princeton University Press, 2015)

Csikszentmihalyi, Mihaly, *Flow: The Psychology of Optimal Experience* (Harper Perennial Modern Classics, 2008)

Davenport, Thomas H. and John C. Beck, *The Attention Economy: Understanding the New Currency of Business* (Harvard Business Review Press, 2001)

Davies, Richard, *Extreme Economies: Survival, Failure, Future – Lessons from the World's Limits* (Bantam Press, 2019)

Elberse, Anita, *Blockbusters: Hit-making, Risk-taking, and the Big Business of Entertainment* (Henry Holt, 2013)

Evans, David S. and Richard Schmalensee, *Matchmakers: The New Economics of Multisided Platforms* (Harvard Business Review, 2016)

Eyal, Nir, *Indistractable: How to Control Your Attention and Choose Your Life* (Bloomsbury Publishing, 2019)

Fishburne, Tim, *Marketoonist: Your Ad Ignored Here: Cartoons from 15 Years of Marketing, Business, and Doodling in Meetings* (Marketoonist, LLC, 2017)

Furnham, Adrian, *50 Psychology Ideas You Really Need to Know* (Quercus, 2014)

Garber, Meghan, 'A Brief History of Applause, the "Big Data" of the Ancient World' (*The Atlantic*, 13 March, 2013)

Harrison, Ann, *Music: The Business*, seventh edition (Virgin Digital, 2017)

Heller, Michael, *Gridlock Economy: How Too Much Ownership Wrecks Markets, Stops Innovation, and Costs Lives* (Basic Books, 2008)

Grant, Adam, *Give and Take: Why Helping Others Drives Our Success* (Weidenfeld & Nicolson, 2014)

Harford, Tim, *The Undercover Economist* (Little Brown, 2006)

Kay, John, *Obliquity: Why Our Goals Are Best Achieved Indirectly* (Profile Books, 2011)

Kay, John and Mervyn King, *Radical Uncertainty: Decision-making for an Unknowable Future* (The Bridge Street Press, 2020)

Krueger, Alan *Rockonomics: What the Music Industry Can Teach Us About Economics* (John Murray, 2019)

Kuznets, Simon, *National Income, 1929–1932. A report to the US Senate, 73rd Congress, 2nd Session.* (United States Government Printing Office, 1934)

Levitt, Stephen and Stephen J. Dubner, *Freakonomics: A Rogue Economist Explores the Hidden Side of Everything* (Penguin, 2007)

Lewis, Michael, *The Big Short: Inside the Doomsday Machine* (W. W. Norton & Company, 2010)

Marcus, Gary and Ernest Davis, *Rebooting AI: Building Artificial Intelligence We Can Trust* (Ballantine Books Inc., 2019)

Mayer-Schonberger, Viktor and Thomas Ramge, *Reinventing Capitalism in the Age of Big Data* (John Murray Press, 2018)

McAfee, R. Preston, *Competitive Solutions: The Strategist's Toolkit* (Princeton University Press, 2009)

McAfee, Andrew, *More from Less* (Simon & Schuster, 2019)

McLuhan, Marshall, *Understanding Media* (Routledge Classics, 2001)

Meyer, Erin, *Culture Map*, International Edition (Public Affairs, 2016)

Minsky, Hyman, *Stabilizing an Unstable Economy* (McGraw-Hill, 2008)

Moulin, Herve, *Fair Division and Collective Welfare* (MIT Press, 2003)

Niven, John, *Kill Your Friends* (Windmill Books, 2014)

Passman, Don, *All You Need to Know About the Music Business*, 10th Edition (Viking, 2020)

Penenberg, Adam, *Viral Loop: The Power of Pass-It-On* (Sceptre, 2010)

Pilling, David, *The Growth Delusion: The Wealth and Well-Being of Nations* (Bloomsbury Publishing, 2018)

Popper, Karl, *Conjectures and Refutations: The Growth of Scientific Knowledge* (Routledge Classics, 2002)

Randolph, Marc, *That Will Never Work* (Little, Brown, 2019)

Rosling, Hans, Ola Rosling and Anna Rosling Rönnlund, *Factfulness: Ten Reasons We're Wrong About the World – and Why Things Are Better Than You Think* (Sceptre, 2018)

Seabrook, John, *No Brow* (Methuen Publishing, 2000)

Seabrook, John, *The Song Machine: How to Make a Hit* (Jonathan Cape, 2015)

Slywotzky, Adrian, *Value Migration: How to Think Several Moves Ahead of the Competition (Management of Innovation and Change)* (Harvard Business School Press, 1995)

Smith, Adam (1776), *An Inquiry into the Nature and Causes of the Wealth of Nations* (University of Chicago Press, 1977).

Smith, Adam (1759), Knud Haakonssen (ed.), *The Theory of Moral Sentiments* (Cambridge University Press, 2002)

Susskind, Richard, *Tomorrow's Lawyers: An Introduction to Your Future* (Oxford University Press, 2017)

Sutherland, Rory, *Alchemy: The Surprising Power of Ideas That Don't Make Sense* (WH Allen, 2019)

Szymanski, Stefan, *Playbooks and Checkbooks: An Introduction to the Economics of Modern Sports* (Princeton University Press, 2009)

Taleb, Nassim Nicholas, *Incerto box set: Antifragile, The Black Swan, Fooled by Randomness, The Bed of Procrustes, Skin in the Game* (Penguin, 2019)

Thaler, Richard, H., *Misbehaving: The Making of Behavioural Economics* (Penguin, 2015)

Thaler, Richard H. and Cass R. Sunstein, *Nudge: Improving Decisions About Health, Wealth and Happiness* (Penguin, 2009)

Varian, Hal and Carl Shapiro, *Information Rules: A Strategic Guide to the Network Economy* (Harvard Business Review Press, 1998)

Varian, Hal, *Intermediate Microeconomics with Calculus: A Modern Approach: Media Update* (W. W. Norton & Company, 2019)

Waldfogel, Joseph, *Digital Renaissance: What Data and Economics Tell Us About the Future of Popular Culture* (Princeton University Press, 2018)

Wu, Tim, *The Attention Merchants: How Our Time and Attention Are Gathered and Sold*, main edition (Atlantic Books, 2017)

Zinsser, William, *On Writing Well*, 30th Anniversary Edition (Harper Perennial, 2016)

## Documentaries and Movies

*All the President's Men* (1976), Wildwood Enterprises

*All Things Must Pass: The Rise and Fall of Tower Records* (2015), FilmRise

*Barbarians at the Gate* (1993), HBO Films (as HBO Pictures), Columbia Pictures Television, Rastar Pictures

*Being There* (1979), BSB; CIP; Lorimar Film Entertainment; NatWest Ventures; New Gold Entertainment (co-production); Northstar Media

*Fog of War* (2003), Sony Pictures Classics

*Kill Your Friends* (2015), Unigram; Altitude Film Entertainment

*The Big Short* (2015), Paramount Pictures; Regency Enterprises; Plan B Entertainment

*Vinyl* (TV series, 2016), Sikelia Productions; Jagged Films; Cold Front Productions; Paramount Television; Home Box Office (HBO)

# ACKNOWLEDGEMENTS

First – I would like to recognise the guidance and support from my former professor, Andrew Hughes-Hallett, who passed away (while this book was in construction) on Hogmanay, 31 December 2019. On graduating from Edinburgh University in 2002, where I specialised in studying the after-effects of German Unification ten years on, he kindly reminded me that unless North and South Korea go for it, I had no job prospects!

Second – Before 'passing go' and 'collecting two hundred pounds', there are two people who I need to thank for making this journey possible; one I probably will never know and the other I've got to know very well. To whoever kindly left their copy of the *Financial Times* on a 35 bus in Edinburgh on the evening of 16 March 2006, I owe you more than just the cover price of the paper – more like a lifetime subscription to Spotify! Second, I was able to embark on this journey thanks to Adam Singer, the former CEO of the Performing Right Society, for responding to my critique of his op-ed in that very same edition of the *Financial Times*. He opened the door for economics to enter the music industry and took a gamble on me to become his 'rockonomist'. I hope this book gives him the assurance that the gamble paid off. It still gives me goosebumps to this day to think that none of this would have happened had I not taken that bus.

Third – For guiding me through my first book, from

inception to completion and all the pain in-between, my thanks to the team: Phil Marino, Vanessa Mobley, Elizabeth Gassman and Elizabeth Garriga (Little, Brown); Ian Marshall, Frances Jessop, Louise Davies, Sue Stephens and Genevieve Barratt (Simon & Schuster); Martin Lubikowski (illustrator); Amelia Atlas and Billy Hollock (ICM Partners). Prior to working with this dream team, Sarah Caro and Diane Coyle (Princeton University Press), Ralph Simon (Mobilium) and David Safir (Music Economics) all played a pivotal role in making this concept crystallise. Respect is due to Paul Bradshaw, Gilles Peterson and the *Straight No Chaser* community for giving me my first big break in the music industry. Any journey begins at the beginning, so hat-tips to Nick Glynn and Henna Silvennoinen (Audible), who explained the role of the agent and connected me with one of the very best: Gordon Wise (Curtis Brown).

Fourth – It was Jim Griffin who introduced me to the phrase 'Tarzan Economics' in a bar in southern Norway in 2007 – and thanks to extortionate Norwegian bar prices I remained sober enough to mentally cling on to it the following morning. Jim's been a source of inspiration ever since, helping me 'sharpen my knife' when constructing arguments and putting forth opinions.

Fifth – For the ass-kicking that was required to get me to embark on this journey in the first place, this cast of characters need crediting: Troy Carter (Founder, Q&A), who told me I was already going to do this even before I'd made up my own mind; Richard Davies (author of *Extreme Economies*), who showed me how it could be done; Lucie Watson, Hagar Graiser and Denzyl Feigelson (Platoon) have been kindred spirits in supporting this from the get-go; Cait O'Riordan (*Financial Times*) spent seven years reminding me this would be doable; Lauren Jarvis (Spotify), whose work ethic reminded me what it takes to actually get sh*t done; and Jill Smayo, who took less than five minutes skim-reading my proposal before telling me it was time to do it. Her LA-based radio station KCRW made night shifts reading manuscripts in the GMT time zone manageable thanks to them being nine hours behind.

Sixth – Back when this journey began, James Anderson, the chief investment officer of Baillie Gifford, took me aside after watching a dour goalless draw between Heart of Midlothian and Ross County, and told me that he had heard that 'writing a book was a terrible idea, it's like playing tennis with yourself'. I got lucky and stumbled on a long list of unique and inspirational tennis players who returned my serve whenever it was called upon. Here they all are: Rebecca Aydin; Sam Blake; Alex Barron; Stewart McKie; Tom Frederikse; Sohit Karol; Matt Locke; David Erlandsson; Ashley Dutton; Nigel Hikmet; Richard Kramer; Daniel Levine; Sam Lourensz and Chris Tynan.

Seventh – While there may not be many 'rockonomists' around, there is an important roll call of economists who have taken the dismal science into new territory and made it matter, each one of them an inspiration: Susan Athey; Pat Bajari; Diane Coyle; Brett Danaher; Andy Haldane; Tim Harford; Karin Kimbrough; Alan Krueger; Stephen Levitt; Preston McAfee; George Magnus; James Pomeroy; Stefan Szymanski; Steve Tadelis; Hal Varian; Joel Waldfogel and finally John Kay – who always reminded me that to be a fan of business is not necessarily the same thing as being a fan of markets.

Eighth – I would like to recognise the direct, indirect and induced influence of the following cast of characters: Vanessa Bakewell; David Bakula; Sir Peter Bazalgette; Emily ffrench Blake; Jon Blaufarb; Tom Broughton; Ed Bugge; Milena Bogdanova Bursztyn; Andrew Bud; Stephen Cannon

(AMB Group); Christelle Chamouton (Bloomsbury Press); Ed Christman; Salman Chaudhry; Jack Cox; James Cridland (Pod News); Russ Crupnick (MusicWatch); Daniel Day (Ofcom); Chris Deering; Stuart Dredge (Music Ally); Bryce Edge (ATC Management); Nigel Elderton (peermusic); John Enoch; Benedict Evans; Joe Fleischer; Adrian Furnham; Chris Gardener; Eric Garland; Scott Galloway; Stephen Garrett and Vince Gilligan (writer of *Breaking Bad*); Seth Gerson (Survios VR); Ally Glerum (MRC Media); Fred Goldring; Bill Gorjance (peermusic); Simmy Grover; Marina Haydn (*The Economist*); Greg Herman (Spotify); Ken Hertz; Alex Holmes (AWS); Courtney Holt; Chris Hufford (Courtyard Management); Crispin Hunt; Seven Ilyas; Tim Ingham (MBW); David Jevons (Oxera); Mitch Kanner; Hannah Karp (*Billboard*); Tim Kent; Sharky Laguana; Anaïs Lempereur; Matt LeMay; Geoff Mayfield; Richard Mahony (Omdia); Mariano Mamertino (LinkedIn); Liam Maxwell (AWS); Geoff Mayfield; Jennifer McCarron (Netflix); Sean McGuire (Oliver and Ohlbaum); Brian Message (ATC Management); Ross Michaels; Simon David Miller; Larry Miller (New York University); Mark Mulligan (MIDiA); Arvind Narayanan; Kenny Ning; Matthew Ogle; Mark Oliver (Oliver and Ohlbaum); Yoshio Osaki (IDG Consulting); Michael Pye; Ralph Peer II (peermusic); Jomar Perez; Shaun Richards; Paul Sanders; Deva Santiago; Michael Small (Mike Gee from the Jungle Brothers); Chris Smith (Barbershop Music); Ruth Simmons (SoundLounge); Rory Sutherland (Ogilvy); Ben Thompson (Stratechery); Chris Tynan; Dobs Vye; Tricia Wang; Rick Webb; Alison Wenham; and Gareth Williams (founder and former CEO of Skyscanner).

Ninth – With more than a decade of working with and for Spotify produces a list of acknowledgments that's longer than any algorithmic playlist – apologies in advance for the skips:

Daniel Ek; Ken Parks; Niklas Ivarsson; Petra Hansson; Angela Watts; Sachin Doshi; Niklas Lundberg; Marc Hazan; Johan Bergqvist; Alex Norström; James Duffett-Smith; Samantha Mandel-Dallal; Alison Bonny; Mark Williamson; Bryan Johnson; Nicholas Lightle; Beck Kloss; Horacio Gutierrez; Emery Simon; Tom Manatos; and finally Chris Bevington, who tragically died in the Stockholm terror attack in April 2017; to this day it still hurts every time I fly to Stockholm knowing he won't ever be there. During my six years as chief economist of PRS for Music, a long list of generous experts took the time to help me climb up a steep learning curve – as with any collecting society the log sheet will be incomplete: Robert Ashcroft; Jez Bell; William Booth; Chris Carey; Tim Chambers; Paul Curran; Jane Dyball; Gary Eggleton; Crispin Evans; Jeremy Fabinyi; Andy Heath; Barney Hooper; Martin Mills; Ellis Rich; Debbie Stones and David Touve.

Tenth – Across all record labels, publishers and trade bodies, I've had some phenomenal teachers who have helped me see around corners: Joseph Cacciola (Warner Music Group); Charles Caldas (Merlin); Steve Cooper (WMG); Mark Dennis (Sony Music Entertainment); Joshua Friedlander (RIAA); Mitch Glazier (RIAA); Adam Granite (Universal Music Group); Chris Green (BPI); John Kennedy; Dennis Kooker (SME); David Leibowitz; Gabriela Lopes (UMG); Martin Mills (Beggars Group); Frances Moore (IFPI); Gadi Oron (CISAC); Mitchel Shymanskey (UMG); and Steve Stoute of United Masters, who told me that I needed to stare into the darkness to get this book into the light.

Last but not least is family, who have been there through thin and thin: David, Isabel, Thomas, Annie and Margaret Page; Carol and Drick Vernon; Johnny, Pauline, Jamie, Katie, Peter and Evelyn Hood; David and Elizabeth Edward; Colin and Renata Whurr; Ralph Pool; Antonio, Leticia, Joaquin, Mari Cruz, Adela and especially my wife, Juana, and daughters, Gabriela and Isabel. The only reason I wanted to work in music was to replicate the achievements of Doreen Loader (1952–2012), who once taught me that the music business was 'so bent it's straight' and Nigel Grainge (1946–2018), who constantly reminded me that 'if you've never served a customer in a record shop, you should never be allowed to work at a record label'.

# INDEX

Page references in *italics* indicate images.